PENNSYLVANIA DIVORCES

Dauphin County, 1788–1867
and
York County, 1790–1860

Eugene F. Throop

HERITAGE BOOKS
2012

HERITAGE BOOKS

AN IMPRINT OF HERITAGE BOOKS, INC.

Books, CDs, and more—Worldwide

For our listing of thousands of titles see our website
at
www.HeritageBooks.com

Published 2012 by
HERITAGE BOOKS, INC.
Publishing Division
100 Railroad Ave. #104
Westminster, Maryland 21157

Other Heritage Books by the author:

CD: Cumberland County, Pennsylvania Divorces, 1789–1860

CD: Lancaster County, Pennsylvania Divorces, 1786–1832

CD: Pennsylvania Divorces

CD: Pennsylvania Divorces: Dauphin County, 1788–1867 and York County, 1790–1860

Cumberland County, Pennsylvania Divorces, 1789–1860

Forest County, Pennsylvania Cemetery Inscriptions

Lancaster County, Pennsylvania Divorces, 1786–1832

International Standard Book Numbers
Paperbound: 978-0-7884-0376-7
Clothbound: 978-0-7884-3407-5

Contents

◆　　◆　　◆

Foreword

◆　　◆　　◆

For over twenty-six years I have been involved in genealogical research for others. During that time it became increasingly apparent that many researchers were overlooking an important aid to their genealogical investigation, and that was the divorce records. Despite the great personal turmoil involved in a divorce case, these records are at times a "gold mine" of information for family historians. Usually, when a woman filed for a divorce she did so "by her next friend," who often was a close male relative such as a father or brother. Many of the witnesses who testified were neighbors or relatives of the divorcing couple, and their relationships were duly noted.

Having been through a divorce myself, I can certainly attest to the emotional toll it has on all directly affected. I'm sure it was no different in the time period my book covers. Often these early divorces came as the unavoidable result of very distressing circumstances such as desertion, extreme cruelty, and/or adultery. I also noted distinct similarities with modern-day divorces such as vindictive wives trying to take their husbands for all they could, and attorneys who played both ends against the middle to get a huge slice of the "pie."

It was amusing to see the strange spellings which I left as they were originally recorded. Some of the justices of the peace were notoriously bad spellers and some were notoriously bad handwriters. For those stuck on the idea that a surname should be spelled one way only, please note how careless clerks and Justices of the Peace were. I saw instances where the same surname was spelled three different ways on a document written by the same individual!

This compilation of Dauphin County and York County divorces is invaluable not only for those interested in the history and genealogies of this area, but many other locations as well. When a husband or wife left their mate, they often went quite a distance.

Hopefully, my readers will forgive me for summarizing most of the records I copied. By doing so, I used fewer pages making it easier to copy and easier to type. I also avoided repeating the same legal terminology over and over. I tried very hard not to miss anything of real value that my readers would want to know.

Unfortunately, much of the valuable information about divorces in these counties is lost, apparently forever. In Dauphin County some of the early divorce records were so poorly microfilmed that I just could not read them and many of the early records are in the index book but missing on the microfilm. In some cases they may have been microfilmed out of place, so perhaps some of these will turn up later. Personally, I didn't have the time needed to read hundreds of reels of microfilm just to see if any were out of place. In York County, Pennsylvania, the situation is even worse. I could find the record of each divorce action, but the original documents which would have given us researchers the really important information such as date of marriage, cause of divorce, names of relatives and neighbors who testified are all missing. So, I could only copy from what is now available.

My special thanks goes to Mary Walter who heads the Archives Dept. of the York County Courthouse. She and her assistants were especially helpful to me in my search. These records are now found in the attic of the York County Courthouse. The earlier records prior to 1810 are from microfilm at the Pennsylvania State Archives at Harrisburg, Pennsylvania.

I'm truly sorry this book will not be as informative as my earlier books on Pennsylvania divorces. It's unfortunate that some of the custodians of courthouse records have in the past thrown away some of what we now know are valuable records of the past, or had them so poorly microfilmed as to render them of no use. But, be that as it may, hopefully my readers will find some useful information from all my efforts.

July 6, 1995
Eugene F. Throop
920 Baltimore St.
Hanover, PA 17331

Abbreviations

Adjd. - Adjurned
afft. - affidavit
ans. - answer
Apr. - April
Argt. - argued
atty. - attorney
Aug. - August
Co. - County
contd. - continued
ct. - court
Dec. - December
def. - defendant
Esq. - Esquire
Feb. - February
Gen. - General
Hon. - Honorable
Jan. - January
Jul. - July
Jun. - June
Jr. - Junior

Mar. - March
Messrs. - plural of Mr.
Md. - Maryland
N.C. - North Carolina
"N.E.I." - "Non Est Inventus"
No. - Number
Nov. - November
Oct. - October
Pa. - Pennsylvania
plf., Pltfs. - plaintiff, Plaintiffs
recd. - received
Rev. - Reverend
S.C. - South Carolina
Sept. - September
sheff. - sheriff
shff. - sheriff
Sr. - Senior
Twp. - Township
Va. - Virginia

Dauphin County, Pennsylvania Divorces, 1788-1867

Apr. 15, 1788 - Subpoena to Catharine Wright to appear in court at Philadelphia, Pa. Jul. 2, 1788 to answer her husband's libel for divorce.

May 22, 1788 - Conviction of Catharine Wright of adultery by a grand Inquest of the county of Dauphin at a Court of Quarter Sessions before Joseph Montgomery, Esq. She committed adultery Apr. 10, 1787 in Dauphin Co., Pa. with Joseph Keller, yeoman, of Dauphin Co.. Both were married as Joseph Keller had a wife named Elizabeth. This act of adultery resulted in a "bastard child". Catharine Wright was sentenced to pay a fine of five pounds, pay costs of prosecution, "and in the mean time be committed." - Copy extracted from records by Alex. Grayson, clerk. Henry Muhlenberg Lutheran minister of Lancaster testified he married Joseph Wright of Manor Twp., Lancaster Co., Pa. Sept. 8, 1784 to Catharine Lick of the borough of Lancaster, Pa.

May 28,1788 - Joseph Wright, yeoman, of Lancaster Co. petitioned Thomas McKean, justice of the Supreme Court of Pa. for a divorce. He married Sept. 8, 1784 Catharine Lick of the boro of Lancaster. "That the said Catharine hath behaved in a very gross and improper manner towards your petitioner hath frequently eloped and hath run your petitioner in debt to a considerable sum, which he hath discharged." They separated in Aug. 1785 and since then she has committed adultery of which she was convicted in Dauphin Co., Pa. Jul. 1, 1788 - Anthony Kelker, Esq. sheriff of Dauphin Co., Pa. testified that he had served subpoena on Catharine Wright May 28, 1788. Testified before Thomas McKean, chief justice of the Supreme Court of Pennsylvania.

Jul. 15, 1788 - Subpoena to Catharine Wright, late of Lancaster Co., Pa. to appear in court in Philadelphia, Pa. Sept. 24, 1788.

Aug. 23, 1788 - Anthony Kelker, Esq. high sheriff of Dauphin Co., Pa. testified he served subpoena on Catharine Wright and left copy of subpoena Aug. 20, 1788. Testified before J. Kean, justice of the Court of Common Pleas of Dauphin Co., Pa.

Sept. 24, 1788 - Supreme Court of Pennsylvania granted Joseph Wright a divorce from his wife Catharine.

Jun. 1, 1789 - petition of Sarah Bossler by her next friend and father John Garber, to the Pennsylvania Supreme Court at Philadelphia, Pa. She married Henry Bossler late of Allen Twp., Cumberland Co., Pa. in Dec. 1781 and had two children by him. In Dec. 1784 he separated from her, leaving the area. He returned in Sept. 1785 when he visited her father's house about two hours and told her father he would not stay with his wife unless her father paid him a sum of money. He made no provision for his wife and children so they have been maintained by her father since her husband's desertion. During their marriage they lived together as man and wife less than twelve months. Testified before William Attlee. Signed by Sarah Bossler and John Garber. Subpoena awarded by court.

Jun. 3, 1789 - John Snyder, yeoman, of West Pennsboro Twp., Cumberland Co., Pa. testified he left a copy of the subpoena for Henry Bossler to appear in court at the dwelling house of Archibald McAlister in Paxton Twp., Dauphin Co., Pa., the last place of abode for Henry Bossler. Henry Bossler had left the state a considerable time ago and is now residing in Georgia.

Jul. 15, 1789 - Commonwealth of Pennsylvania issued a subpoena to Henry Bossler, late of Allen Twp., Cumberland Co., Pa. to appear in court at Philadelphia, Sept. 24, 1789 to answer his wife's libel for a divorce.

Jul. 25, 1789 - Charles Leeper, sheriff of Cumberland Co., Pa. testified he made the required three days of proclamation at the Cumberland County Courthouse for Henry Rossler to appear in court to answer his wife's libel for a divorce.

Oct. 7, 1789 - Commonwealth of Pennsylvania issued subpoena for Henry Bossler, late of Allen Twp., Cumberland Co., Pa. to appear in court in Philadelphia, Pa. Jan. 2, 1790 to answer the libel of his wife for divorce.

Jan. 2, 1790 - Thomas Buchanan, Esq., sheriff of Cumberland Co., Pa. testified he made the required three days of proclamation for Henry Bossler to appear in court to answer his wife's libel for a divorce.

Jan. 2, 1790 - James Ash, Esq., sheriff of Philadelphia Co., Pa. claimed he made the required three days proclamation for the appearance in court of Henry Bossler to answer his wife's libel for a divorce. He made it at the new courthouse, in the public markets and in two public newspapers.

Jan. 2, 1790 - The Commonwealth of Pennsylvania appointed John Jordan, Ephraim Steel, John Agnew and William Lyon or any two of them to be commissioners to take testimony in the case of Sarah Bossler vs. Henry Bossler, libel in divorce.

Apr. 15, 1790 - Commonwealth of Pennsylvania issued a subpoena to Henry Bossler late of Allen Twp., Cumberland Co., Pa., to appear in court in Philadelphia, Pa. Jul. 2, 1790 to answer the libel of his wife Sarah Bossler for a divorce.

Apr. 22, 1790 - Deposition of John Garber of West Pennsborough Twp., Cumberland Co., Pa. before John Jordan and Ephraim Steel.

He said that Sarah Bossler was his daughter and he was present at her marriage Dec. 1781 in his house in Paxton Twp., Lancaster Co., Pa. to Henry Bossler. They lived together as man and wife at his house at intervals for eleven or twelve months during which time his daughter always lived in his house. Henry Bossler left his wife without any provisions for her maintenance in Dec. 1784. He returned to her twice, first in Sept. 1785 for five or six days. After his wife had a son he stayed one day. The second time he returned was in Jun. 1786 when he visited for about two hours and he requested from him one hundred guineas which he was refused. The money seemed to be the only reason for his visit. He also testified "Henry Bossler has for several years past resided in Georgia where it has been reported that he has intermarried with a widow."

Apr. 22, 1790 - Deposition of Mary Garber wife of John Garber. She was present at her daughter's wedding to Henry Bossler in 1781 in Paxton Twp., Lancaster Co., Pa. by Rev. McKandel now of Lancaster Co., Pa. They had a son and a daughter. He left for three years later and returned only twice but at neither occasion had "connection with the said Libellant as his wife." Her daughter and her two children have been provided for by her husband as Henry Bossler made no provision for them. Henry Bossler wrote his wife a letter in the German language in which he said he would never return to his wife unless her father gave him three hundred or four hundred pounds. She personally saw this letter and read it. Signed by Mary Garber.

Undated decree of divorce for Sarah Bossler and Henry Bossler.

Oct. 19, 1790 - Subpoena to James Harris late of Lower Paxton Twp., Dauphin Co., Pa. to appear before the Supreme Court of Pennsylvania at Philadelphia, Pa. Jan. 3, 1791 to answer his wife's libel for a divorce.

Nov. 17, 1790 petition of Jane Harris by her next friend Robert Clark. She married May 23, 1791 James Harris of Lower Paxton Twp., then Lancaster Co., Pa. now Dauphin Co., Pa. Shortly after their marriage he "gave himself up to dissolute and idle courses." In the latter end of Nov. 1791 he deserted her. Soon afterward she had a child and her husband made no provision for her. She hath frequently wrote her husband inviting him to return but he never has nor told her he would provide for her "as a good husband ought to do." Her husband's father has informed her by letter that James Harris lives in North Carolina with another woman as his wife and has several children reputed to be his.

Dec. 6, 1790 - James Clunie, sheriff testified he could not find James Harris in Dauphin Co., Pa. and left a copy of the subpoena at his last abode the house of Michael Frantz Nov. 29, 1790.

Apr. 15, 1791 - Court appoints Joseph Montgomery, Esq. and Alexander Grayson, Esq. of Harrisburg to take depositions in the case of James Harris.

Apr. 15, 1791 - Subpoena issued to James Harris, late of Lower Paxton Twp., Dauphin Co., Pa. to appear before the Supreme Court at Philadelphia, Pa. Jul. 2, 1791 to show cause why his wife Jane should not have a divorce.

May 20, 1791 - John McCleary swears he could not find James Harris in Dauphin Co., Pa. and left a copy of subpoena at the dwelling house of Michael Frantz his last place of abode there May 16, 1791.

May 27, 1791 - Deposition of James Colier of Paxton Twp., Dauphin Co., Pa., held at house of Samuel Grahams, innholder at the Sign of the Federal Arms in the borough of Harrisburg. He had known Jane Harris since he was six years of age and her husband James Harris since about the time of his marriage to Jane. Jane was Jane Hutchison and she married James Harris in her mother's house in Paxton Twp. about the middle of May 1779. He "saw them married and put to bed together and that they lived some months together at the house of her mother as man and wife". James left his wife "with child" at her mother's house. He didn't know why he left or where he went. He has not seen James Harris since but he had seen a letter he sent his wife about two years ago. He said he resided in South Carolina and he expected to see her in a few months. The letter was not dated and he didn't recollect what place in South Carolina it was from. He had also heard that James Harris lives in South Carolina with another woman. He wrote a letter back to James Harris for his wife in answer. He wrote it for her at her insistence directed to the father of the said James Harris requesting him to forward it to his son in which "letter she desired him to return and upbraided him with his inconstancy and neglect and told him of her own faithfulness to her marriage tye (sic)". He knows of no provision made by James Harris for his wife and child nor of any invitation made by him for his wife to "cohabit with him".

May 27, 1791 - Deposition of Richard Fulton of Paxton Twp., Dauphin Co., Pa., aged 27 years. He had known Jane Harris, formerly Jane Hutchinson, about 14 years and James Harris about 12 years ago. He was not present at their marriage but saw them at meeting together and knew they were regarded as man and wife. He knew James deserted his pregnant wife and about six months later "she was delivered of a female child." He doesn't know why he left unless it was because he was in debt and has heard he went to South Carolina with another woman. He has heard Jane Harris declare she had written to her husband and has always understood it was her wish that he should return to her. He knows of no provision made by James Harris for his wife nor "does not know that the said James Harris hath refused to return and live with the said Jane."

May 28, 1791 - Deposition of Rev. John Elder, minister of the gospel in the congregation of Paxton, Dauphin Co., Pa., aged 81 years. He knew Jane Harris since she was a child and knew James Harris about 2 months prior to their marriage. Jane was Jane Hutchison and she married James Harris at her brother's house, where her mother also lived, May 27, 1779. They lived together there about seven or eight months. In the fall of 1779, James deserted his wife and shortly thereafter she had a child. He believed "he left her on account of his being much in debt and that it was said he went to Virginia and from there to South Carolina." To the best of his knowledge James has never returned to Pa., but he has heard he lives in either N.C. or S.C. with another woman not his wife. He believes James Harris left no provision for his wife and child. Jane Harris informed him "that she had received a letter from the father of the said James giving her to understand she had nothing to expect from her said husband as he was married to and living with another woman."

Jul. 2, 1791 - James Clunie, sheriff of Dauphin Co., Pa., testified he made public proclamation at Dauphin Co. Courthouse three several days in May 1791 term for James Harris.

Jul. 2, 1791 - James Ash, sheriff of Philadelphia Co., Pa., testified he published notice for the appearance of James Harris in *Dunlap's American Daily Advertiser* and *Halls & Sellers Gazette* and made public declaration at three market days at old courthouse and in open court.

Undated - Supreme Court of Pennsylvania grants Jane Harris a divorce from James Harris.

Feb. 25, 1793 - Petition of Henry Stoner of Lower Paxton Twp., Dauphin Co., Pa., before Jasper Yeates, judge of the Supreme Court of Pennsylvania. He married May 3, 1792 Magdalena Stoler of Heidleberg Twp., Dauphin Co., Pa., a single woman. At the time of their marriage he considered her a virtuous woman, but since she committed adultery with Jacob Kline. He signed his name in German script. Notation on the front of this document - "7 Sept. 95 abated by Pltfs. death."

Apr. 11, 1795 - Commonwealth of Pennsylvania issued subpoena to David Bealert, husband of Mary Bealert to appear in court in Philadelphia, Pa. Sept. 7, 1795. Issued by Thomas McKean, Esq. chief justice of the Supreme Court of Pennsylvania.

Jun. 17, 1795 - Petition of Mary Bealert now working in the city of Philadelphia wife of David Bealert of Middletown, Dauphin Co., Pa., ropemaker, by her next friend Jacob Keighler. She was born in Pa. and residing there all her life. She married Aug. 1, 1768 David Bealert. He willfully deserted her in Dec. 1788 without just cause and she wants a divorce. Her petition was signed by Mary Bealert, Thomas McKean and Edward Burd, Esq., prothonotary of the

Supreme Court.

Sept. 7, 1795 - James McIntire of Upper Merion Twp., Montgomery Co., Pa., schoolmaster, testified he delivered subpoena to David Bealert Jul. 7, 1795 at Harrisburg, Pa.

Nov. 7, 1795 - Commonwealth of Pennsylvania subpoena to David Bealert to appear in court at Philadelphia, Dec. 14, 1795 on libel of divorce issued by Thomas McKean, Esq., chief justice of Supreme Court at Philadelphia. Signed by Edward Shippen.

Dec. 5, 1795 - Deposition of John McDonald, stone cutter of the city of Philadelphia who testified he saw David Bealert living on Shelly's Island about three miles below Middletown, Pa., Nov. 20, 1795 and believes he still resides there. Testified before Alexander James, Esq.

Dec. 14, 1795 - John McDonald of the city of Philadelphia, stone-cutter, testified that he gave a copy of subpoena to David Bealert at Shelly's Island on the Susquehanna River about three miles below Middletown in Dauphin Co., Pa., Nov. 20, 1795.

Dec. 14, 1795 - Deposition of Jacob Kinsley, shoemaker of the city of Philadelphia. About twelve years ago he knew David and Mary Bealert who then lived in Philadelphia and for two or three years after that. They had four children. About eight years ago or upwards David Bealert abandoned his wife and children. Enclosed marriage certificate certified David Bealer and Mary Fultz Spinsner (sic) both of Philadelphia were married Aug. 5, 1767 by Henry Muhlenberg. Witnessed by William Levering, Jr., Jacob Bealert and Nathan Levering.

Dec. 16, 1795 - William Levering of Roxborough Twp., Philadelphia Co., Pa., blacksmith, testified before Alexander James, Esq., that he was present along with Jacob Bealert and Nathan Livering when David and Mary Bealert were married by Rev. Henry Muhlenberg in the city of Philadelphia. Rev. Muhlenberg has since died. Rev. Muhlenberg signed his name to the marriage certificate and so did the witnesses William Levering, Jacob Bealert and Nathan Levering.

Dec. 18, 1798 - David Bealert being three times solemnly called and he not appearing his wife Mary was granted a divorce.

Mar. 13, 1800 - Susannah Miller by her next friend Abraham Wolf offered her petition before Joseph Henry, president of the Court of Common Pleas of Dauphin Co., Pa., that she was married Dec. 1, 1798 to Samuel Miller. They lived together five months "and that during that time he never had connection with her - nor carnally did know her." Samuel Miller confessed to her he was impotent and incapable of procreation. She signed her petition by mark and Abraham Wolf signed using his initials A.W.

Mar. 17, 1800 - Subpoena to Samuel Miller to appear in court Philadelphia first Monday of Sept. 1800. John Carothers, sheriff testified he served subpoena and it was twenty miles.

Dec. 8, 1800 - Subpoena to Samuel Miller to appear in court Philadelphia first Monday of Mar. 1801. John Carothers, sheriff, testified that he served the subpoena Feb. 7, 1801 sixteen miles.

Sept. 19, 1801 - Subpoena to Barbara Mayer to appear in court on the second Monday of Dec. 1801 in Philadelphia to answer a libel of divorce.

Oct. 13, 1801 - Petition of Rudolph Myer of Somerset Co., Pa. He married his present wife Barbara in May 1776 and they lived together fourteen years and "for a considerable time past given herself up to adulterous practices."

Dec. 14, 1801 - John Mayer testified he served subpoena on Barbara Mayer on or before Nov. 23, 1801. He signed as Johannes Mayer.

Dec. 14, 1801 - Subpoena to Barbara Mayer to appear in court Philadelphia on third Monday of Mar. 1802.

Dec. 15, 1801 - Court appointed John Tome and John Gloninger to take depositions in this case.

Dec. 23, 1801 - Jacob Mayer of Dauphin Co., Pa., testified he has known John Mayer since infancy and became acquainted with Barbara Mayer at her father's house in Heidleburg Twp., Lancaster Co., Pa., and at her brother-in-law John Mayer's house in Heidleburg Twp. about two years before the marriage of John and Barbara. He was present at their wedding about 26 years ago in the Mennonite meetinghouse in Lebanon Twp. then in Lancaster Co., by Frederick Kauffman, a Mennonite Minister, since deceased. They lived as man and wife about 14 or 15 years. It was "common report" and "generally believed" that Barbara committed adultery with Benjamin Young of Heidleburg Twp. now in Dauphin Co. Barbara deserted her husband about 11 or 12 years ago when they lived in York Co. and eloped without any just cause.

Dec. 23, 1801 - Deposition of Henry Mayer of Lebanon Twp., Dauphin Co., Pa., farmer. He had known John Mayer since infancy and Barbara Mayer about two years before her marriage while she lived in her father's house. They were married about 26 years ago by Frederick Kauffman, since deceased, in a Mennonite meetinghouse and lived as man and wife about 15 years. It was commonly believed Barbara had committed adultery with Benjamin Young "as she herself had made oath thereof before a justice of the peace as he this affirmant is informed." About eight or nine years ago Barbara told him she was married to Frederick Fuhrman. About two months later he was at Frederick Fuhrman's house and noted they lived together. She left John Mayer about eleven years ago while they lived in York Co., Pa.

Dec. 23, 1801 - Deposition of John Shenk of Heildleburg Twp., Dauphin Co., Pa., miller. He had known John Mayer since infancy and Barbara Mayer since shortly before her marriage to John. He was present at their wedding about 25 or 26 years ago in a Mennonite meeting house in Lebanon Twp. by Frederick Kauffman. They lived together 14 or 15 years. After Barbara left her husband she had a child and Benjamin Young was reported to be the father.

Dec. 24, 1801 - Deposition of George Hoke of Warwick Twp., York Co., Pa., farmer, that he "is little acquainted with the Libellant, that he has been acquainted with the defendant about 7 or 8 years." Barbara Mayer told him that her daughter living with her was the daughter of Benjamin Young. He knows this girl and she is about 11 or 12 years old. He also knows Frederick Fuhrman and he "further told this affirmant that he Fuhrman did sleep with her the Defendant and he would sleep with her if Rudolph Mayer was presant." Frederick Fuhrman and Barbara Mayer have lived together in his neighborhood about three years just as if they were man and wife.

Dec. 24, 1801 - Deposition of Henry Sheffer, Esq. of Heidleburg Twp., Dauphin Co., Pa. He had known John Mayer about 20 years and Barbara Mayer since she was a child and lived with her father who was a near neighbor of his. John and Barbara Mayer lived together about 14 or 15 years. About 10 or 11 years ago Barbara made oath before him that she had a bastard child and the father of the child was Benjamin Young of Heidleburg Twp. He issued a warrant and as he understood the affair was settled. At the time she pressed charges against Benjamin Young her husband lived in York County. He knew Frederick Fuhrman and Barbara Mayer have lived together for seven or eight years.

Mar. 15, 1802 - Supreme Court of Pennsylvania granted the divorce.

Dec. 1798 - Court of Quarter Sessions of Dauphin Co., Pa. Dec. Sessions 1798 convicted David Miskimmins, yeoman of Dauphin Co., Pa. that on Nov. 6, 1798 at Hanover Twp., Dauphin Co., Pa. he beat up his wife Jane. He was convicted of assault and battery and sentenced to one month in the Dauphin Co., Pa. jail and pay costs of case. Signed by Joshua Elder, clerk.

Jul. 16, 1799 - Orphans Court Division of property of the late William Sawyer, late of Londonderry Twp., Dauphin Co., Pa. between William Sawyer, eldest son, Jane Miskimmons, Mary Sawyer, wife of William Crane, Margaret Sawyer, wife of Alexander McKinney, and Elizabeth Sawyer wife of Alexander Wier.

Dec. 3, 1801 - Petition of Jane Miscimmins by her next friend William Sawyer before William Maclay, associate judge of the Court of Common Pleas of Dauphin Co., Pa. She married Oct. 18, 1785 David Miscimmins. From Jan. 1, 1795 he has abused her and endangered her life causing her to leave him. She has lived in Pa. since her birth. Signed by mark.

Sept. 11, 1802 - Subpoena to David Miscinnins to appear in court on the first Monday of Dec. 1802. Samuel Elder, sheriff of Dauphin Co., Pa. reported "not found in my bailiwick."

Dec. 6, 1802 - Subpoena on David Miscinnius to appear in court on the first Monday of Mar. 1803. Samuel Elder, sheriff of Dauphin Co., Pa. reported he could not find David in Dauphin Co., Pa.

Mar. 25, 1803 - Court appointed Joshua Elder of Harrisburg, Pa. to take depositions in this case.

Jun. 23, 1802 - Deposition of Jane Martin who knew both parties. They lived in West Hanover Twn., Dauphin Co., Pa., and she was employed by them as a domestic helper. About seven years ago David Miskimmons became "very frequently intoxicated with strong liqour." His wife tried hard to please him but he struck her on the face, pulled her hair, threw buckets of water on her and her young child and otherwise abused her. She left their employ as she couldn't tolerate his behavior. At times David forced his wife out of his house and kept her out for a length of time. In Jul. 1801 she left his house with her young child and fled to neighbors. A few days later he sent the other three children to his wife Jane. Since then she has supported herself and family by her industry and kindness of neighbors. He shortly left the county. He had no property of his own but his wife had some by inheritance. "The said David is a man much addicted to drunkeness and when drunk a very refractory bad tempered man. And that this Deponent being well acquainted with the said Jane the Libellant knows her to be an honest sober inoffensive and industrious woman." She signed by mark.

Jun. 23, 1803 - Deposition of Peter Hann before Joshua Elder. He gave testimony that in the summer of 1801 David Miskimmons came to his house to try to persuade his wife Jane to return to his house. He admitted beating her while drunk and promised to behave better in the future. David's wife twice came to his house in west Hanover Twp. to gain refuge from her husband. "Her hair was very much torn when she came." "The said David is a man of a quarelsome character and mischeifeous (*sic*). That Jane Miscimmons is a peaceable inoffensive and industrious woman."

Jun. 23, 1803 - Deposition of David Ferguson of West Hanover Twp., Dauphin Co., Pa. before Joshua Elder that "he was for about eight years past acquainted with David Miskimmins and Jane his wife. That the general character of the said David is not a good one. That he is a lazy worthless man fond of strong drink and that he abandoned and left his wife the above libellant and their children some time ago and that he this deponent does not know where he the said David is gone to reside. That he this deponent as far as comes to his knowledge believes the above libellant to be a prudent sober woman."

Jun. 23, 1803 - Deposition of Martha Rippeth of West Hanover Twp., Dauphin Co., Pa. In Jul. 1801 Jane Miscimmins came to her house very late at night because she had fled from the abuse of her husband. Her hair was very torn and her head was cut and bruised as was several other parts of her body. "That the bad and gross treatment of the said David to his said wife was of the most beastly and cruel kind, and notorius of the whole County, that the said David is a man of bad character and has left his said wife Jane with four children to be supported alone by the industry of herself via the said Jane and the kindness of her neighbors. That she this deponent is well acquainted with the Libellant and knows her to be a peaceable inoffensive sober and industrious woman." Martha Rippeth signed her deposition by mark.

Jun. 23, 1803 - Deposition of Robert Freekleton of West Hanover Twp., Dauphin Co., Pa., well acquainted with David and Jane Miscimmins. By his ill treatment they separated two or three times. By the persuasion of the neighbors she returned and tried to live with him. She finally was obliged to leave him to protect her own life. David called on him to then try to persuade his wife to return. He admitted drink was the cause of the problem but promised to reform. He refused this request because he did not trust his promises. Robert Freekleton signed this deposition by mark.

Jun. 23, 1803 - Deposition of John Finney of West Hanover Twp., Dauphin Co., Pa. David Miscimmins rented a house from him in Apr. 1799 for one year and came with his wife and family. David Miscimmins had just been released from prison after being convicted of assault and battery on his wife. He behaved well until the following winter during which time he was under oath not to take any strong drink. He then started to drink at every opportunity. When he became drunk he was "neither company for man nor beast which situation he was in then almost every day." Jane Miscinnins came to his house in the middle of the night saying she could not live with him anymore. She later returned to her husband and they lived together until the summer of 1801 when the abuse grew worst. He had heard that David came to his wife when sober and pleaded for her to return. Jane went home with him twice "and the deponent says he has seen the said David drunk the next day after he made the promise that he would take an oath not to get drunk again. That this deponent has caught the said defendant burning his own goods, that the said defendant when drunk appears to have a pleasure in tormenting his family, and that the defendant's wife Jane was and appeared to be a peaceable sober and industrius woman."

Jul. 30, 1803 - Deposition of William Logan that he was present at the marriage of David Miscimmins and Jane Miscimmins (late Jane Sayers widow and relict of William Sayers late of Londonderry Twp. in the county of Dauphin deceased) the marriage took place at Jane's house in Londonderry Twp. about sixteen years ago by Rev. M. Kurtz.

Sept. 17, 1803 - Subpoena to David Miscimmins to appear in court Dec. 31, 1803 John Barker, sheriff of Philadelphia Co., Pa. testified that he had made proclamation on three market days at courthouse and gave notice in a public newspaper in Philadelphia, Pa.

Dec. sessions 1801 court of Oyer and Terminer, Dauphin Co., Pa. before Judge John Joseph Henry, inquest found Ann Roop of Middleton, Pa., wife of George Roop of Middleton, Pa. Millright, at Nov. 1, 1799, and at divers other times between Nov. 1, 1799 and Mar. 1, 1801 committed adultery with George Toot. She permitted George Toot to father a bastard child "on the body of her the said Ann." Mar. 13, 1802, she was found guilty of adultery and bastardy and sentenced to pay a fine of $1.00 to the Commonwealth, the costs of the trail and be confined in Dauphin Co., Pa. jail for three months.

Mar. 16, 1802 - Petition before the judge of the Court of Common Pleas of Lancaster Co., Pa. of George Roupe of Middletown, Dauphin Co., Pa. who was married about fourteen years ago to Ann Cassell. He accused her of adultery with George Toot and mentioned that she was found guilty by trial.

Sept. 18, 1802 - Subpoena to Ann Roup to appear in court in Philadelphia, Pa. Jan. 1, 1803, to answer the libel of her husband for a divorce.

Dec. 11, 1802 - Ann Roup testified that she was read the subpoena. She signed by mark.

Mar. 26, 1803 - The Supreme Court of Pennsylvania granted George Roupe a divorce from his wife Ann Roupe.

Dec. 1804 #12 Dauphin Co., Pa. Appearance Docket filed 1804 Jacob Hummel, defendant in divorce vs. Margaret Humel, plaintiff. Original papers now missing.

Mar. 1805 #56 Dauphin Co., Pa. Appearance Docket filed 1805 Hannah Eicholtz, defendant in divorce vs. John Eicholtz, plaintiff. Original papers now missing.

Feb. 1808 #34 Dauphin Co., Pa. Appearance Docket filed 1808 Catharine Brightbill, defendant in divorce vs. Michael Brightbill, plaintiff. Feb. 2, 1808, petition of Catharine Brightbill said that she married Michael Brightbill Mar. 16, 1806, and he later deserted her.

Sept. 1809 #36 Dauphin Co., Pa. Appearance Docket filed 1809, Philip Dietrich, defendant in divorce vs. Sarah Dietrich, plaintiff. Original papers now missing.

Dec. 1809 #23 Dauphin Co., Pa. Appearance Docket filed 1809 Philip Dietrich, defendant in divorce vs. Sarah Dietrich, plaintiff.

Original papers now missing.

Apr. 1810 #13 Dauphin Co., Pa. Appearance Docket filed 1810, Philip Dietrich, defendant in divorce vs. Sarah Dietrich, plaintiff. Original papers now missing.

Sept. 1810 #49 Dauphin Co., Pa. Appearance Docket filed 1810, Henry Summers, defendant in divorce vs. Margaret Summers, plaintiff. Apr. 30, 1810, petition of Margaret Summers by her father and next friend Charles Chamberlin. Margaret Summers stated that she married Henry Summers May 1, 1802. She accused him of adultery. Divorce subpoena was issued May 1, 1810.

Feb. 1811 #4 Dauphin Co., Pa. Appearance Docket filed 1811, Elizabeth Hanna, plaintiff in divorce vs. William R. Hanna, defendant. Original papers now missing.

Apr. 1811 #8 Dauphin Co., Pa. Appearance Docket filed 1811, Elizabeth Hanna, plaintiff in divorce vs. William R. Hanna, defendant. Original papers now missing.

Feb. 1812 #27 Dauphin Co., Pa. Appearance Docket filed 1812, Hugh McClauchlin, defendant in divorce vs. Mary McClauchlin, plaintiff. Dec. 6, 1811, petition of Mary McClauchlin by her next friend John Norton. She stated that she married Hugh McClauchlin Jan. 22, 1803. He mistreated her and frequently left her for long periods of time. In Nov. 1807 he was committed to Dauphin Co., Pa. jail for two years for larceny and he has not lived with her since that time.

Feb. 1812 #28 Dauphin Co., Pa. Appearance Docket filed 1812 Catharine Welsh, plaintiff in divorce vs. Michael Welsh, defendant. She petitioned the court Nov. 30, 1811, that she married Michael Welsh Mar. 3, 1798, and he deserted her without any just cause Jul. 1, 1798.

Feb. 1812 #29 Dauphin Co., Pa. Appearance Docket filed 1812 Phebe Ridge, plaintiff in divorce vs. Thomas Ridge, defendant. Sept. 5, 1811, petition of Phebe Ridge by her next friend James Murphy stated that she married Thomas Ridge in Mar. of 1807, and he abused her and she accused him of "turning her out of doors." Divorce subpoena was issued Dec. 7, 1811. Phebe Ridge signed her petition "by mark".

May 1812 #13 Dauphin Co., Pa. Appearance Docket filed 1812, Hugh McClauchlin, defendant in divorce vs. Mary McClauchlin, plaintiff. Original papers now missing.

May 1812 #58 Dauphin Co., Pa. Appearance Docket filed 1812 Catharine Welsh, plaintiff in divorce vs. Michael Welsh, defendant. Original papers now missing.

Nov. 1813 #41 Dauphin Co., Pa. Appearance Docket filed Oct. 1813 Eve Uhrich, plaintiff in divorce vs. Peter Uhrich, defendant. Original papers now missing.

May 1815 #23 Dauphin Co., Pa. Appearance Docket filed 1815 Robert Parker, defendant in divorce vs. Eleanor Parker, plaintiff. Original papers now missing.

Sept. 1815 #95 Dauphin Co., Pa. Appearance Docket filed Jul. 22, 1815. Elizabeth Hummell, plaintiff in divorce vs. Samuel Hummell, defendant. Original papers are illegible apparently because of poor quality microfilming.

Dec. 1815 #9 Dauphin Co., Pa. Appearance Docket filed Sept. 11, 1815. John Brestle, defendant in divorce vs. Mary Brestle, plaintiff. Original papers now missing.

Dec. 1815 #13 Dauphin Co., Pa. Appearance Docket filed Sept. 1815 Mary Dentler nee Smith, defendant in divorce vs. Soloman Dentler, plaintiff. Original papers now missing.

Dec. 1815 #21 Dauphin Co., Pa. Appearance Docket filed 1815 Dinah Hagerman, plaintiff in divorce vs. William Hagerman, defendant. Original papers now missing.

Apr. 1816 #45 Dauphin Co., Pa. Appearance Docket filed Mar. 1816. George Elsman, defendant in divorce vs. Margaret Elsman, plaintiff. The defendant pleaded not guilty to his wife's charges of abuse and insisted that his action did not cause her to leave him.

Sept. 1816 #122 Dauphin Co., Pa. Appearance Docket filed Jul. 15, 1816. Elizabeth Bowerman, plaintiff in divorce vs. William Bowerman, defendant. Original papers missing.

May 1817 #82 Dauphin Co., Pa. Appearance Docket filed Mar. 13, 1817. John A. Williams, defendant in divorce vs. Mary Williams, plaintiff. Original papers missing.

May 1817 #83 Dauphin Co., Pa. Appearance Docket filed Mar. 13, 1817. Daniel Campbell, defendant in divorce vs. Elizabeth Campbell, plaintiff.
Feb. 6, 1817 petition of Elizabeth Campbell formerly Elizabeth Ewalt of Harrisburg, Pa. by her next friend John Benjamin. She said

she was born in Pa. and married Daniel Campbell about twelve years ago and he deserted her over two years ago. She signed her petition "by mark".

May 1817 #84 Dauphin Co., Pa. Appearance Docket filed Mar. 13, 1817. Augustus Massaul, defendant in divorce vs. Eliza Massaul, plaintiff. Original papers now missing.

May 1817 #85 Dauphin Co., Pa. Appearance Docket filed Mar. 13, 1817. Mary Wollison, plaintiff in divorce vs. William Wollison, defendant. Original papers now missing.

May 1817 #98 Dauphin Co., Pa. Appearance Docket filed Mar. 20, 1817. Catharine Dewitt, plaintiff in divorce vs. William Dewitt, defendant. Original papers now missing.

Sept. 1817 #33 Dauphin Co., Pa. Appearance Docket filed May 20, 1817. John A. Williams, defendant in divorce vs. Mary Williams, plaintiff. Original papers now missing.

Sept. 1817 #34 Dauphin Co., Pa. Appearance Docket filed May 20, 1817. Augustus Massaul, defendant in divorce vs. Elizabeth Massaul, plaintiff. Original papers now missing.

Sept. 1817 #35 Dauphin Co., Pa. Appearance Docket filed May 20, 1817. Daniel Campbell, defendant in divorce vs. Elizabeth Campbell, plaintiff. Original papers now missing.

Sept. 1817 #57 Dauphin Co., Pa. Appearance Docket filed Jun. 1817. Peter Fox, defendant in divorce vs. Elizabeth Fox, plaintiff. Original papers now missing.

Sept. 1817 #193 Dauphin Co., Pa. Appearance Docket filed Aug. 1, 1817. Catharine Dewitt, plaintiff in divorce vs. William Dewitt, defendant. Original papers now missing.

May 1818 #30 Dauphin Co., Pa. Appearance Docket filed Feb. 21, 1818. Mary Reigart, plaintiff in divorce vs. Thomas Reigart, defendant. Original papers now missing.

May 1818 #111 Dauphin Co., Pa. Appearance Docket filed Mar. 1818. Nancy Swartz nee Bumbarger, defendant in divorce vs. Samuel Swartz, plaintiff. Original papers now missing.

Jun. 1818 #16 Dauphin Co., Pa. Appearance Docket filed May 8, 1818. Mary Reigart, plaintiff in divorce vs. Thomas Reigart, defendant. Original papers now missing.

Jun. 1818 #23 Dauphin Co., Pa. Appearance Docket filed May 15, 1818. James Dunlap, defendant in divorce vs. Mary Dunlap, plaintiff. Original papers now missing.

Oct. 1818 #161 Dauphin Co., Pa. Appearance Docket filed Sept. 2, 1818. James Dunlap, defendant in divorce vs. Mary Dunlap, plaintiff. Original papers now missing.

Dec. 1818 #26 Dauphin Co., Pa. Appearance Docket filed Oct. 31, 1818. Amelia Gray, plaintiff in divorce vs. George Gray, defendant. Petition of Amelia Gray by her brother and next friend William Duck stated that she married George Gray Jan. 31, 1814 and he deserted her in Jun. of 1816.

Mar. 1819 #21 Dauphin Co., Pa. Appearance Docket filed Dec. 28, 1818. Amelia Gray, plaintiff in divorce vs. George Gray, defendant. Original papers now missing.

Mar. 1820 #118 Dauphin Co., Pa. Appearance Docket filed Feb. 11, 1820. John McCreight, defendant in divorce vs. Mary McCreight, plaintiff. Original papers now missing.

May 1820 #84 Dauphin Co., Pa. Appearance Docket filed Jan. 1820. Daniel Stahl, defendant in divorce vs. Eve Stahl, plaintiff. Original papers now missing.

Jun. 1820 #12 Dauphin Co., Pa. Appearance Docket filed Mar. 16, 1820. John McCreight, defendant in divorce vs. Mary McCreight, plaintiff. Original papers now missing.

Jun. 1820 #30 Dauphin Co., Pa. Appearance Docket filed Mar. 21, 1820. Daniel Stahl, defendant in divorce vs. Eve Stahl, plaintiff. Original papers now missing.

Mar. 1821 #52 Dauphin Co., Pa. Appearance Docket filed Jan. 6, 1821. Catharine Miller, plaintiff in divorce vs. Henry Miller, defendant. Original papers now missing.

Mar. 1821 #77 Dauphin Co., Pa. Appearance Docket filed Jan. 18, 1821. Bernard Hoffman, defendant in divorce vs. Elizabeth Hoffman, plaintiff. Original papers now missing.

Jun. 1821 #30 Dauphin Co., Pa. Appearance Docket filed Mar. 26, 1821. Catharine Miller, plaintiff in divorce vs. Henry Miller, defendant. Original papers now missing.

Jun. 1821 #174 Dauphin Co., Pa. Appearance Docket filed May 8, 1821. Barbara Buchmeyer, plaintiff in divorce vs. John Buchmeyer, defendant. Original papers now missing.

Mar. 1822 #38 Dauphin Co., Pa. Appearance Docket filed Dec. 31, 1821. Martin Moyer, defendant in divorce vs. Nancy Moyer, plaintiff. Original papers now missing.

Mar. 1822 #39 Dauphin Co., Pa. Appearance Docket filed Dec. 31, 1821. Joseph S. Marshall, plaintiff in divorce vs. Mary Marshall, defendant. Original papers now missing.

Jun. 1822 #22 Dauphin Co., Pa. Appearance Docket filed Mar. 25, 1822. Eliza Chapman, plaintiff in divorce vs. John Chapman, defendant. Feb. 28, 1822 petition of Eliza Chapman by her next friend Casper Waggoner stated that she married John Chapman Jun. 8, 1817 but he deserted her in the fall of 1819. Eliza Chapman signed her petition "by mark." Subpoena issued for Jun. 1822 Term of Court.

Jun. 1822 #23 Dauphin Co., Pa. Appearance Docket filed Mar. 25, 1822. Jacob Baker, defendant in divorce vs. Barbara Baker. Petition for a divorce by Barbara Baker by her next friend John Miller. On Oct. 24, 1822 the sheriff testified that he could not find John Baker in his bailiwick.

Jun. 1822 #24 Dauphin Co., Pa. Appearance Docket filed Mar. 25, 1822. Leonard Gingerich, plaintiff in divorce vs. Catharine Gingerich nee Zimmerman. Original papers now missing.

Jun. 1822 #85 Dauphin Co., Pa. Appearance Docket filed Apr. 23, 1822. Martin Moyer, defendant in divorce vs. Mary Moyer, plaintiff. Original papers now missing.

Jun. 1822 #86 Dauphin Co., Pa. Appearance Docket filed Apr. 23, 1822. Joseph S. Marshall, plaintiff in divorce vs. Mary Marshall, defendant. Plaintiff objects to the taking of an appeal by the defendant.

Aug. 1822 #16 Dauphin Co., Pa. Appearance Docket filed Jul. 2, 1822. Barbara Baker, plaintiff in divorce vs. Jacob Baker, defendant. Petition of Barbara Baker by her next friend John Uhler for a divorce from her husband Jacob Baker. Alias subpoena issued Jul. 1, 1822. Sheriff reported Jacob Baker was not found in his bailiwick Oct. 24, 1822.

Aug. 1822 #27 Dauphin Co., Pa. Appearance Docket filed Jul. 9, 1822. Daniel Sullivan, defendant in divorce vs. Eliza Sullivan, plaintiff. Original papers now missing.

Nov. 1822 #6 Dauphin Co., Pa. Appearance Docket filed Aug. 21, 1822. Mary Lebo, plaintiff in divorce vs. Peter Lebo, defendant. Original papers now missing.

Nov. 1822 #81 Dauphin Co., Pa. Appearance Docket filed Oct. 14, 1822. Daniel Sullivan, defendant in divorce vs. Eliza Sullivan, plaintiff. Original papers now missing.

Aug. 1823 #8 Dauphin Co., Pa. Appearance Docket filed Apr. 24, 1823. Mary Carroll, plaintiff in divorce vs. William Carroll. Apr. 16, 1823 petition of Mary Carroll by her next friend Jacob Dubbs in which she stated she married William Carroll May 26, 1818. She accused him of adultery and that he deserted her in Apr. of 1819.

Aug. 1823 #9 Dauphin Co., Pa. Appearance Docket filed Apr. 21, 1823. Apr. 19, 1823 petition of Elizabeth Kline by her next friend George Uschlander. She married William Kline Sept. 11, 1820 and he deserted her in Mar. of 1821. She signed her petition "by mark." Subpoena was issued Apr. 21, 1823.

Aug. 1823 #10 Dauphin Co., Pa. Appearance Docket filed May 24, 1823. May 24, 1823 petition of Catharine Fritz by her next friend John Bigler. She married John Fritz more than forty years ago and he deserted her about twenty-seven years ago. She signed her petition "by mark."

Aug. 1823 #89 Dauphin Co., Pa. Appearance Docket filed May 24, 1823. Catharine Fritz, plaintiff in divorce vs. John Fritz, defendant. Original papers now missing.

Nov. 1823 #17 Dauphin Co., Pa. Appearance Docket filed Aug. 29, 1823. Mary Carrol, plaintiff in divorce vs. William Carrol, defendant. Original papers now missing.

Nov. 1823 #82 Dauphin Co., Pa. Appearance Docket filed Nov. 1, 1823. William Kline, defendant in divorce vs. Elizabeth Kline, plaintiff. Original papers now missing.

Nov. 1824 #21 Dauphin Co., Pa. Appearance Docket filed Aug. 1824. Sophia Mahen, plaintiff in divorce vs. William Mahen, defendant. Original papers now missing.

Jan. 1826 #61 Dauphin Co., Pa. Appearance Docket filed Dec.

28, 1825. Catharine Size, plaintiff in divorce vs. John Size, defendant. Original papers now missing.

Jan. 1826 #61 Dauphin Co., Pa. Appearance Docket filed Dec. 28, 1825. Peter Hawk, defendant in divorce vs. Susanna Hawk, plaintiff. Original papers are now missing.

Apr. 1826 #112 Dauphin Co., Pa. Appearance Docket filed Mar. 23, 1826. Catharine Size, plaintiff in divorce vs. John Size, defendant. Original papers now missing.

Apr. 1826 #113 Dauphin Co., Pa. Appearance Docket filed Mar. 23, 1826. Peter Hawk, defendant in divorce vs. Susanna Hawk, plaintiff. Original papers now missing.

Aug. 1826 #7 Dauphin Co., Pa. Appearance Docket filed Jul. 13, 1826. James Stamp, defendant in divorce vs. Rosamond Stamp, plaintiff. Apr. 1, 1826 petition of Rosamond Stamp by her next friend John H. Hartwig. She married James Stamp Sept. 23, 1820 and she accused him of abuse and failing to provide for her and her children.

Aug. 1826 #95 Dauphin Co., Pa. Appearance Docket filed Jun. 13, 1826. John Rough, plaintiff in divorce vs. Elizabeth Rough, defendant. Apr. 29, 1826 petition of John Rough of Hanover Twp., Dauphin Co., Pa. He married in Dec. of 1806 his present wife Elizabeth and she left him over two years ago without any just cause.

Nov. 1826 #40 Dauphin Co., Pa. Appearance Docket filed Sept. 1826. James Stamp, defendant in divorce vs. Rosamond Stamp, plaintiff. Original papers are now missing.

Nov. 1826 #41 Dauphin Co., Pa. Appearance Docket filed Sept. 1826. Henry Stahl, plaintiff in divorce vs. Margaret Stahl, defendant. Sept. 23, 1826 petition of Henry Stahl of the borough of Harrisburg, Pa. He married his present wife, Margaret, Nov. 18, 1821. He accused her of adultery and of deserting him.

Nov. 1826 #55 Dauphin Co., Pa. Appearance Docket filed Oct. 1826. Elizabeth Rough nee Forney, defendant in divorce vs. John Rough, plaintiff. Original papers are now missing.

Nov. 1826 #57 Dauphin Co., Pa. Appearance Docket filed Oct. 1826. Mary Willi, plaintiff in divorce vs. Samuel Willi, defendant. Jul. 20, 1826 petition of Mary Willi by her next friend Andrew Krause stated she married Samuel Willi who deserted her without any just cause. Mary Willi signed the petition "by mark."

Jan. 1827 #46 Dauphin Co., Pa. Appearance Docket filed Dec. 2, 1826. Mary Willi, plaintiff in divorce vs. Samuel Willi, defendant. Original papers are now missing.

Aug. 1828 #61 Dauphin Co., Pa. Appearance Docket filed Jul. 1828. Eleanor Walker, defendant in divorce vs. Henry Walker, plaintiff. May 29, 1828 petition of Henry Walker stated that he married his present wife Eleanor Jan. 28, 1822 and he accused her of adultery.

Aug. 1828 #125 Dauphin Co., Pa. Appearance Docket filed Jul. 9, 1828. Ann Brown, plaintiff in divorce vs. Christian Brown, defendant. Jul. 1828 petition of Ann Brown by her next friend Conrad Knessley. She married in Jun. of 1817 Christian Brown and he deserted her in Mar. of 1826. She signed her petition "by mark."

Nov. 1828 #24 Dauphin Co., Pa. Appearance Docket filed Sept. 12, 1828. Charles Cuff, plaintiff in divorce vs. Mahaley Jane Cuff, defendant. Aug. 16, 1828 petition of Charles Cuff for a divorce. He married Apr. 8, 1823 Mahaley Jane Brown and she deserted him in Feb. of 1824. He signed the petition "by mark." Court issued a subpoena Aug. 20, 1828.

Nov. 1828 #25 Dauphin Co., Pa. Appearance Docket filed Sept. 11, 1828. Ann Brown, plaintiff in divorce vs. Christian Brown, defendant. Original papers now missing.

Jan. 1829 #27 Dauphin Co., Pa. Appearance Docket filed Dec. 3, 1828. Charles Cuff, plaintiff in divorce vs. Mahaley Jane Cuff, defendant. Original papers now missing.

Apr. 1829 #52 Dauphin Co., Pa. Appearance Docket filed Feb. 11, 1829. Amanda B. Catlin, plaintiff in divorce vs. Charles Catlin, defendant. Feb. 10, 1829 petition of Amanda B. Catlin by her next friend Silas Marsh. She married Nov. 18, 1816 Charles Catlin and he deserted her May 21, 1823.

Apr. 1829 #58 Dauphin Co., Pa. Appearance Docket filed Feb. 17, 1829. Daniel Stahl, defendant in divorce vs. Eve Stahl, plaintiff. Subpoena issued Aug. 29, 1829. Divorce granted Dec. 3, 1829.

Aug. 1829 #31 Dauphin Co., Pa. Appearance Docket filed May 8, 1829. Daniel Stahl, defendant in divorce vs. Eve Stahl, plaintiff. Original papers now missing.

Aug. 1829 #40 Dauphin Co., Pa. Appearance Docket filed May 18, 1829. Elizabeth Hummel, plaintiff in divorce vs. Samuel Hummel, defendant. Apr. 17, 1829 petition of Elizabeth Hummel by her next friend John Brubaker. She married Samuel Hummel Nov. 21, 1816. She accused him of abuse which forced her to leave him Aug. 16, 1828. She signed her petition "by mark."

Aug. 1829 #111 Dauphin Co., Pa. Appearance Docket filed Jul. 1, 1829. Amanda B. Catlin, plaintiff in divorce vs. Charles Catlin. Original papers now missing.

Aug. 1829 #127 Dauphin Co., Pa. Appearance Docket filed Jul. 10, 1829. Jacob Keyser, plaintiff in divorce vs. Mary Keyser, defendant. Jul. 8, 1829 petition of Jacob Keyser of Middletown, Dauphin Co., Pa. He married Mary Reiley in 1807 and they had five children. He accused her of adultery and deserting him over four years ago.

Nov. 1829 #78 Dauphin Co., Pa. Appearance Docket filed Oct. 21, 1829. Jacob Keyser, plaintiff in divorce vs. Mary Keyser, defendant. Original papers now missing.

Jan. 1830 #8 Dauphin Co., Pa. Appearance Docket field 1829. John Mattes, defendant in divorce vs. Sophia Mattes, plaintiff. Sept. 15, 1829 petition of Sophia Mattes by her next friend John Conrad. She married John Mattes who she accused of endangering her life and deserting her in Jun. of 1827. She signed her petition "by mark." Subpoena issued Nov. 16, 1829.

Apr. 1830 #75 Dauphin Co., Pa. Appearance Docket filed Feb. 20, 1830. John Mattes, defendant in divorce vs. Sophia Mattes plaintiff. Original papers now missing.

Aug. 1830 #107 Dauphin Co., Pa. Appearance Docket filed Jun. 14, 1830. James Barret, defendant in divorce vs. Priscilla Barret, plaintiff. Jun. 12, 1830 petition of Priscilla Barret by her next friend George Espy. She married James Barret in Apr. of 1825 and he deserted her Apr. 16, 1825.

Aug. 1830 #137 Dauphin Co., Pa. Appearance Docket filed Jun. 23, 1830. Adam Shaffner, plaintiff in divorce vs. Mary Shaffner, defendant. Jun. 12, 1830 petition of Adam Shaffner of Lower Paxton Twp., Dauphin Co., Pa. who married in Dec. of 1825 Mary Shitz who deserted him over two years ago. Subpoena issued Jun. 21, 1830.

Aug. 1830 #167 Dauphin Co., Pa. Appearance Docket field Jul. 6, 1830. Hetty Roop, plaintiff in divorce vs. Joseph Roop, defendant. Jul. 6, 1830 petition of Hetty Roop by her next friend John Hatfield. She married Joseph Roop Dec. 25, 1823 and he deserted her in Jun. of 1828. Subpoena issued Jul. 8, 1830.

Nov. 1830 #37 Dauphin Co., Pa. Appearance Docket filed Sept. 28, 1830. Hetty Roop, plaintiff in divorce vs. Joseph Roop, defendant. Original papers now missing.

Aug. 1830 #27 Dauphin Co., Pa. Appearance Docket filed Apr. 28, 1831. Elizabeth Harman, plaintiff in divorce vs. Philip Harman, defendant. Apr. 25, 1830 petition of Elizabeth Harman by her next friend Matthias Deibler. She married Philip Harman in 1800 and he left her eighteen or twenty years ago. He now has children by another woman and they lived in the same twp. as she does. She signed her petition "by mark." Subpoena issued Apr. 28, 1831.

Aug. 1831 #75 Dauphin Co., Pa. Appearance Docket filed Jun. 3, 1831. Elizabeth Orendorf, plaintiff in divorce vs. John Orendorf, defendant. Jun. 3, 1831 petition of Elizabeth Orendorf by her next friend Philip Stiller. She married about forty years ago Dr. John Orendorf. By his rude treatment he drove her out in Sept. of 1830. She returned in Mar. of 1831 but his violence forced her to leave again. Elizabeth Orendorf signed her petition "by mark." Subpoena issued Jun. 3,1831.

Apr. 1832 #193 Dauphin Co., Pa. Appearance Docket filed Mar. 7, 1832. John Moyer, defendant in divorce vs. Magdalena Moyer, plaintiff. Mar. 6, 1832 petition of Magdalena Moyer of Mifflin Twp., Dauphin Co., Pa. by her next friend Nicholas Hoffman. She married John Moyer but he left her over two years ago taking with him the money and real estate that she had before their marriage and leaving her destitute. He also took the $80.00 a year she received from the estate of her late husband Jacob Dietrich. Magdalena Moyer signed her petition "by mark." Subpoena issued Mar. 7, 1832.

Nov. 1832 #6 Dauphin Co., Pa. Appearance Docket filed Aug. 28, 1832. Cornelius Baskins, plaintiff in divorce vs. Martha Baskins, defendant. Aug. 27, 1832 petition of Conrad Baskins of Halifax Twp., Dauphin Co., Pa. who had lived in Pa. since his birth. He married in Feb. of 1818 Martha Kessler. He accused her of adultery. Subpoena issued Aug. 27, 1832. Depositions were to be taken on the third Monday of Nov. 1832.

Nov. 1832 #73 Dauphin Co., Pa. Appearance Docket filed Oct. 1832. Alexander Burney, defendant in divorce vs. Rachel Burney, plaintiff. Sept. 26, 1832 petition of Rachel Burney by her next friend William Cochran. She married in Jul. of 1828 Alexander Burney who deserted her in the fall of 1829. Subpoena issued Sept. 28, 1832.

Nov. 1832 #74 Dauphin Co., Pa. Appearance Docket filed Oct. 1832. Clarinda Updegrove, defendant in divorce vs. Thomas Updegrove, plaintiff. Oct. 1, 1832 petition of Thomas Updegrove stated that he married Clarinda Mar. 14, 1826. She deserted him in Jun. of 1830. Subpoena issued Oct. 1, 1832.

Jan. 1833 #4 Dauphin Co., Pa. Appearance Docket filed Nov. 1832. Elizabeth Moyer, plaintiff in divorce vs. Thomas Moyer, defendant. Original papers now missing.

Jan. 1833 #34 Dauphin Co., Pa. Appearance Docket filed Nov. 1832. Clarinda Updegrove, defendant in divorce vs. Thomas Updegrove, plaintiff. Original papers now missing.

Jan. 1833 #35 Dauphin Co., Pa. Appearance Docket filed Nov. 1832. Alexander Burney, defendant in divorce vs. Rachel Burney, plaintiff. Original papers now missing.

Apr. 1833 #35 Dauphin Co., Pa. Appearance Docket filed Feb. 1833. Mary Knight, plaintiff in divorce vs. Richard Knight, defendant. Dec. 26, 1832 petition of Mary Knight by her next friend George Boyer. She married in 1816 Richard Knight. She accused him of "adulterous practices with divers persons." He drove her from his house in the fall of 1828 and failed to give her any support. A subpoena was issued Dec. 26, 1832.

Nov. 1833 #24 Dauphin Co., Pa. Appearance Docket filed Aug. 31, 1833. Michael Crum, defendant in divorce vs. Martha Crum, plaintiff. Original papers now missing.

Jan. 1834 #44 Dauphin Co., Pa. Appearance Docket filed Dec. 7, 1833. Amanda Feighery, plaintiff in divorce vs. Michael Feighery, defendant. Sept. 22, 1833 petition of Amanda Feighery by her next friend Philo B. Parsons. She married Michael Feighery Jul. 16, 1827 and he deserted her Aug. 24, 1830.

Apr. 1834 #25 Dauphin Co., Pa. Appearance Docket filed Feb. 4, 1834. Martin Rowe, defendant in divorce vs. Susannah Rowe, plaintiff. Dec. 30, 1833 petition of Susannah Rowe by her next friend David Ressel. She married in Jan. of 1833 Martin Rowe and he left her in Feb. of 1833. She had a male child born from this union and she requested a divorce and alimony. Susannah Rowe signed her petition "by mark." Subpoena issued Jan. 27, 1834.

Apr. 1834 #119 Dauphin Co., Pa. Appearance Docket filed Mar. 1834. Amanda Feighery, plaintiff in divorce vs. Michael Feighery, defendant. Original papers now missing.

Apr. 1834 #121 Dauphin Co., Pa. Appearance Docket filed Mar. 11, 1834. Ann Harman, defendant in divorce vs. Daniel Harman, plaintiff. Mar. 10, 1834, petition of Daniel Harman of Millersburg, Upper Paxton Twp., Dauphin Co., Pa. He married in Apr. of 1832, Ann Hunter. He accused her of adultery and requested a divorce.

Apr. 1834 #145 Dauphin Co., Pa. Appearance Docket filed Mar. 19, 1834. John Tinney, defendant in divorce vs. Sarah Tinney, plaintiff. Aug. 5, 1834, petition of John Tinney regarding the libel of Sarah Tinney by her next Nancy Simmerton for a divorce. They were married in 1833. He denies her accusations of abuse.

Apr. 1834 #149 Dauphin Co., Pa. Appearance Docket filed Mar. 19, 1834. John P. Meader, defendant in divorce vs. Margaret Meader, plaintiff. Mar. 19, 1834, petition of Margaret Meader nee Margaret Franklin by her next friend Jonathan Franklin. She married John P. Meader Aug. 18, 1830. He deserted her Feb. 22, 1832. Subpoena was issued Mar. 21, 1834.

Aug. 1834 #45 Dauphin Co., Pa. Appearance Docket filed May 1834. Ann Harman, defendant in divorce vs. Daniel Harman, plaintiff. Alias Subpoena was issued Aug. 28, 1834, for the third Monday of Nov. 1834 with a notice of such to be placed in the Harrisburg, Pa. newspaper for four consecutive weeks prior to that third Monday of Nov. 1834.

Aug. 1834 #195 Dauphin Co., Pa. Appearance Docket filed Jul. 11, 1834. Margaret Loop, plaintiff in divorce vs. Peter C. Loop, defendant. Jul. 5, 1834, petition of Margaret Loop by her next friend Samuel Garmon stated that she married Peter C. Loop Jun. 14, 1812. He abused her and she left him in 1815. Subpoena was issued Jul. 7, 1834.

Aug. 1834 #211 Dauphin Co., Pa. Appearance Docket filed Jul. 1834. Elizabeth Stouffer, plaintiff in divorce vs. Jacob Stouffer, defendant. Jul. 19, 1834, petition of Elizabeth Stouffer by her next friend Ephriam Heller both of Swatara Twp., Dauphin Co., Pa. She married Jacob Stouffer in Sept. of 1804 and he deserted her in Mar. of 1822.

Nov. 1834 #101 Dauphin Co., Pa. Appearance Docket filed Sept. 26, 1834. Elizabeth Stouffer, plaintiff in divorce vs. Jacob Stouffer, defendant. Original papers now missing.

Apr. 1835 #48 Dauphin Co., Pa. Appearance Docket filed Feb. 10, 1835. Elizabeth Alward, plaintiff in divorce vs. John Alward, defendant. May 11, 1835 petition of John Alward that the charges of abuse to his wife were not true and his wife had no just cause to leave him.

Apr. 1835 #57 Dauphin Co., Pa. Appearance Docket filed Feb. 16, 1835. Barbara Imshoffstall, defendant in divorce vs. Jonas Imshoffstall, plaintiff. Jan. 21, 1835 petition of Jonas Imshoffstall of Lykens Twp., Dauphin Co., Pa. He married his present wife Barbara in Jun. of 1831 and she deserted him "a considerable time past."

Apr. 1835 #87 Dauphin Co., Pa. Appearance Docket filed Mar. 11, 1835. Susanna Grove, plaintiff in divorce vs. William Grove, defendant. Mar. 5, 1835 petition of Susanna Grove of Hanover Twp., Dauphin Co., Pa. by her next friend Soloman Uriah. She married Oct. 1, 1827 William Grove of Hanover Twp., Dauphin Co., Pa. and he separated from her in Dec. of 1831. She signed her petition "by mark."

Nov. 1835 #48 Dauphin Co., Pa. Appearance Docket filed Oct. 17, 1835. Nancy Pleasant, plaintiff in divorce vs. William Pleasant, defendant. Oct. 17, 1835 petition of Nancy Pleasant by her next friend Philip A. Jones stated that she married William Pleasant in 1822 and he deserted her in 1826. She signed the petition "by mark." Subpoena issued Oct. 17, 1835.

Jan. 1836 #39 Dauphin Co., Pa. Appearance Docket filed Dec. 22, 1835. Nancy Pleasant, plaintiff in divorce vs. William Pleasant, defendant. Original papers now missing.

Apr. 1836 #10 Dauphin Co., Pa. Appearance Docket filed Feb. 2, 1836. Adam Kettering, defendant in divorce vs. Catharine Kettering, plaintiff. Jan. 16, 1836 petition of Catharine Kettering by her next friend Adam Grittinger stated she married Adam Kettering Feb. 15, 1828. She accused him of "adultery with a certain Elizabeth Stouffer" causing her to leave him. Subpoena issued Feb. 2, 1836 for the first day of Apr. 1836 term.

Aug. 1836 #22 Dauphin Co., Pa. Appearance Docket filed May 17, 1836. Ann Maria Dorsey, plaintiff in divorce vs. Henry Dorsey, defendant. Apr. 1, 1836 petition of Ann Maria Dorsey by her next friend Jacob Stroman. She married Henry Dorsey Apr. 10, 1829 and he deserted her in the spring of 1833. Subpoena issued Aug. 2, 1836.

Aug. 1836 #36 Dauphin Co., Pa. Appearance Docket filed Jun. 7, 1836. Margaret Pool, plaintiff in divorce vs. Nathaniel Pool, defendant. May 30, 1836 petition of Margaret Pool by her next friend

Henry F. Ginsley stated she married Nathaniel Pool Aug. 31, 1831 and he deserted her Jul. 25, 1833. Subpoena issued May 31, 1836.

Jan. 1837 #29 Dauphin Co., Pa. Appearance Docket filed Dec. 21, 1836. Owen Quinn, defendant in divorce vs. Susanna Quinn, plaintiff. Dec. 13, 1836 petition of Susanna Quinn by her next friend Henry Fox. She stated that she married Owen Quinn Jun. 26, 1834 and he deserted her Oct. 1, 1836. Subpoena issued Dec. 14, 1836.

Apr. 1837 #16 Dauphin Co., Pa. Appearance Docket filed Feb. 23, 1837. Owen Quinn, defendant in divorce vs. Susanna Quinn, plaintiff. Original papers now missing.

Aug. 1837 #1 Dauphin Co., Pa. Appearance Docket filed Apr. 20, 1837. Margaret Greer, plaintiff in divorce vs. Philip Greer, defendant. Apr. 20, 1837 petition of Margaret Greer by her next friend and father Peter Rickabaugh. She stated that she married Philip Greer Dec. 8, 1836. Since then she has been informed her husband was lawfully married to Mary Ann Fowler in the city of Boston, Mass. May 23, 1830. Philip Greer and his wife Mary Ann lived as husband and wife four, five or six years. Mary Ann Greer was still his wife when he married her (Margaret) and Mary Ann was still living as of Apr. 14, 1837 and is believed to be living yet. Subpoena issued Apr. 20, 1837.

Jan. 1838 #22 Dauphin Co., Pa. Appearance Docket filed Dec. 9, 1837. Rebecca Matter, plaintiff in divorce vs. Michael Matter, Jr., defendant. Original papers now missing.

Aug. 1838 #4 Dauphin Co., Pa. Appearance Docket filed Apr. 19, 1838. Daniel Prosser, plaintiff in divorce vs. Elvira Prosser, defendant. Apr. 18, 1838 petition of Daniel Prosser stated that he married Elvira Bixby Mar. 3, 1833. He accused her of adultery with (Rollie?) Lawton. Subpoena issued Apr. 19, 1838.

Aug. 1838 #36 Dauphin Co., Pa. Appearance Docket filed Jun. 1, 1838. James Resley, defendant in divorce vs. Mary Resley, plaintiff. May 25, 1838 petition of Mary Resley by her next friend Jacob Mason. She said she married James Resley Nov. 25, 1833 and he deserted her Nov. 26, 1833. Subpoena issued Jun. 1, 1838. Court granted a divorce Jan. 21, 1839.

Nov. 1838 #7 Dauphin Co., Pa. Appearance Docket filed Aug. 31, 1838. Elizabeth Styer, plaintiff in divorce vs. Michael Styer, defendant. Jul. 17, 1838 petition of Elizabeth Styer by her next friend Henry Fox. She stated she married Michael Styer Aug. 11, 1831 and he deserted her May 31, 1835. Subpoena issued Aug. 31, 1838.

Nov. 1838 #9 Dauphin Co., Pa. Appearance Docket filed Sept. 3, 1838. Daniel Prosser, plaintiff in divorce vs. Elvira Prosser, defendant. Original papers now missing.

Nov. 1838 #10 Dauphin Co., Pa. Appearance Docket filed Sept. 4, 1838. James Resley, defendant in divorce vs. Mary Resley, plaintiff. Original papers now missing.

Nov. 1838 #58 Dauphin Co., Pa. Appearance Docket filed Nov. 5, 1838. Daniel Hatton, defendant in divorce vs. Esther Hatton, plaintiff. Oct. 23, 1838 petition of Esther Hatton by her next friend Solomon Urish. She stated that she married Daniel Hatton Oct. 27, 1836 and he deserted her Oct. 27, 1836 (that same day). She signed her petition "by mark."

Nov. 1838 #59 Dauphin Co., Pa. Appearance Docket filed Nov. 5, 1838. Agnes Mitchell, plaintiff in divorce vs. William Mitchell, defendant. Oct. 19, 1838 petition of Agnes Mitchell by her next friend James B. Small stated that she married William Mitchell Feb. 2, 1827 and he deserted her in Aug. of 1829.

Jan. 1839 #62 Dauphin Co., Pa. Appearance Docket filed Jan. 3, 1839. Elizabeth Styer, plaintiff in divorce vs. Michael Styer, defendant. Original papers now missing.

Jan. 1839 #63 Dauphin Co., Pa. Appearance Docket filed Jan. 3, 1839. Daniel Hatton, defendant in divorce vs. Esther Hatton, plaintiff. Original papers now missing.

Jan. 1839 #64 Dauphin Co., Pa. Appearance Docket filed Jan. 3, 1839. Agnes Mitchell, plaintiff in divorce vs. William Mitchell, defendant. Original papers now missing.

Nov. 1839 #56 Dauphin Co., Pa. Appearance Docket filed Oct. 15, 1839. Catherine Hawk, plaintiff in divorce vs. George Michael, Hawk defendant. Oct. 7, 1839 petition of Catherine Hawk by her next friend Frederick Harner stated she married George Michael Hawk Aug. 2, 1819. She accused him of abusing her especially in the last four months they lived together thus forcing her to leave him Aug. 17, 1839. Catherine Hawk signed her petition "Citty Hawk." Subpoena issued Oct. 14, 1839.

Apr. 1840 #57 Dauphin Co., Pa. Appearance Docket filed Feb. 21, 1839. Peter Roberts, plaintiff in divorce vs. Catharine Roberts, defendant. Feb. 21, 1840 petition of Peter Roberts stated that he married his present wife Catherine about eight years ago. He accused her of adultery. Subpoena issued Feb. 21, 1840.

Apr. 1840 #75 Dauphin Co., Pa. Appearance Docket filed Mar. 2, 1840. Elizabeth Loy, plaintiff in divorce vs. John Loy, defendant. Mar. 6, 1840 petition of Elizabeth Loy stated that she married John Loy in 1826 and he deserted her without any just cause in 1836. Elizabeth Loy signed her petition "by mark."

Aug. 1840 #19 Dauphin Co., Pa. Appearance Docket filed Apr. 29, 1840. Elizabeth Martin, plaintiff in divorce vs. James Martin, defendant. Apr. 20, 1840 petition of Elizabeth Martin by her next friend George Brubaker. She married James Martin Apr. 12, 1838 and he deserted her Apr. 21, 1838. Elizabeth Martin signed her petition "by mark."

Nov. 1840 #15 Dauphin Co., Pa. Appearance Docket filed Aug. 17, 1840. Barbara Lentz, defendant in divorce vs. Frederick Lentz, plaintiff. Aug. 17, 1840 petition of Frederick Lentz stated that over forty years ago he married Barbara (Koeminch? Koemmel?). He stated that she deserted him in 1804 and about two years thereafter "undertook to marry herself to Isaac (Dunlap?) with whom she cohabited as man and wife for years." This petition was written in very poor handwriting making it very hard for me to accurately abstract.

Jan. 1841 #57 Dauphin Co., Pa. Appearance Docket filed Dec. 20, 1840. Barbara Lentz, defendant in divorce vs. Frederick Lentz, plaintiff. Original papers now missing.

Jan. 1841 #92 Dauphin Co., Pa. Appearance Docket filed Jan. 13, 1841. Christiana Kendig, defendant in divorce vs. John Kendig, plaintiff. Original papers now missing.

Apr. 1841 #1 Dauphin Co., Pa. Appearance Docket filed May 11, 1841. Jacob Ehrgott, defendant in divorce vs. Salome Ehrgott, plaintiff. On May 3, 1841 depositions were taken before Mordecai McKinley, Esq. at his office in the borough of Harrisburg, Pa.
Michael Ehrgott testified he was upwards of twenty-two years of age and a nephew of the libellant and respondent. He came to this town between three and four years ago. At that time his aunt and uncle were considered as man and wife. She left him last November after he had whipped her. Jacob Ehrgott is a gardener and keeps a nursery and attends a market twice a week. Michael Ehrgott boarded with his uncle about two years and worked for his uncle during that time. He had known him to sell two or three dollars sometimes more and sometimes less.

Deposition of John Wener of Middletown, Dauphin Co., Pa. aged nearly thirty-two years of age. He lived with Jacob Ehrgott one year and two months and left him about last Christmas. Jacob Ehrgott and Salome Ehrgott lived together as man and wife. He saw him whip her at least two or three times, and heard her scream. When he is sober he is a good-hearted man. "When he is drunk he is bad. He was drunk pretty often." He feels Jacob Ehrgott has more debts than property. During the summer he keeps two hands which he pays half a dollar a day and boarding of $8.00 or $9.00 a month and boarding. He heard Jacob Ehrgott say he would pay off all his debts and live like a gentleman. On the last day of December he told him of his wife leaving him.

Deposition of Peter Kretter aged thirty years and a resident of Harrisburg. He lives with Jacob Ehrgott and works for him. Last fall he worked for him at $9.00 a month and boarding. Since the first of Apr. he gets sixteen dollars a month which he is to get until the first of Nov. Jacob Ehrgott sold this spring a hundred trees at twenty-five cents apiece.

Deposition of Christian Rutterspach aged fifty-two years and a resident of Harriburg, Pa. He had known Jacob Ehrgott five or six years. He heard him say he made eight dollars last spring selling trees and fifteen dollars of that was in cash. Jacob Ehrgott kept tavern at the Black Horse sign in the tavern where Umberger now keeps. He sold out this spring and now boards at Umbergers. He sold his bed, cupboard and chairs on Saturday for twenty-five dollars.

Court decreed this divorce final May 8, 1841.

Aug. 1841 #91 Dauphin Co., Pa. Appearance Docket filed Jun. 26, 1841. Rosanna Clark, plaintiff in divorce vs. Edward Clark, defendant. Jun. 25, 1841 petition of Rosanna Clark stated that she married Edward Clark in Aug. of 1837 and he later deserted her.

Aug. 1841 #93 Dauphin Co., Pa. Appearance Docket filed Jun. 28, 1841. Caroline Wolfersberger, defendant in divorce vs. Levi Wolfersberger, plaintiff. Jun. 28, 1841 petition of Levi Wolfersberger of Hanover Twp., Dauphin Co., Pa. merchant. He stated that he married Caroline R. Witt Mar. 26, 1839 and she deserted him Jun. 1, 1839.

Nov. 1841 #14 Dauphin Co., Pa. Appearance Docket filed Aug. 23, 1841. Barbara Howalt, plaintiff in divorce vs. George Howalt, defendant. Original papers are now missing.

Nov. 1841 #25 Dauphin Co., Pa. Appearance Docket filed Aug. 27, 1841. Mary Ann Yocum, plaintiff in divorce vs. Isaac Yocum, defendant. Original papers now missing.

Nov. 1841 #26 Dauphin Co., Pa. Appearance Docket filed Aug. 27, 1841. Caroline Wolfersberger, defendant in divorce vs. Levi Wolfersberger, plaintiff. Original papers are now missing.

Jan. 1842 #54 Dauphin Co., Pa. Appearance Docket filed Dec. 17, 1841. Isaac Yocum, defendant in divorce vs. Mary Ann Yocum, plaintiff. Original papers are now missing.

Jan. 1842 #56 Dauphin Co., Pa. Appearance Docket filed Dec. 18, 1841. Rosanna Clark, plaintiff in divorce vs. Edward Clark, defendant. Original papers are now missing.

Jan. 1842 #57 Dauphin Co., Pa. Appearance Docket filed Dec. 8, 1841. Barbara Howalt, plaintiff in divorce vs. George Howalt, defendant. Original papers are now missing.

Apr. 1842 #29 Dauphin Co., Pa. Appearance Docket filed Feb. 4, 1842. Margaret Pool, plaintiff in divorce vs. Nathaniel Pool, defendant. Feb. 2, 1842 petition of Margaret Pool by her next friend Henry F. Gensley stated that she married Nathaniel Pool Aug. 31, 1831. He deserted her in Dec. of 1839. Subpoena issued Feb. 4, 1842.

Apr. 1842 #44 Dauphin Co., Pa. Appearance Docket filed Feb. 10, 1842. Charles Webner, plaintiff in divorce vs. Harriet Webner, defendant. Mar. 7, 1842 Court appointed Frederick Hummel and John Houser, Esq. to take depositions in this case Mar. 29, 1842 for Frederick Hummel and Apr. 5, 1842 for John Houser, Esq. both at their office in Harrisburg, Pa.

Mar. 7, 1842 deposition of Rev. Henry Wagner, Pastor of the German Reformed Church of the borough of Lebanon who presented a true copy of the Church Record- "Married - on the 28th December 1833, by the Rev. Henry Krah, Mr. Charles Webner to Miss Harriet Salady."

Mar. 29, 1842 deposition of William Rann aged about thirty-six years. He knew both parties about four years and stated "I did not think she behaved as she ought to. From her behavior I am of the opinion that she had criminal connection with a certain George Murphy." William Rann signed his deposition "by mark."

Mar. 29, 1842 deposition of Sarah Rann aged about thirty-one years who had known both parties about four years. She stated that Mrs. Webner "often told me that she would never take up with her husband the Libellant but that she would consider him George Murphy as her husband. She told me that her youngest child which she called George was the son of George Murphy. She told me even she went away from her husband's house that she was going to hunt him George Murphy up. I have know (*sic*) doubt myself that Harriet Webner hat (*sic*) criminal connections with George Murphy and further this deponent saith not." Sarah Rann signed her deposition "by mark."

Apr. 1842 #71 Dauphin Co., Pa. Appearance Docket filed Feb. 26, 1842. Elizabeth Kling, plaintiff in divorce vs. Henry Kling, defendant. Feb. 3, 1842, petition of Elizabeth Kling by her next friend Abraham Martin stated that she married Henry Kling, tailor, late of Harrisburg, Pa. Aug. 17, 1837. He deserted her in Dec. of 1839. Subpoena issued Feb. 7, 1842. Elizabeth Kling signed her petition "by mark."

Apr. 1842 #105 Dauphin Co., Pa. Appearance Docket filed Mar. 15, 1842. Anna Maria Ort, plaintiff in divorce vs. Conrad Ort, defendant. Mar. 14, 1842, petition of Anna Maria Ort by her next friend Charles White stated that she married Jan. 1, 1830 Conrad Ort late of Mifflin Twp., Dauphin Co., Pa. He deserted her in Jan. of 1834. Subpoena issued Mar. 15, 1842.

Aug. 1842 #19 Dauphin Co., Pa. Appearance Docket filed Apr. 29, 1842. Margaret Pool, plaintiff in divorce vs. Nathaniel Pool, defendant. Court ordered sheriff to place notice of divorce action for four successive weeks in newspaper and appointed C.A. Snyder, Esq. of Harrisburg, Pa. to take depositions Aug. 22, 1842. Nov. 10, 1842, deposition of Henry F. Gensley stated that Nathaniel Pool deserted his family three years and seven months ago and has not visited them or provided for them thereafter. Nov. 10, 1842, deposition of Matthew Wilson who testified that Henry F. Gensley had told the true facts.

Aug. 1842 #76 Dauphin Co., Pa. Appearance Docket filed May 26, 1842. Anna Maria Ort, plaintiff in divorce vs. Conrad Ort, defendant. Original papers are now missing.

Jan. 1843 #4 Dauphin Co., Pa. Appearance Docket filed Nov. 23, 1842. John Croffert, plaintiff in divorce vs. Magdalena Croffert, defendant. Oct. 7, 1842, petition of John Croffert who married Dec. 5, 1819, Magdalena Ronberger late of Lykens Twp., Dauphin Co., Pa. She deserted him in Aug. of 1839. Subpoena issued Nov. 23, 1842.

Aug. 1842 #62 Dauphin Co., Pa. Appearance Docket filed May 20, 1843. John Hinds, defendant in divorce vs. Mary Hinds, plaintiff. May 16, 1843, petition of Mary Hinds by her next friend Samuel R. Dunlap. She married John Hinds in Sept. 1841. He abused her and she left him May 8, 1843. Mary Hinds signed her petition "by mark."

Aug. 1843 #79 Dauphin Co., Pa. Appearance Docket filed May

26, 1843. George M. Haag, plaintiff in divorce vs. Catherine Haag, defendant. Original papers are now missing.

Jan. 1844 #20 Dauphin Co., Pa. Appearance Docket filed Dec. 8, 1843. Barbara Hummel, defendant in divorce vs. Joseph Hummel, plaintiff. Oct. 16, 1843, petition of Joseph Hummel of Halifax Twp., Dauphin Co., Pa. stated he married his present wife Barbara, May 9, 1841, and she deserted him over two years ago.

Jan. 1844 #50 Dauphin Co., Pa. Appearance Docket filed Dec. 19, 1843. Clarissa Singer, plaintiff in divorce vs. Samuel Singer, defendant. Original papers are now missing.

Apr. 1844 #25 Dauphin Co., Pa. Appearance Docket filed Jan. 29, 1844. Simon Yeager, plaintiff in divorce vs. Sarah Yeager, defendant. Dec. 25, 1843, petition of Simon Yeager stated that he married his present wife Sarah Feb. 2, 1841 and she deserted him "a day almost immediately following their marriage." Court granted him a divorce Jan. 15, 1844.

Apr. 1844 #26 Dauphin Co., Pa. Appearance Docket filed Jan. 29, 1844. John Williams, defendant in divorce vs. Maria Williams, plaintiff. Jan. 15, 1844, petition of Maria Williams by her next friend George Molson stated that she married John Williams and he deserted her in May of 1838. Maria Williams signed her petition "by mark." Subpoena issued Jan. 16, 1844.

Aug. 1844 #2 Dauphin Co., Pa. Appearance Docket filed Apr. 16, 1844. Catherine Knauff nee Peters, defendant in divorce vs. David Knauff, plaintiff. Original papers are now missing.

Aug. 1844 #30 Dauphin Co., Pa. Appearance Docket filed Jun. 1, 1844 John Gruver, defendant in divorce vs. Mary Gruver, plaintiff. Mar. 5, 1844, petition of Mary Gruver by her next friend Samuel Manuel. She married John Gruver Jan. 10, 1834, who by cruel and barbarous treatment endangered her life. He deserted her about two years ago and is now in Dauphin county jail for larceny on a two year sentence which will expire about Apr. 20, 1845. Mary Gruver signed her petition "by mark."

Aug. 1844 #81 Dauphin Co., Pa. Appearance Docket filed Jul. 29, 1844. John Williams, defendant in divorce vs. Maria Williams, plaintiff. Original papers are now missing.

Nov. 1844 #10 Dauphin Co., Pa. Appearance Docket filed Aug. 31, 1844. Catharine Segraves, plaintiff in divorce vs. Charles Segraves, defendant. Aug. 16, 1844, petition of Catharine Segraves by her next friend Jacob H. Swartz stated that she married Charles Segraves Feb. 5, 1837. He deserted her in Mar. of 1842 and he "is now living with Mary Horst, who it is said has had two children by him the said Charles Segraves." Subpoena issued Aug. 19, 1844.

Nov. 1844 #36 Dauphin Co., Pa. Appearance Docket filed Oct. 14, 1844. Elizabeth Umberger, defendant in divorce vs. John Umberger, plaintiff. Oct. 10, 1844 petition of John Umberger who stated that he married Elizabeth Mar. 12, 1840. She deserted him in Nov. 1841 almost three years ago. Subpoena issued Oct. 10, 1844.

Nov. 1844 #49 Dauphin Co., Pa. Appearance Docket filed Oct. 24, 1844. John Gruver, defendant in divorce vs. Mary Gruver, plaintiff. Original papers are now missing.

Nov. 1844 #54 Dauphin Co., Pa. Appearance Docket filed Nov. 2, 1844. Levi Woolfinger, plaintiff in divorce vs. Mary Ann Woolfinger nee Williams, defendant. Original papers are now missing.

Nov. 1844 #67 Dauphin Co., Pa. Appearance Docket filed Nov. 5, 1844. George McCauley, plaintiff in divorce vs. Molly McCauley, defendant. Jul. 31, 1844 petition of Molly McCauley by her next friend John Bechtold stated that she married George McCauley in 1839. He deserted her in the beginning of Jun. 1840. Subpoena issued Aug. 20, 1844.

Jan. 1845 #9 Dauphin Co., Pa. Appearance Docket filed Nov. 30, 1844. Levi Woolfinger, plaintiff in divorce vs. Mary Ann Woolfinger nee Williams, defendant. Original papers are now missing.

Jan. 1845 #16 Dauphin Co., Pa. Appearance Docket filed Dec. 6, 1844. Ann Gusswiler, plaintiff in divorce vs. Daniel Gusswiler, defendant. Dec. 3, 1844 petition of Ann Gusswiler late Ann Carpenter by her next friend Henry Zimmerman stated that she married Daniel Gusswiler Sept. 16, 1841 by Rev. John Ulrich of Carlisle, Pa. Her husband deserted her Aug. 15, 1841. She accused him of personal abuse and unkind treatment.

Jan. 1845 #57 Dauphin Co., Pa. Appearance Docket filed Jan. 9, 1845. Elizabeth Umberger, defendant in divorce vs. John Umberger, plaintiff. Original papers are now missing.

Jan. 1845 #64 Dauphin Co., Pa. Appearance Docket filed Jan. 13, 1845. John Heimer, plaintiff in divorce vs. Mary Heimer, defendant. Nov. 28, 1844 petition of John Heimer stated that he married his present wife Mary, Jun. 19, 1833. He accused her of adultery. Subpoena issued Nov. 28, 1844.

Apr. 1845 #7 Dauphin Co., Pa. Appearance Docket filed Jan. 25, 1845. George McCauley, plaintiff in divorce vs. Molly McCauley, defendant. Original papers are now missing.

Apr. 1845 #41 Dauphin Co., Pa. Appearance Docket filed Mar. 14, 1845. Jacob Fortney, defendant in divorce vs. Rachel Fortney, plaintiff. Original papers are now missing.

Apr. 1845 #51 Dauphin Co., Pa. Appearance Docket filed Mar. 22, 1845. Ann Gusswiler, plaintiff in divorce vs. Daniel Gusswiler, defendant. Original papers are now missing.

Aug. 1845 #82 Dauphin Co., Pa. Appearance Docket filed Jun. 2, 1845. Henry T. Coleman, defendant in divorce vs. Louisa E. Coleman, plaintiff. May 6, 1845 petition of Lucinda E. Coleman by her next friend and brother Joseph (Foulton?) stated that she married Henry T. Coleman Feb. 11, 1832. She accused him of a failure to provide for her, unkind treatment and personal abuse as well as deserting her Nov. 1, 1844.

Aug. 1845 #83 Dauphin Co., Pa. Appearance Docket filed Jun. 28, 1845. Mary Cook, plaintiff in divorce vs. Patrick Cook, defendant. Apr. 22, 1845 petition of Mary Cook by her next friend John Haas and she stated that she married Patrick Cook Jan. 27, 1834. He deserted her without any just cause Aug. 24, 1842. Mary Cook signed her petition "by mark."

Aug. 1845 #142 Dauphin Co., Pa. Appearance Docket filed Aug. 6, 1845. Richard Pople, plaintiff in divorce vs. Susan Pople nee McNight, defendant. Apr. 19, 1845 petition of Richard Pople stated he married Susan McNight in 1829. He accused her of adultery and deserting him over two years ago. Richard Pople signed his petition "by mark." Subpoena issued May 2, 1845.

Jan. 1846 #36 Dauphin Co., Pa. Appearance Docket filed Dec. 22, 1845. Richard Pople, plaintiff in divorce vs. Susan Pople nee McNight, defendant. Original papers are now missing.

Jan. 1846 #36 Dauphin Co., Pa. Appearance Docket filed Dec. 23, 1845. James Battis, defendant in divorce vs. Martha Battis, plaintiff. Nov. 25, 1845 petition of Martha Battis by her next friend James Pople. She stated that she married James Battis in 1841 and he deserted her in 1842. Martha Battis signed her petition "by mark."

Jan. 1846 #72 Dauphin Co., Pa. Appearance Docket filed Jan. 9, 1846. Henry T. Coleman, defendant in divorce vs. Louisa E. Coleman, plaintiff. Original papers are now missing.

Jan. 1846 #73 Dauphin Co., Pa. Appearance Docket filed Jan. 9, 1846. Mary Cook, plaintiff in divorce vs. Patrick Cook, defendant. Original papers are now missing.

Apr. 1846 #138 Dauphin Co., Pa. Appearance Docket filed Apr. 25, 1846. John Himer, plaintiff in divorce vs. Mary Himer, defendant. Original papers are now missing.

Nov. 1846 #2 Dauphin Co., Pa. Appearance Docket filed Aug. 19, 1846. Mary Cooper, plaintiff in divorce vs. Philip Cooper, defendant. Jul. 20, 1846 petition of Mary Cooper who stated that she married Philip Cooper Mar. 28, 1844. He deserted her more than two years ago. Mary Cooper signed her petition "by mark."

Nov. 1846 #52 Dauphin Co., Pa. Appearance Docket filed Oct. 20, 1846. Catharine Buseres, plaintiff in divorce vs. Martin Buseres, defendant. Sept. 23, 1846 petition of Catharine Buseres by her next friend Daniel Farling. She stated that she married Martin Buseres Aug. 23, 1838. She suffered such indignities to her person that she was force to leave him Aug. 18, 1845. Catharine Buseres signed her petition "by mark."

Nov. 1846 #53 Dauphin Co., Pa. Appearance Docket filed Oct. 24, 1846. Julian Kendig, plaintiff in divorce vs. John Kendig, defendant. Oct. 23, 1846 petition of Julian Kendig of the borough of Harrisburg, Pa. She stated that she married John Kendig Oct. 21, 1821 and he deserted her in Oct. of 1843 and is now in the Eastern Penitentiary upon a conviction of robbery and larceny in Lancaster Co., Pa. John Kendig had "conducted himself in a most brutal manner for the past three years." Julian Kendig signed her petition "by mark."

Jan. 1847 #50 Dauphin Co., Pa. Appearance Docket filed Dec. 31, 1846. Julian Kendig, plaintiff in divorce vs. John Kendig, defendant. Original papers are now missing.

Apr. 1847 #26 Dauphin Co., Pa. Appearance Docket filed Feb. 19, 1847. Lewis Burtle, defendant in divorce vs. Susan Margaret Burtle, plaintiff. Jan. 12, 1847 petition of Susan Margaret Burtle who stated that she married Lewis Burtle in Jul. of 1844 in the Borough of Harrisburg, Pa. She left him in the fall of 1846. Her husband had a continual habit of drunkenness followed by cruel and barbarous treatment of herself. She signed her petition "by mark."

Apr. 1847 #41 Dauphin Co., Pa. Appearance Docket filed Mar. 10, 1847. Benjamin F. Shue, defendant in divorce vs. Sarah Shue, plaintiff. Mar. 10, 1847 petition of Sarah Shue by her next friend Samuel Midlan. She stated that she married Benjamin F. Shue Mar. 2, 1845. He abused her and she was forced to leave him Feb. 13, 1847. Subpoena issued Mar. 10, 1847.

Aug. 1847 #74 Dauphin Co., Pa. Appearance Docket filed Jul. 8, 1847. Emeline Stephenson, plaintiff in divorce vs. Thomas Stephenson, defendant. Jul. 3, 1847 petition of Emeline Stephenson by her next friend Charles T. Muench. She stated that she married Sept. 11, 1845 Thomas Stephenson who deserted her over two years ago without any just cause. Emeline Stephenson signed her petition "by mark."

Nov. 1847 #11 Dauphin Co., Pa. Appearance Docket filed Aug. 21, 1847. Christian Weygandt, defendant in divorce vs. Mary Weygandt, plaintiff. Aug. 5, 1847 petition of Mary Weygandt by her next friend Elizabeth Gensley before B. McClenachan, justice of the peace in Schuylkill Co., Pa. Mary Weygandt had married Christian Weygandt in 1834 and he deserted her in 1836 without any just cause. Subpoena issued Aug. 21, 1847.

Nov. 1847 #15 Dauphin Co., Pa. Appearance Docket filed Aug. 21, 1847. Elizabeth Jones, plaintiff in divorce vs. Josiah Jones, defendant. Aug. 21, 1847 petition of Elizabeth Jones by her next friend David Dennis. She stated that she married Josiah Jones Sept. 13, 1845 and on Nov. 9, 1846 and at other times he abused her and endangered her life causing her to leave him in Mar. of 1847. Elizabeth Jones requested a divorce and alimony of a third of his estate and future income. She signed her petition "by mark."

Jan. 1848 #23 Dauphin Co., Pa. Appearance Docket filed Nov. 26, 1847. Christian Weygandt, defendant in divorce vs. Mary Weygandt, plaintiff. Original papers are now missing.

Aug. 1848 #34 Dauphin Co., Pa. Appearance Docket filed May 30, 1848. Catharine Hushener, defendant in divorce vs. William Hushener, plaintiff. She was born Catharine Culp and she denied the charges made by her husband in a libel for divorce. She claimed that Henry Means did not commit adultery with her but he was only a friend and he left for the West some twelve years ago. Catharine Hushener signed her petition "by mark."

Nov. 1848 #10 Dauphin Co., Pa. Appearance Docket filed Sept. 7, 1848. Susan Sessamon, plaintiff in divorce vs. Thomas Sessamon, defendant. Sept. 2, 1848 petition of Susan Sessamon by her next friend Thomas Benjamin. She stated that she married Thomas Sessamon Jul. 28, 1825 and from the time of his marriage he never supported his family, he abused her and his children. He knocked her down and beat her till she was black and "choked her till she was strangled." Susan Sessamon signed her petition "by mark." Subpoena issued Sept. 8, 1848.

Jan. 1849 #9 Dauphin Co., Pa. Appearance Docket filed Dec. 1, 1848. Ann Elizabeth Johns, plaintiff in divorce vs. John Henry Johns, defendant. Original papers are now missing.

Apr. 1849 #27 Dauphin Co., Pa. Appearance Docket filed Feb. 7, 1849. Abraham Boyer, plaintiff in divorce vs. Catharine Boyer. Feb. 7, 1849 petition of Abraham Boyer who stated that he married Catharine Shreck Apr. 1, 1842. She deserted him the very next day. Court granted him a divorce May 15, 1850.

Apr. 1849 #35 Dauphin Co., Pa. Appearance Docket filed Feb. 13, 1849. Jacob Buffington, plaintiff in divorce vs. Rebecca Buffington, defendant. Feb. 12, 1849 petition of Jacob Buffington stated that in Feb. of 1843 he married Rebecca Alspach who deserted him Feb. 7, 1846.

Apr. 1849 #42 Dauphin Co., Pa. Appearance Docket filed Feb. 20, 1849. Susannah Huber, defendant in divorce vs. John Huber, plaintiff. Feb. 19, 1849 petition of John Huber of Dauphin Co., Pa. who married Susannah Daniel in Mar. "he thinks in the year of our Lord one Thousand Eight Hundred and Forty Four." She deserted him in May of 1846. Subpoena issued Feb. 19, 1849.

Aug. 1849 #19 Dauphin Co., Pa. Appearance Docket filed May 8, 1849. Elizabeth Garverich, plaintiff in divorce vs. John Garverich, defendant. Apr. 17, 1849 petition of Elizabeth Garverich who married John Garverich Dec. 19, 1829. He deserted her Jun. 18, 1846. Elizabeth Garverich signed her petition "by mark."

Aug. 1849 #20 Dauphin Co., Pa. Appearance Docket filed May 9, 1849. Mary Main, defendant in divorce vs. George Main, plaintiff. May 7, 1849 petition of George Main who stated that he married Mary Allen Oct. 27, 1844. He accused her of adultery with one Daniel Giken "and divers other persons."

Aug. 1849 #60 Dauphin Co., Pa. Appearance Docket filed Jun.

25, 1849. Abraham Boyer, plaintiff in divorce vs. Catharine Boyer, defendant. Original papers are now missing.

Nov. 1849 #39 Dauphin Co., Pa. Appearance Docket filed Oct. 16, 1849. Elizabeth Robison, late Elizabeth Cork, plaintiff in divorce vs. Greenbury Robison, defendant. Oct. 12, 1849 petition of Elizabeth Robison by her next friend Curry Taylor stated that she married Greenbury Robison Dec. 3, 1842. He deserted her Nov. 2, 1843. Subpoena issued Oct. 15, 1849. Court granted her a divorce May 15, 1850.

Jan. 1850 #14 Dauphin Co., Pa. Appearance Docket filed Nov. 28, 1849. Abraham McNeal, defendant in divorce vs. Juliann McNeal, plaintiff. Nov. 26, 1849 petition of Juliann McNeal by her next friend Frederick Hake. She stated that she married Abraham McNeal Mar. 2, 1834. She accused him of adultery with Susana Ray and that he turned "his wife out of doors" in 1849 and "at divers and various times" he abused her. Finally over six months ago he deserted her. Subpoena issued Nov. 26, 1849. Court granted Juliann McNeal a divorce Aug. 23, 1851 and ordered that Abraham McNeal pay all the costs.

Jan. 1850 #44 Dauphin Co., Pa. Appearance Docket filed Dec. 26, 1850. Elizabeth Robinson, plaintiff in divorce vs. Greenbury Robinson, defendant. Original papers are now missing.

Apr. 1850 #23 Dauphin Co., Pa. Appearance Docket filed Feb. 8, 1850. Anna Ohmer, plaintiff in divorce vs. Jacob S. Ohmer, defendant. Jan. 15, 1850 petition of Anna Ohmer by her next friend John Snyder stated that she married Jacob S. Ohmer Nov. 19, 1847. He deserted her over two years ago. She was born in Pa. and has lived there ever since. Subpoena issued Feb. 7, 1850.

Apr. 1850 #53 Dauphin Co., Pa. Appearance Docket filed Mar. 2, 1850. Margaret Cover, plaintiff in divorce vs. Samuel Cover, defendant. Mar. 1, 1850 petition of Margaret Cover by her next friend Jacob Seider stated she married Samuel Cover. He deserted her Oct. 5, 1847 and Margaret Cover wanted a divorce. She signed her petition "by mark". Subpoena issued Mar. 1, 1850 for the next term.

Aug. 1850 #6 Dauphin Co., Pa. Appearance Docket filed Apr. 26, 1850. Joseph Manley, plaintiff in divorce vs. Sarah Manley, defendant. Apr. 8, 1850 petition of Joseph Manley stated that he married Sarah Dewees Mar. 12, 1847. He accused her of adultery with John T. Gaynov. They separated in Jul. of 1849. Subpoena issued Apr. 22, 1850.

Aug. 1850 #7 Dauphin Co., Pa. Appearance Docket filed Apr. 26, 1850. Anna Ohmer, plaintiff in divorce vs. Jacob S. Ohmer, defendant. Original papers are now missing.

Aug. 1850 #29 Dauphin Co., Pa. Appearance Docket filed May 16, 1850. Nancy F. Cook, plaintiff in divorce vs. James M. Cook, defendant. Apr. 18, 1850 petition of Nancy F. Cook late Nancy F. Young by her next friend Amos W. Young stated that she married James M. Cook Sept. 11, 1847. Her husband deserted her Apr. 8, 1848.

Aug. 1850 #68 Dauphin Co., Pa. Appearance Docket filed Jul. 8, 1850. Margaret Cover, plaintiff in divorce vs. Samuel Cover, defendant. Original papers are now missing.

Aug. 1850 #80 Dauphin Co., Pa. Appearance Docket filed Jul. 17, 1850. Franklin Lee, plaintiff in divorce vs. Sarah Lee, defendant. Jul. 17, 1850 petition of Franklin Lee of Harrisburg, Pa., silver plater, who stated that he married Sarah Frantz Feb. 16, 1850. He accused her of adultery. Subpoena issued Jul. 17, 1850. Aug. 29, 1850 Sarah Lee by her attorney Thomas J. Jordan answered the libel of Franklin Lee and denied his accusation of adultery and said that she was a true, chaste and faithful wife. Dec. 4, 1850 the Court granted Franklin Lee a divorce from his wife Sarah Lee.

Nov. 1850 #17 Dauphin Co., Pa. Appearance Docket filed Sept. 2, 1850. Joseph Manley, plaintiff in divorce vs. Sarah Manley, defendant. Original papers are now missing.

Nov. 1850 #18 Dauphin Co., Pa. Appearance Docket filed Sept. 2, 1850. Samuel Trump, plaintiff in divorce vs. Sarah Trump, defendant. Jul. 26, 1850 petition of Samuel Trump stated that in 1845 he married Sarah Mick. They lived together for five months then she deserted him without any just cause in 1846. Subpoena issued Sept. 2, 1850.

Jan. 1851 #25 Dauphin Co., Pa. Appearance Docket filed Dec. 23, 1850. Richard Walton, defendant in divorce vs. Sarah Walton, plaintiff. Dec. 21, 1850 petition of Sarah Walton by her next friend Levi Adams stated that she married Richard Walton Apr. 20, 1841. He deserted her without any just cause Nov. 4, 1846. Sarah Walton signed her petition "by mark." Subpoena issued Dec. 23, 1850. Alias subpoena issued for third Monday of Aug. 1850 and four weeks of notice to be published in *The Keystone*.

Apr. 1851 #103 Dauphin Co., Pa. Appearance Docket filed Mar. 26, 1851. Richard Walton, defendant in divorce vs. Sarah Walton, plaintiff. Original papers are now missing.

Apr. 1851 #119 Dauphin Co., Pa. Appearance Docket filed Apr. 2, 1851. John Wesley Galey, plaintiff in divorce vs. Mary Ann Galey, defendant. Mar. 17, 1851 petition of John Wesley Galey by his attorney John J. Schulie. He stated that he married Mary Ann Morris Oct. 15, 1840 and his wife left him several times in 1849 and "offered him many insults and indignities." Over eight months ago she left him for good and is now living with John Burd. Subpoena issued Mar. 25, 1851.

Aug. 1851 #15 Dauphin Co., Pa. Appearance Docket filed May 3, 1851. Catharine Blattenberger, plaintiff in divorce vs. Isaac Blattenberger, defendant. Apr. 23, 1851 petition of Catharine Blattenberger formerly Catherine Wolf by her next friend Matilda Mayers, late Matilda Wolf. She stated that she married Isaac Blattenberger Mar. 15, 1837 who deserted her over fourteen years ago.

Aug. 1851 #19 Dauphin Co., Pa. Appearance Docket filed May 5, 1851. Catharine Sprigman, plaintiff in divorce vs. Henry Sprigman, defendant. Apr. 2, 1851 petition of Catharine Sprigman by her next friend Manning Shankland stated that she married Henry Sprigman Dec. 4, 1826. Her husband abused her and forced her to leave him Mar. 31, 1851. Subpoena issued May 5, 1851 for Aug. 7, 1851. Court granted divorce Nov. 25, 1851.

Aug. 1851 #58 Dauphin Co., Pa. Appearance Docket filed Jun. 18, 1851. Catharine Matter, defendant in divorce vs. Joseph Matter, plaintiff. Apr. 3, 1851 petition of Joseph Matter of Wisconisco Twp., Dauphin Co., Pa., who married in 1832 Catharine (Gerger?). She deserted him Mar. 15, 1837. For part of her absence she cohabited with and had criminal intercourse with George Sallade of Dauphin Co., Pa. whom she sued for fornication and bastardy. Subpoena issued Jun. 18, 1851.

Nov. 1851 #1 Dauphin Co., Pa. Appearance Docket filed Aug. 18, 1851. Catharine Weaver, plaintiff in divorce vs. John M. Weaver, defendant. Aug. 15, 1851 petition of Catharine Weaver by her next friend John Gouber. She stated that she married John M. Weaver Dec. 13, 1837 and he deserted her without any just cause Sept. 16, 1847. Catharine Weaver signed her petition "by mark." Subpoena issued Aug. 18, 1851.

Nov. 1851 #8 Dauphin Co., Pa. Appearance Docket filed Aug. 25, 1851. Michael Shank, defendant in divorce vs. Mary Shank, plaintiff. Aug. 22, 1851 petition of Mary Shank by her next friend George L. McClure which stated that she married Michael Shank Oct. 26,

1848. He deserted her without any just cause Aug. 12, 1851. "The said Michael is much addicted to the drinking of ardent spirits, that for the last two years he has been almost constantly intoxicated and during that time he has by continued ill treatment rendered the condition of your libellant intolerable." Mary Shank signed her petition "by mark." Subpoena issued Aug. 23, 1851.

Nov. 1851 #11 Dauphin Co., Pa. Appearance Docket filed Sept. 2, 1851. Clarissa M. Singer, plaintiff in divorce vs. Samuel Singer, defendant. Sept. 1, 1851 petition of Clarissa M. Singer by her next friend John H. Fox stated that she married Samuel Singer Jun. 13, 1839. He abused her and thereby forced her to leave him in Nov. of 1844. Subpoena issued Sept. 2, 1851.

Nov. 1851 #12 Dauphin Co., Pa. Appearance Docket filed Sept. 2, 1851. Elizabeth Seiders, defendant in divorce vs. Henry Seiders, plaintiff. Jun. 9, 1851 petition of Henry Seiders who stated that he married Jun. 20, 1844 Elizabeth his present wife. He accused her of adultery with John Outts and said that they separated Dec. 1, 1844. Subpoena issued Sept. 2, 1851.

Jan. 1852 #7 Dauphin Co., Pa. Appearance Docket filed Nov. 21, 1851. Catharine Fauver, defendant in divorce vs. George Fauver, plaintiff. Feb. 21, 1852 Court appointed Daniel A. Muench, Esq., justice of the peace to take depositions at his office in Halifax Twp., Dauphin Co., Pa., Apr. 19, 1852 between 10 A.M. and 4 P.M. Apr. 19, 1852 Nicholas Boyer, Esq. who was subpoenaed to appear failed to appear but he did testify on May 1, 1852 that he married George and Catharine Fauver May 20, 1841 and "at that time said Catharine lived with her father Daniel Miller. Deponent further says that to the best of his knowledge said George Fauver and Catharine his wife, have not lived together as husband and wife, since their marriage and that said Catharine has been living with her father since their marriage and is still living there and further saith not." Apr. 19, 1852 deposition of Jacob E. Snyder of Jackson Twp., Dauphin Co., Pa. taken at the office of Daniel A. Muench, justice of the peace at Fisherviller Jackson Twp., Dauphin Co., Pa. He stated "that he had lived with Daniel Miller the father of Catharine Fauver, the defendant, and that he was from the fall of 1850, to the spring of the ensuing year, living with the said Daniel Miller, where said Catharine Fauver had her home. Deponent in conversation with said Catharine, heard her say that she would go to live with her husband George Fauver, provided he would leave his mother's house and after Mrs. Fauver (plaintiff's mother) had died, said defendant told deponent that her husband Geo. Fauver had been with her and requested her to come and live with him, but that she had told him that she would never live with him and further saith not."

Jun. 10,1852 Deposition made at the office of Daniel A. Muench, justice of the peace at Fisherville, Jackson Twp., Dauphin Co., Pa. stated "Elizabeth Fauver, of Jefferson Township, Dauphin County being first duly sworn saith that in the spring of A.D. 1847, on her way to the town of Halifax, deponent called at the house of Daniel Miller where Catharine Fauver the defendant had her home and in a certain conversation they had together, concerning George Fauver (the plaintiff) said Catharine remarked that she did not care if George would look for another wife, and get married, so that she the defendant might get clear of him, that she would look out for herself and so might he, and she was satisfied if he would do so for, she would never live with her said husband as long as she lived. Said Catharine did not assign any reason or cause at that time why she would not live with her husband, deponent further saith not." She signed her deposition "by mark". Aug. 19, 1852 court granted the divorce.

Jan. 1852 #12 Dauphin Co., Pa. Appearance Docket filed Nov. 26, 1851. Daniel Fessler, defendant in divorce vs. Rebecca Fessler, plaintiff. Nov. 11, 1851 petition of Rebecca Fessler by her next friend William Reiley Fessler. She stated that she married Daniel Fessler in Mar. of 1827. He deserted her in Feb. of 1844. Rebecca Fessler was of Harrisburg, Pa. when she submitted her petition and she signed "by mark." Subpoena issued Nov. 17, 1851.

Jan. 1852 #25 Dauphin Co., Pa. Appearance Docket filed Dec. 3, 1851. Catharine Weaver, plaintiff in divorce vs. John M. Weaver, defendant. Court ordered on Apr. 28, 1852 the sheriff to made proclamation of divorce notice for defendant to appear for one week in one newspaper printed in Harrisburg, Pa. Aug. 14, 1852 E. Williams, sheriff reported that he had published this proclamation in the *Whig State Journal.*

Apr. 1852 #6 Dauphin Co., Pa. Appearance Docket filed Jan. 22, 1852. Jonas Imshoffstall, plaintiff in divorce vs. Susanna Imshoffstall, defendant. Jan. 22, 1852 petition of Jonas Imshoffstall of Lyken Twp., Dauphin Co., Pa. He married on "the (left blank) day of June or" in the summer of 1836 Susanna Umholtz. She deserted him over two years ago. Subpoena issued Jan. 22, 1852.

Apr. 1852 #8 Dauphin Co., Pa. Appearance Docket filed Jan. 23, 1852. Caroline Sheeley, plaintiff in divorce vs. John Sheeley, defendant. Jan. 17, 1852 petition of Caroline Sheeley by her next friend Jacob Baab stated that she married John Sheeley Jul. 4, 1848. He deserted her over two years ago. Subpoena issued Jan. 23, 1852.

Apr. 1852 #9 Dauphin Co., Pa. Appearance Docket filed Jan. 23, 1852. Michael Shank, defendant in divorce vs. Mary Shank, plaintiff. Jan. 14, 1852 petition of Mary Shank by her next friend George L. McClure. She stated that she married Michael Shank and he abused her causing them to separate Aug. 20, 1851. She signed her petition "by mark." Subpoena issued Jan. 23, 1852. Court granted her a divorce May 8, 1852.

Apr. 1852 #51 Dauphin Co., Pa. Appearance Docket filed Feb. 20, 1852. John Tipin, defendant in divorce vs. Mary Tipin, plaintiff. Feb. 16, 1852 petition of Mary Tipin by her next friend Joseph Novinger stated that she married John Tipin Nov. 23, 1845. He deserted her Jun. 1, 1846. She signed her petition "by mark." Subpoena issued Feb. 20, 1852. Nov. 23, 1852 Court granted her a divorce.

Apr. 1852 #80 Dauphin Co., Pa. Appearance Docket filed Mar. 18, 1852. Daniel Fessler, defendant in divorce vs. Rebecca Fessler, plaintiff. Aug. 14, 1852 Sheriff E.C. Williams reported that he had not placed proclamations in newspaper because plaintiff refused to pay for the publication notice that the Court on May 22, 1852 had ordered the sheriff to publish in one newspaper for four successive weeks.

Apr. 1852 #81 Dauphin Co., Pa. Appearance Docket filed Mar. 18, 1852. Charles Seiler, plaintiff in divorce vs. Nancy Seiler, defendant. Mar. 12, 1852 petition of Charles Seiler who married Nancy Spencer Dec. 26, 1833. They lived together as man and wife for twelve years and then she deserted him without any just cause Dec. 25, 1845. Subpoena issued Mar. 18, 1852.

Apr. 1852 #112 Dauphin Co., Pa. Appearance Docket filed Apr. 3, 1852. Samuel Trump, plaintiff in divorce vs. Sarah Trump, defendant. Apr. 3, 1852 petition of Samuel Trump stated that he married Sarah Mick Nov. 17, 1845. She deserted him without any just or reasonable cause about the middle of May 1846. Samuel Trump signed his petition "by mark." Subpoena issued Apr. 3, 1852.

Aug. 1852 #3 Dauphin Co., Pa. Appearance Docket filed Apr. 26, 1852. Abraham Fegly, defendant in divorce vs. Sarah Fegly, plaintiff. Apr. 26, 1852 petition of Sarah Fegly late Sarah Trotman by her next friend George Hoffman. She married Apr. 9, 1849 Abraham Fegely who deserted her without any just cause Mar. 17, 1850. She also accused him of abusing her while they lived together. Sarah Fegely signed her petition "by mark."

Aug. 1852 #4 Dauphin Co., Pa. Appearance Docket filed Apr. 26, 1852. John Tipen, defendant in divorce vs. Mary Tipen, plaintiff. Aug. 19, 1852 the court ordered the sheriff to make proclamation of the subpoena.

Aug. 1852 #10 Dauphin Co., Pa. Appearance Docket filed Apr. 28, 1852. Caroline Sheeley, plaintiff in divorce vs. John Sheeley, defendant. Original papers are now missing.

Aug. 1852 #48 Dauphin Co., Pa. Appearance Docket filed May 27, 1852. Elizabeth Jones, plaintiff in divorce vs. Josiah Jones, defendant. May 21, 1852 petition of Elizabeth Jones by her next friend Robert Murphy stated that she married Josiah Jones Sept. 30, 1845. He abused her and she left him Apr. 1, 1852. Subpoena issued May 27, 1852.

Aug. 1852 #74 Dauphin Co., Pa. Appearance Docket filed Jul. 6, 1852. Daniel Witzell, defendant in divorce vs. Rehecca C. Witzell, plaintiff. Jul. 3, 1852 petition of Rebecca C. Witzell by her next friend George O'Neil stated that she married Daniel Witzell Nov. 7, 1843. He abandoned her and his family in 1847. Subpoena issued Jul. 5, 1852.

Nov. 1852 #4 Dauphin Co., Pa. Appearance Docket filed Aug. 17, 1852. Reuman Smallwood, plaintiff in divorce vs. Juliann Smallwood, defendant. Reuman Smallwood's petition stated that he married Juliann Yeates Nov. 25, 1850. She deserted him without any just cause May 10, 1851 and later she committed adultery "with a certain Bratten." Reuman Smallwood signed his petition "by mark."

Nov. 1852 #5 Dauphin Co., Pa. Appearance Docket filed Aug. 17, 1852. Mary Eppler, defendant in divorce vs. Tobias Eppler, plaintiff. Aug. 17, 1852 petition of Tobias Eppler of Londonderry Twp., Dauphin Co., Pa. He married Mary Lehman either May 30, 1832 or May 30, 1833 and she deserted him without any just or reasonable cause Jul. 8, 1850.

Nov. 1852 #6 Dauphin Co., Pa. Appearance Docket filed in 1852. Abraham Fegely, defendant in divorce vs. Sarah Fegely, plaintiff. Nov. 18, 1852 the court ordered that divorce proclamation be made.

Nov. 1852 #20 Dauphin Co., Pa. Appearance Docket filed Aug. 31, 1852. Daniel Witzell, defendant in divorce vs. Rebecca Witzell, plaintiff. Dec. 2, 1852 court ordered sheriff to publish in one Harrisburg newspaper the subpoena for divorce. Sheriff reported that he took the notice to the printers Dec. 21, 1852.

Nov. 1852 #21 Dauphin Co., Pa. Appearance Docket filed Aug. 30, 1852. Catharine Kinderknecht, defendant in divorce vs. George Kinderknecht. Aug. 24, 1852 petition of George Kinderknecht stated that he married in 1848 Catharine McCord. They lived together for five months then she deserted him. He accused her of adultery of having a child by someone unknown to him. Subpoena issued Aug. 31, 1852.

Nov. 1852 #68 Dauphin Co., Pa. Appearance Docket filed Oct. 14, 1852. Amelia S. Mase, defendant in divorce vs. John Mase, plaintiff. Oct. 8, 1852 petition of John Mase stated that he married Amelia S. Goldden Dec. 8, 1846. In pursuance of business and with a view to better his condition he has been living for the past few years in Lebanon and Dauphin Counties, Pa. By correspondence his wife has known where he was but remained absent. They have been separated over two years. Subpoena issued Oct. 9, 1852. Apr. 17, 1853 court ordered the sheriff to make proclamation of divorce for four successive weeks prior to May 17, 1853. May 17, 1853 Sheriff E.C. Williams reported it was published in the *Whig State Journal.*

Jan. 1853 #5 Dauphin Co., Pa. Appearance Docket filed Nov. 18, 1852. Frederick Shupp, plaintiff in divorce vs. Catharine Shupp, defendant. Nov. 16, 1852 petition of Frederick Shupp stated that he married Catharine Harten Nov. 18, 1850 and she deserted him without any just or reasonable cause over two years ago. Subpoena issued Nov. 18, 1852.

Jan. 1853 #6 Dauphin Co., Pa. Appearance Docket filed Nov. 18, 1852. Ann M. Durgin, plaintiff in divorce vs. John Durgin, defendant. Oct. 18, 1852 petition of Anna Maria Durgin by her next friend Josiah Jones stated that she married John Durgin Nov. 25, 1847 and without any just or reasonable cause he deserted her Oct. 4, 1850. Subpoena issued Nov. 18, 1852. (Note: Aug. 1852 #48 divorce of Josiah Jones! Wonder if there is a story behind these two divorce actions!)

Jan. 1853 #11 Dauphin Co., Pa. Appearance Docket filed Nov. 24, 1852. Amelia S. Mase, defendant in divorce vs. John Mase, plaintiff. Original papers are now missing.

Jan. 1853 #25 Dauphin Co., Pa. Appearance Docket filed Dec. 9, 1852. Joseph H. Bates, defendant in divorce vs. Mary Sophia Bates, plaintiff. Dec. 9, 1852 petition of Mary Sophia Bates by her next friend James Finney stated that she married Joseph H. Bates Aug. 11, 1811. He deserted her without any just or reasonable cause Sept. 1, 1849. Subpoena issued Dec. 9, 1852.

Apr. 1853 #1 Dauphin Co., Pa. Appearance Docket filed Jan. 19, 1853. Jeremiah Kirk, plaintiff in divorce vs. Nancy Kirk late Nancy Sillyman, defendant. Jan. 17, 1853 petition of Jeremiah Kirk stated that he married Nancy Sillyman Mar. 14, 1820. She deserted him without any just or reasonable cause Jan. 15, 1851. Subpoena issued Jan. 10, 1853.

Apr. 1853 #12 Dauphin Co., Pa. Appearance Docket filed Jan. 27, 1853. Mary Ann Weltcher, plaintiff in divorce vs. Saren E. Weltcher, defendant. Jan. 24, 1853 petition of Mary Ann Weltcher by her next friend Chambers C. Mullin stated that the married Saren E. Weltcher Sept. 184- (rest of the date left blank.) He abused her and forced her to leave him. Subpoena issued Jan. 27, 1853.

Apr. 1853 #30 Dauphin Co., Pa. Appearance Docket filed Feb. 21, 1853. Catharine Howard, defendant in divorce vs. Peter Howard, plaintiff. Feb. 21, 1853 petition of Peter Howard stated that he married in Jan. of 1838 Catharine Stump. He accused her of adultery with George Shride and John Shoe "and divers other persons unknown." He left her in Mar. of 1852.

Apr. 1853 #35 Dauphin Co., Pa. Appearance Docket filed Feb. 25, 1853. Annie Nathans, plaintiff in divorce vs. George Nathans, defendant. Feb. 24, 1853 petition of Annie Nathans by her next friend Edward Bennett stated that she married George Nathans in Dec. of 1844. By cruel and barbarous treatment he caused her to leave him in the latter end of Dec. of 1846. Annie Nathans signed her petition "by mark." Subpoena issued Feb. 25, 1853.

Apr. 1853 #49 Dauphin Co., Pa. Appearance Docket filed Mar. 9, 1853. Nancy Allyn, plaintiff in divorce vs. John Q. Allyn, defendant. Mar. 1, 1853 petition of Nancy Allyn by her next friend George F. Wehover stated that she was married to John Q. Allyn Sept. 26, 1850 by Rev. David Sterrett Pastor of the Waynesboro Church in Mifflin Co., Pa. Her husband never lived with her except for a few weeks in Nov. of 1850. Subpoena issued Mar. 1, 1853.

Apr. 1853 #57 Dauphin Co., Pa. Appearance Docket filed Mar. 18, 1853. Elizabeth Hughes, plaintiff in divorce vs. William Hughes, defendant. Original papers are now missing.

Apr. 1853 #60 Dauphin Co., Pa. Appearance Docket filed Mar. 19, 1853. Lucetta Rush, defendant in divorce vs. Jacob Rush, plaintiff. Mar. 5, 1853 petition of Jacob Rush of Dauphin Co., Pa. who stated that he married his present wife Lucetta May 7, 1850 and she deserted him without any just or reasonable cause over two years ago. Subpoena issued Mar. 19, 1853. Dec. 24, 1853 the court ordered the sheriff to make proclamation. Sheriff E.C. Williams reported that proclamation was published in *The Whig State Journal* Dec. 26, 1853.

Apr. 1853 #61 Dauphin Co., Pa. Appearance Docket filed Mar. 19, 1853. Susan Lang, plaintiff in divorce vs. Joseph Osborn Lang, defendant. Petition of Susan Lang by her next friend Soloman Vance stated that she married Apr. 28, 1836 Joseph Osborn Lang of the borough of Harrisburg, Pa. He deserted her in Apr. of 1856. Susan Lang signed her petition "by mark." Subpoena issued Mar. 19, 1853. Aug. 29, 1853 the court ordered William Kline, Esq. to take depositions at his office in Harrisburg, Pa. on Saturday Nov. 24, 1853 between 10 A.M. and 5 P.M. in the case of Susan Lang by her next friend Soloman Vance vs. Joseph Osborn Lang. Aug. 29, 1853 the court changed the time to Dec. 11, 1853 between 10 A.M. and 6 P.M.

Aug. 1853 #8 Dauphin Co., Pa. Appearance Docket filed May 2, 1853. Susan Lang, plaintiff in divorce vs. Joseph Osborne Lang, defendant. Original papers are now missing.

Aug. 1853 #9 Dauphin Co., Pa. Appearance Docket filed May 2, 1853. Lucetta Rush, defendant in divorce vs. Jacob Rush, plaintiff. Original papers are now missing.

Aug. 1853 #15 Dauphin Co., Pa. Appearance Docket filed May 6, 1853. George Kaylor, defendant in divorce vs. Susanna Kaylor, plaintiff. May 5, 1853 petition of Susanna Kaylor by her next friend Philip K. Auxer stated that she married George Kaylor Jan. 29, 1844. He abused her and thereby forced her to leave him Mar. 23, 1853. She petitioned for a divorce and alimony and she signed her petition "by mark."
Sept. 13, 1853 - "Dauphin County Sct. Susanna Kaylor by her next friend Philip K. Auxer vs. George Kaylor: In the Common Pleas of Dauphin County No. 15 Aug. Term 1853 Subpoena in Divorce - George Kaylor the respondent in the above stated case, saving and reserving to himself the manifold errors and inconsistencies, and imperfections in the libel of the said Susanna by her next friend Philip K. Auxer, praying for a divorce, set forth for answer thereto, or to as much thereof, as he is advised it is necessary for him to answer, admits that the said Susanna the libellant aforesaid on the day she has set forth in her said Libel - was bound with this respondent in the holy bonds of matrimony and protest that the said Libellant has not demeaned herself as a dutiful and loving wife but the indolgence of a capricious temper, and selffishness (*sic*) has greatly disturbed his peace. The respondent avers that he has always since the said marriage conducted himself as a husband ought to do

towards the said Susanna, that he never offered any indignity to the person of the said Susanna, or did any thing to the said Susanna to render her condition intolerable or life burthensome, or so as to force her to withdraw from his house and family - but avers that the said Susanna, without warning respondent; boldly, and cruelly withdrew from his bed and board without any just cause. And the said respondent for further plea saith that before his intermarriage with the said Susanna viz on the 25th day of January one thousand eight hundred and forty four, he paid the said Susanna the sum of one hundred Dollars in consideration whereof; the said Susanna before respondent on the day and year last aforesaid, entered into marriage articles of agreement to that purport, that after the soleminzation of their intended marriage, the said respondant should permit and allow the said Susanna to hold possession and enjoy a certain house and lot of ground whereof she was seized in Elizabethtown, Lancaster County and certain household and kitchen furniture, which she sold as seperate property, with power to the said Susanna to dispose of the same by a last will and Testament and further provided that if the said Susanna was joined with your respondent in the holy bonds of matrimony, and should cohabit and live with your respondent, during life, in the event of said Susanna surviving your respondent she should receive the annual sum of forty dollars out of the estate of your respondent which sum the said Susanna covenanted and agreed should be in lieu of and in full satisfaction of dower and such thirds as she would be entitled to at common law as your respondent's widow, or by act of assembly, out of the estate real or personal of your respondent, and also in bar and full satisfaction of all personal estate of the said George Kaylor which she the said Susanna might otherwise claim by virtue of the statue of distributions of Intestate's estate - in case the said respondent should happen to die intestate. Your respondent further shows that the said Susanna having without just cause, and under circumstances of gross unkindness, and quietly withdrawn from the society and deserted the present house of your respondent, the said Susanna thereby violated the spirit and meaning of said marriage articles of agreement, and has forfieted all those rights estate and privlege as intended to be secured to her by the Samer wherefore your respondent prays that the said libel may be dismissed at the costs of the said Susanna." (signed George Kaylor) "Dauphin County sect. Personally appeared before the subscriber a Justice of the Peace in and for said County, George Kaylor, respondent in the above stated case, and on being qualified according to law, did depose and say, that the facts set forth in the above answer are true in substance and in fact. Sworn and subscribed before me the thirteenth day of September A.D. 1853." (signed George Kaylor and W. Kline)

Jan. 3, 1854 - "Plaintiff's Specification - The Plaintiff by her council David Mumma, Esq. hereby gives notice that on the trial of the above case she will prove repeated acts of cruelty and indignities offered to the person of the Plaintiff by the defendent between the 4th of Apr. 1848 and the 24th of Mar. 1853 as follows to wit, the said George Kaylor the defendant aforesaid did at various times and places between the dates aforesaid make repeated efforts to seduce one Mary Auxer a daughter of Susanna Kaylor, his wife, and conduct himself in a most outrageous manner toward the said Mary Auxer, on one occastion having got to bed with the said Mary Auxer by force and against the will of the said Mary with his clothes off in his the said George Kaylor's own house in the Borough of Harrisburg. And that the said George Kaylor defendant aforesaid did, between the dates afforesaid (sic) commit an assult upon the said Mary Auxer, at the house of the said Mary in the County of Lancaster, by laying his hand upon her and in a rude manner did throw her upon a bed and attempt forcibly and violently to have connection with the said Mary a daughter of the Plaintiff in this case, who is the lawful wife of the said defendant and was at that time living with the defendant as his wife. And that the said Mary Auxer communicated above facts to the Plaintiff. That the said George Kaylor defendant aforesaid did at various times between the dates aforesaid attempt to seduce one Barbara Small, a sister of the said Susanna Kaylor, the Plaintiff in this case. That the said George Kaylor between the dates aforesaid called at the home of the said Barbara Small in Lancaster County, the husband of the said Barbara being abscent (sic) from home, and did there commit an assault upon the said Barbara, by laying his hand upon her person, and rudely and violently attempted to have connection with her, and that the said Barbara Small communicated to the Plaintiff in the above stated case, the facts that the defendant had committed the aforesaid outrages upon her between the dates aforesaid, that the said George Kaylor, Defendent in the aforestated case, did between the dates aforesaid attempt to seduce one Catherine Hoover by repeatedly coming to her house in the absence of her husband, and offering her money as well as by laying hand upon her person in a 'rude manner and keeping her against her will, and the said Catherine Hoover informed the Plaintiff, Susanna Kaylor, of the conduct of the said George Kaylor toward her the said Catherine, between the dates aforesaid, that the said George Kaylor, the defendent in the aforesaid stated case, did, between the dates aforesaid, at various time and places, and in the presence of divers persons, slander, insult, and abuse the said Susanna Kaylor (his wife) the plaintiff in this case by charging her with being a thief and of having stolen money from him, also with having stolen a bond from him, and thereby sorely distressing the said Susanna by disgracing her among her neighbors and friends. That the aforesaid charges and insults were frequently made by the said defendant in the presence of the said Plaintiff, and that the Plaintiff frequently manifested great distress on account thereof." -- "Libel in Divorce -

The Plaintiff in the above stated case by her council David Mumma hereby gives notice that the reply in the trial of the above case, gives in evidence the following facts in addition to those stated in the statement filed January 3, 1854. That the defendent George Kaylor attempted to seduce Mary Auxer by getting into bed with her on the morning of the fifth of Apr. 1848 in defendant's own home in Harrisburg. That the defendant George Kaylor attempted to seduce said Mary Auxer in the year 1850 at the home of her husband Philip K. Auxer in Elizabethtown, Lancaster County, by trying to persuade her to accompany him to Lancaster and then go to bed with him and pass there as man and wife. That the defendent, George Kaylor, attempted to seduce Mary Auxer in the year 1850 at the house of her husband Philip K. Auxer in the village of Elizabethtown, Lancaster County by proposing to take a walk and in passing an alley attempted to persuade her to go with him into it and let him have connection with her. That George Kaylor, the above defendant attempted to seduce Mary Auxer at the house of her husband Philip K. Auxer in Lancaster County in the year 1850, or between the dates of the first of Apr. 1848 and the Fourth of Mar. 1853, by commiting a violent assault upon her person by throwing her forcibly upon a bed and attempting to have connection with her by force. That George Kaylor the defendant aforesaid did in the year 1850 between Christmas and New Year charge Susanna Kaylor his wife before Mary Auxer her daughter and her husband Philip K. Auxer and their family at the home of said Auxer in Lancaster County, with stealing fifty dollars of money, which charge then and there made greatly distressed said Susanna the Libelant in this case. That the above stated facts were communicated to Susanna Kaylor the Libelant in this case, by the said Mary Auxer in the month of Apr. 1851, and that the said Susanna laboured under great distress of mind in connection thereof up to time of cursing George Kaylor. That George Kaylor the defendant in the above stated case did between the 4th of Apr. 1848 and the 24th of Mar. 1853, attempt to seduce Barbara Small, a sister of Susanna Kaylor his wife at her home in Conoy Township, Lancaster County and committed a violent assault upon the said Barbara Small by laying his hand upon her person and to force her to have connection with him. That the above stated facts were communicated to the Libellant in this case between the dates aforesaid. That George Kaylor the defendant attempted to seduce one Catherine Hoover living in the tenant house of the said George Kaylor in Londonderry Township, Dauphin County by offering her money if she would consent to let him have crimminal connection with her between the first of Mar. 1852 and the 24th of Mar. 1854, and that the said George Kaylor between the dates aforesaid changed the libellant his wife with having stolen between two and three hundred dollars from him, and that the said Catherine Hoover communicated the aforesaid facts to the said Susanna Kaylor, whereupon she the said Susanna became much distressed in her mind in consequence thereof. That George Kaylor admited that he got into bed with Mary Auxer in his own home in Harrisburg. That this admission was made in the office of John J. Walborn, Esq. in Middletown, Dauphin County, on the seventeenth of November 1853 before Henry Dechtmoyer, Adam Gross, George Pearer and George Byrod. That the said George Kaylor defendant aforesaid between the first of Apr. 1850 and the 24th of Mar. 1853 at his own house and at other places charged Susanna Kaylor his wife the Libellant in this case with being a thief and of having stolen money from him. That said charges were made to and in the presence of George Pearer, Adam Gross, Henry Dechtmoyer, (Jaris?) P. Smith, Jacob W. Holtz, and Jacob R. Hoover and that the said charges were frequently made in the presence of the said Susanna Kaylor the Libellant in this case and that she became much distressed in her mind in consequence thereof."

Jan. 20, 1854 - George Kaylor's attorney Hamilton Alricks informed Susanna Kaylor's attorney David Mumma that her libel of accusing George Kaylor of abuse and adultery must be backed up with exact names, dates and circumstances.

Mar. 27, 1854 - "Susanna Kaylor by her next friend Philip K. Auxer vs. George Kaylor: In the Court of Common Pleas of Dauphin County No. 15 Aug. Term 1853 Mar. 27, 1854, It is ordered and decreed by the Court that Susanna Kaylor be divorced from the bed and board of her husband George Kaylor and it is also ordered and decreed that the said George Kaylor pay to the said Susanna Kaylor the sum of One hundred Dollars per annium for her reasonable alimony to commence and be computed from this day the same to be payable half yearly so long as this divorce continues unless the husband complies with the provisions of the act of assembly. It is also ordered that the said George Kaylor pay to the said Susanna Kaylor the Sum of One hundred and twenty five dollars for her reasonable expenses in attending to and carrying on this suit, including the amount paid to council and for her boarding and other expenses whilst attending thereto and also that the said George Kaylor pay all the costs of the suit including the attendance of Plaintiff's witnesses subpoening the same all the docket costs and the expense of taking the Depositions before the Commissioner. And the court being of opinion that there is no property belonging to the defendant within this County on which the Plaintiff can have a sufficient Lien for the security of said money and from the evidence laid before this Court it also being of opinion that the defendant has sufficient estate and means to secure the payment of the sum above ordered and is likely to remove the same out of the reach of the process of this Court it is ordered that the said George Kaylor give security by Bond with at least one sufficient surety to be approved by the Court Conditioned and in the form presented by the act of assembly or by the Deposit in Court of a suffient sum of money to secure the payment of the alimony as the same may fall due and the performance of this decree and that the said surety be given or deposit made on or before the 7th day of Apr. next. By the Court."

undated - "In the matter of the application of Susanna Kaylor for alimony. It is evidenced that the circumstances of George Kaylor are as follows:

Land sale for	6337.90
Personal Property for	369.00
	6706.90
The debts due by Kaylor	1354.07
	5352.83

The above considered for the present purpose only:

Deft. objects to any decree of alimony being made in this case on account of the prenuptial contract which he says bars all claim thereto. The court is of opinion that the writing has no such effect and is no bar to alimony though a less amount (rest of this document is too faded to properly read)."

Aug. 1853 #32 Dauphin Co., Pa. Appearance Docket filed May 18, 1853. Jeremiah Kirk, plaintiff in divorce vs. Nancy Kirk, late Nancy Sillyman defendant. Sept. 6, 1853 court directed the sheriff to publish proclamation in one Dauphin Co., Pa. newspaper for libellant to appear in court. Oct. 31, 1853 Sheriff E.C. Williams testified that he did as he was commanded.

Nov. 1853 #2 Dauphin Co., Pa. Appearance Docket filed Aug. 29, 1853. George Sheesley, defendant in divorce vs. Mary Sheesley, plaintiff. Aug. 27, 1853 petition of Mary Sheesley by her next friend Ludwig Lenkert stated that she married George Sheesley Feb. 18, 1834. He deserted her without any just cause Apr. 3, 1851 and she signed her petition "by mark." Subpoena issued in this suit Aug. 29, 1853.

Nov. 1853 #3 Dauphin Co., Pa. Appearance Docket filed Aug. 29, 1853. Catharine Ricker, plaintiff in divorce vs. John S. Ricker, defendant. Aug. 24, 1853 petition of Catharine Ricker by her next friend John Snyder stated that she was the wife of John S. Ricker of Swartara Twp., Dauphin Co., Pa. They were married in Aug. 1833 and "that since the first day of Jan. last A.D. 1853 the said John S. Ricker her husband has on two different occasions treated her by cruel and barbarous treatment and offered such indignities to her person by striking and violently kicking her, and on one of these occasions throwing her off the porch of the house to the ground, by which she was so severely injuried as to be confined to her bed from the effects of divers wounds inflicted by her husband and was under the care and medical treatment of physcians, that the last time injury was thus inflicted upon her person was about the first day of July and that by this barborous treatment the said Catharine was forced to withdraw from the house and family of her said husband, and has been for nearly two months past residing with her father the said John Snyder in Frankfort Township, Cumberland County in this state. That the said Catherine is now dependant upon her said Father for support, whilst her said husband owns and resides upon a valuable real estate about six miles from Harrisburg in said Township of Swatara in which real estate he carries on a large Tannery as well as farming. Your petitioner therefore by her next friend further prays the court to grant her a divorce from bed and board and also to allow her such alimony as her husband's circumstances will admit of. And for that purpose to issue a subpoena to the said John S. Ricker requiring him to appear and answer this complaint, according to law." Catherine Ricker signed her petition "by mark." Subpoena issued Aug. 29, 1853.

Nov. 1853 #5 Dauphin Co., Pa. Appearance Docket filed Aug. 31, 1853. Elizabeth Gregg, defendant in divorce vs. Richard Gregg, plaintiff. Apr. 27, 1853 petition of Richard Gregg of the borough of Harrisburg stated that he married Elizabeth Greenawalt Jul. 12, 1851. He was never able to have sexual intercourse with her and "nor does he believe that any man possesed of ordinary virale development could have such connection with her." He mentioned "her peculiarly contracted physical formation." Subpoena issued in this case Aug. 31, 1853.

Nov. 1853 #16 Dauphin Co., Pa. Appearance Docket filed Sept. 2, 1853. George Hoffman, Jr., plaintiff in divorce vs. Caroline Hoffman, defendant. Aug. 31, 1853 petition of George Hoffman, Jr. stated that he married Caroline Borrell Aug. 9, 1851. She deserted him over two years ago. Subpoena issued Sept. 1, 1853.

Jan. 1854 #15 Dauphin Co., Pa. Appearance Docket filed Dec. 6, 1853. George Sheesley, defendant in divorce vs. Mary Sheesley, plaintiff. On May 15, 1854 the court ordered the sheriff to make proclamation. Sheriff E.C. Williams testified that he had sent the proclamation to the printers.

Jan. 1854 #17 Dauphin Co., Pa. Appearance Docket filed Dec. 7, 1853. George Hoffman, Jr., plaintiff in divorce vs. Caroline Hoffman, defendant. On Feb. 16, 1854 court ordered sheriff to make proclamation of alias subpoena.

Sept. 1854 #7 Dauphin Co., Pa. Appearance Docket filed Apr. 28, 1854. J.A. Rumberger, plaintiff in divorce vs. Jonathan Rumberger, defendant. Apr. 14, 1854 petition of J.A. Rumberger by her next friend Joseph Horn stated that she married Jonathan Rumberger Jul. 28, 1849 and he deserted her without any just or reasonable cause Feb. 1, 1851. Court granted her a divorce Feb. 1, 1855.

Nov. 1854 #3 Dauphin Co., Pa. Appearance Docket filed Sept. 7, 1854. Annie E. Cannan, defendant in divorce vs. James A. Cannan, plaintiff. Sept. 2, 1854 petition of James A. Cannan stated that he married Annie E. Zahm Sept. 16, 1852. She deserted him without any just or reasonable cause Dec. 11, 1852. Subpoena issued Sept. 7, 1854.

Nov. 1854 #10 Dauphin Co., Pa. Appearance Docket filed Sept. 19, 1854. Elizabeth Hughes, defendant in divorce vs. William Hughes, plaintiff. Original papers are now missing.

Jan. 1855 #3 Dauphin Co., Pa. Appearance Docket filed Nov. 24, 1854. Annie E. Cannan, defendant in divorce vs. James A. Cannan. Apr. 28, 1855 court appointed C.A. Snyder, Esq. to take depositions in this case at his office on Third Street in Harrisburg, Pa. Nov. 13, 1855 between the hours of 10 a.m. and 4 p.m.

Apr. 1855 #2 Dauphin Co., Pa. Appearance Docket filed Jan. 15, 1855. Louisa Miller, plaintiff in divorce vs. Frederick Miller, defendant. Jan. 15, 1855 petition of Louisa Miller by her next friend John Cramer stated that she married Frederick Miller Mar. 27, 1842. Her husband "offered such indignities to the person of the said petitioner to render her condition untolerable" causing her to leave him. Subpoena issued Jan. 15, 1855.

Apr. 1855 #20 Dauphin Co., Pa. Appearance Docket filed Jan. 24, 1855. Sarah Ann Frank, plaintiff in divorce vs. William Frank, defendant. Jan. 19, 1855 petition of Sarah Ann Frank of East Hanover Twp., Dauphin Co., Pa. by her next friend Mordecai Miller stated that she married William Frank Oct. 12, 1847 and he deserted her Mar. 1, 1849 without any just or reasonable cause. Sarah Ann Frank signed her petition "by mark."

Apr. 1855 #66 Dauphin Co., Pa. Appearance Docket filed Feb. 22, 1855. Catharine Ramler, plaintiff in divorce vs. Jacob Ramler, defendant. Feb. 17, 1855 petition of Catharine Ramler of South Hanover Twp., Dauphin Co., Pa. by her next friend John H. Nunamaker stated she married Jacob Ramler Nov. 13, 1847. He deserted her without any just or reasonable cause in Jan. of 1850. Catharine

Ramler signed her petition "by mark." Subpoena issued Feb. 23, 1855.

Apr. 1855 #71 Dauphin Co., Pa. Appearance Docket filed Feb. 23, 1855. Lewis Burkle, defendant in divorce vs. Christianna Burkle, plaintiff. Feb. 22, 1855 petition of Christianna Burkle by her next friend George Seidle stated that she married Lewis Burkle Mar. 7, 1850. Her husband "offered such indignities and outrages to the person of this petitioner as to render her life burdensome and condition intolerable." She therefore left her husband Dec. 25, 1859 (Nice Christmas present!).

Apr. 1855 #72 Dauphin Co., Pa. Appearance Docket filed Feb. 24, 1855. Jacob Miller, defendant in divorce vs. Rebecca Miller, plaintiff. Feb. 21, 1855 petition of Rebecca Miller by her next friend George Runyan stated that she married Jacob Miller Sept. 7, 1851. He deserted her without any just or reasonable cause Sept. 8, 1851. Subpoena issued Feb. 24, 1855.

Apr. 1855 #129 Dauphin Co., Pa. Appearance Docket filed Mar. 24, 1855. Anthony Burns, defendant in divorce vs. Catharine Burns, plaintiff. Petition of Catharine Burns of the borough of Harrisburg, Pa. by her next friend Nicholas Stockly stated that she married Anthony Burns Oct. 17, 1853 and lived with him until Jan. 1, 1855. Subpoena issued Mar. 29, 1855.

Aug. 1855 #2 Dauphin Co., Pa. Appearance Docket filed Apr. 23, 1855. Abraham Brinzer, defendant in divorce vs. Elizabeth Brinzer, plaintiff. Aug. 6, 1855 petition of Abraham Brinzer answering the libel of Elizabeth Brinzer by her next friend John Sheetz filed Apr. 23, 1855. He acknowledges their marriage of May 7, 1848 but denies her accusations of abuse and accuses his wife of possessing a violent temper.

Aug. 1855 #3 Dauphin Co., Pa. Appearance Docket filed Apr. 23, 1855. Charlotte E. Thomas, plaintiff in divorce vs. Richard Thomas, defendant. Apr. 13, 1855 petition of Charlotte E. Thomas by her next friend George Chester stated that she married Richard Thomas Sept. 12, 1850. Her husband deserted her without any just or reasonable cause Jan. 10, 1852. Subpoena issued Apr. 23, 1855.

Aug. 1855 #4 Dauphin Co., Pa. Appearance Docket filed Apr. 24, 1855. Eliza Lyttle, defendant in divorce vs. George W. Lyttle, plaintiff. Feb. 27, 1855 petition of George W. Lyttle stated that he married Eliza Eckert Jun. 17, 1849. She deserted him without any just or reasonable cause Feb. 3, 1853. Subpoena issued Apr. 24, 1855.

Aug. 1855 #7 Dauphin Co., Pa. Appearance Docket filed Apr. 26, 1855. Catharine Ramler, plaintiff in divorce vs. Jacob Ramler, defendant. Original papers are now missing.

Aug. 1855 #8 Dauphin Co., Pa. Appearance Docket filed Apr. 28, 1855. John Christy, defendant in divorce vs. Sarah Jane Christy, plaintiff. Apr. 27, 1855 petition of Sarah Jane Christy by her next friend Jeremiah Cunningham stated that she married John Christy Aug. 28, 1850 and he deserted her Mar. 15, 1853. Sarah Jane Christy signed her petition "by mark." Subpoena issued Apr. 28, 1855.

Aug. 1855 #10 Dauphin Co., Pa. Appearance Docket. Sarah Ann Frank, plaintiff in divorce vs. William Frank, defendant. Sept. 5, 1855 court orders the sheriff of Dauphin Co., Pa. to make proclamation of divorce.

Aug. 1855 #40 Dauphin Co., Pa. Appearance Docket filed May 12, 1855. Jacob Miller, defendant in divorce vs. Rebecca Miller, plaintiff. Original papers are now missing.

Aug. 1855 #124 Dauphin Co., Pa. Appearance Docket filed Jul. 27, 1855. Jefferson Nunemacher, plaintiff in divorce vs. Mary Nunemacher, defendant. Jul. 23, 1855 petition of Jefferson Nunemacher of Harrisburg, Pa. stated that Apr. of 1853 he married Mary Cox. He accused her of adultery with Thomas C. Sedgwick and signed his petition "by mark." Subpoena issued Jul. 24, 1855.

Aug. 1855 #125 Dauphin Co., Pa. Appearance Docket filed Jul. 27, 1855. Samuel Glassbrenner, defendant in divorce vs. Susanna Glassbrenner, plaintiff. Jul. 19, 1855 petition of Susanna Glassbrenner by her next friend Samuel Hanshue stated that she married Samuel Glassbrenner Jan. 25, 1855. Her husband abused her, endangered her life and she therefore left him Jul. 8, 1855. Jan. 30, 1856 Samuel Glassbrenner petitioned the Court for a new trial. Previously in an undated document he had denied his wife's charges of abuse and claimed he was a good husband to her. May 5, 1856 petition of Susanna Glassbrenner for her husband to pay her expenses for obtaining a divorce from bed and board and for alimony as she had no property or means of income to pay this. May 15, 1856 court granted Susanna Glassbrenner a divorce from the bed and board of Samuel Glassbreener who was to pay her $50.00 a year for alimony until they reconcile and he treat her "as a good husband ought to do." The court also ordered him to pay costs of suit, costs of witnesses' attendance, and to pay his wife twenty dollars for her attendance.

Nov. 1855 #27 Dauphin Co., Pa. Appearance Docket filed Sept. 13, 1855. Jacob Baab, plaintiff in divorce vs. Sarah Ann Baab, defendant. Aug. 11, 1855 petition of Jacob Baab stated that he married Sarah Ann McDonald in Dec. of 1849 and she deserted him Jun. 3, 1853 without any just or reasonable cause.

Nov. 1855 #39 Dauphin Co., Pa. Appearance Docket filed Sept. 21, 1855. Jefferson Nunemacher, plaintiff in divorce vs. Mary Nunemacher, defendant. Original papers are now missing.

Nov. 1855 #41 Dauphin Co., Pa. Appearance Docket filed Sept. 24, 1855. Charlotte E. Thomas, plaintiff in divorce vs. Richard Thomas, defendant. Original papers are now missing.

Jan. 1856 #2 Dauphin Co., Pa. Appearance Docket filed Nov. 20, 1855. Catharine Howard, plaintiff in divorce vs. Peter Howard, defendant. Nov. 4, 1855 petition of Catharine Howard by her next friend John Stump stated that she married Peter Howard Jan. 11, 1835 and he deserted her Mar. 14, 1852 without any just or reasonable cause. Catharine Howard signed her petition "by mark." Subpoena issued Nov. 19, 1855.

Jan. 1856 #13 Dauphin Co., Pa. Appearance Docket filed Nov. 26, 1855. John G. Sauppe, defendant in divorce vs. Mary Sauppe, plaintiff. Nov. 26, 1855 petition of Mary Sauppe by her next friend George Kile stated that she married John G. Sauppe Nov. 21, 1850 and he "turned her out of doors" May 10, 1855 and at other times abused her. Mary Sauppe signed her petition "by mark." Subpoena issued Nov. 26, 1855.

Jan. 1856 #62 Dauphin Co., Pa. Appearance Docket filed Jan. 2, 1856. Jacob Baab, plaintiff in divorce vs. Sarah Ann Baab, defendant. Original papers are now missing.

Apr. 1856 #94 Dauphin Co., Pa. Appearance Docket filed Mar. 17, 1856. Charles Smith, defendant in divorce vs. Leah Smith, plaintiff. Mar. 3, 1856 petition of Leah Smith by her next friend Frederick Karper stated that she married Charles Smith Mar. 4, 1852. He deserted her without any just or reasonable cause May 27, 1852. Leah Smith signed her petition "by mark." Subpoena issued Mar. 17, 1856.

Aug. 1856 #19 Dauphin Co., Pa. Appearance Docket filed May 6, 1856. Elizabeth Hughes, defendant in divorce vs. William Hughes, plaintiff. Apr. 2, 1857 Elizabeth Hughes denies she deserted William Hughes Sept. 3, 1852 without a just or reasonable cause and she petitioned for a trial by jury. Oct. 26, 1859 court orders plaintiff to pay defendant for all her expenses involved in trial including her witnesses and all court costs. Oct. 29, 1859 Sheriff J.M. Eyster reports order was served on William Hughes.

Aug. 1856 #22 Dauphin Co., Pa. Appearance Docket filed May 9, 1856. Charles Smith, defendant in divorce vs. Leah Smith, plaintiff. Original papers are now missing.

Aug. 1856 #32 Dauphin Co., Pa. Appearance Docket filed May 15, 1856. Ann Duck, plaintiff in divorce vs. Franklin M. Duck, defendant. Mar. 22, 1856 petition of Ann Duck by her next friend and father Christian Brubaker. She stated that she married Franklin M. Duck Dec. 13, 1852 and he deserted her without any just or reasonable cause Sept. 3, 1855. Subpoena issued May 15, 1856.

Aug. 1856 #118 Dauphin Co., Pa. Appearance Docket filed Jul. 24, 1856. Elizabeth C. Kilwell, plaintiff in divorce vs. John H. Kilwell, defendant. Jul. 24, 1856 petition of Elizabeth C. Kilwell by her next friend Eleazer Light. She is a daughter of Christian Light, farmer of Lebanon Co., Pa. and lived all her life in Pa. She married John H. Kilwell Sept. 18, 1851. She accused him of adultery with Mary Ann Rouch of which he was convicted and imprisoned for in Dauphin Co. Jail. He was sentenced Sept. 4, 1855. Subpoena issued Jul. 24, 1853.

Aug. 1856 #135 Dauphin Co., Pa. Appearance Docket filed Aug. 13, 1856. Henry Rineold, defendant in divorce vs. Margaret Rineold, plaintiff. Jul. 13, 1856 petition of Margaret Rineold by her next friend G.W. Miller in which she stated she married Henry Rineold in Apr. 1851. He deserted her without any just or reasonable cause in Oct. of 1851. Margaret Rineold signed her petition "by mark." Subpoena issued Aug. 13, 1856.

Nov. 1856 #9 Dauphin Co., Pa. Appearance Docket filed Aug. 29, 1856. Frederick Miller, plaintiff in divorce vs. Louisa Miller, defendant. Aug. 27, 1856 petition of Frederick Miller stated that he married his present wife Louisa in Mar. of 1842 and she deserted him in Mar. of 1854 without any just or reasonable cause. Subpoena issued Aug. 29, 1856.

Nov. 1856 #10 Dauphin Co., Pa. Appearance Docket filed Dec. 29, 1856. Henry Rineold, defendant in divorce vs. Margaret Rineold, plaintiff. Dec. 3, 1856 court appointed C.A. Snyder, Esq. to take depositions in this case at his office in Harrisburg, Pa. Dec. 29, 1856 between 10 A.M. and 1 P.M. and Mr. Snyder was notified of this Dec. 11, 1856.

Nov. 1856 #33 Dauphin Co., Pa. Appearance Docket filed Sept. 17, 1856. Ann Duck, plaintiff in divorce vs. Franklin M. Duck, defendant. Feb. 8, 1858 court appointed Charles A. Snyder, Esq., a commissioner to take depositions in this divorce case.

Jan. 1857 #2 Dauphin Co., Pa. Appearance Docket filed Nov. 18, 1856. Henry Lehman, defendant in divorce vs. Mary A. Lehman, plaintiff. Undated petition of Mary A. Lehman for an order requiring her husband to pay her expenses for counsel, "boarding, maintenance, and that of an infant child." She mentions that her husband had real estate in Middletown valued at $1,500.00 besides notes at hand and other money she believes to the sum of $1,200.00. Subpoena issued Nov. 18, 1856. Alias subpoena issued May 16, 1857 for Jun. 29, 1857.

Jan. 1857 #14 Dauphin Co., Pa. Appearance Docket filed Nov. 24, 1856. Abraham Brenser, plaintiff in divorce vs. Elizabeth Brenser, defendant. Nov. 12, 1856 petition of Abraham Brenser of Londonderry Twp., Dauphin Co., Pa. stated that he married Elizabeth Sheets May 7, 1854 and she deserted him without any just or reasonable cause Jul. 29, 1854.

Jan. 1857 #85 Dauphin Co., Pa. Appearance Docket filed Jan. 5, 1857. Solomon B. Bowerman, plaintiff in divorce vs. Margaret Bowerman, defendant. Sept. 2, 1857 petition of Margaret Bowerman for a trial by jury. She also testified that she was a kind and affectionate wife.

Apr. 1857 #2 Dauphin Co., Pa. Appearance Docket filed Jan. 19, 1857. Christiana Wortz, defendant in divorce vs. Jacob Wortz, plaintiff. Jan. 7, 1857 petition of Jacob Wortz stated that he married Christiana Maily Sept. 1, 1847. He accused her of adultery with James W. Chester. They separated Sept. of 1852. Subpoena issued Jan. 19, 1857.

Apr. 1857 #13 & 15 Dauphin Co., Pa. Appearance Docket filed Feb. 4, 1857. Benjamin Bowman, plaintiff in divorce vs. Mary Bowman, defendant. Jan. 30, 1857 petition of Benjamin Bowman, Farmer, of Upper Swatara Twp., Dauphin Co., Pa. stated that he married Mary Leiter Oct. 14, 1847 and she deserted him without any just or reasonable cause Aug. 1, 1854. Subpoena issued Feb. 4, 1857. Sept. 1857 answer of Mary Rowman agreed that they were married Oct. 14, 1847. She said her husband abused her "and while she was unwell and in an unrit condition to take care of herself, he, the said Benjamin Bowman, had her taken from his said Benjamin Bowman's house and put out onto the public highway.

Nov. 21, 1859 petition of Mary Bowman stated "She was sent

away from her said husband from his house and left on the public highway while in delicate health and since that time he the said Benjamin has totally neglected her and refused to receive her into his house or contribute to her support, but has compelled her to work out for a living. That she has no means of her own to support herself or to bear the expenses incident to the trial of the proceeding commensed against her. That said Benjamin Bowman her husband posseses means to the amout of at least one thousand Dollars all of which was made out of their mutual savings, from some extent out of property of your petitioner held in her own right which was sold by him and the money retained in his possession. That having filed her answer to his petition for a divorce she now prays your honorable Court to grant a rule on said Benjamin Bowman to appear in Court on such time as your honors may think proper to show cause why he should not pay or contribute such sums of money to her support and the payment of her expenses in the proceedings now pending against her as your honour shall deem proper and she now prayeth." Mary Bowman signed her petition "by mark." Mar. 26, 1859 petition of Benjamin Bowman stated that he married Mary Lyter about eleven years ago and she deserted him without any just or reasonable cause about five years ago. May 2, 1859 subpoena issued in this case. Sept. 7, 1859 court ordered Benjamin Bowman to pay his wife $20.00 to pay her council fees. Dec. 19, 1859 Subpoena issued for Benjamin Bowman to appear in court Jan. 16, 1860 to show cause why he should not contribute to the support of his wife. Jan. 7, 1860 Subpoena served on Benjamin Bowman by Sheriff Jacob M. Eyster. Feb. 13, 1860 court granted Benjamin Bowman a divorce from Mary Bowman.

Apr. 1857 #36 Dauphin Co., Pa. Appearance Docket filed Feb. 21, 1857. Joanna Black, defendant in divorce vs. William E. Black, plaintiff. Feb. 12, 1857 petition of William E. Black for a divorce stated that he married Joanna Lemon Feb. 24, 1855 but "hath not cohabited with her from that time to the present." He accused her of adultery. Subpoena issued Feb. 21, 1857. (Note: Of great interest in this regard is case no. 21 Apr. 1855 term in which a Malinda First sued William E. Black for $2,000 because he promised to marry her but not only failed to do so but married another woman on Jan. 24, 1855!!! This apparently involves the same William E. Black but one or the other accidentally got the marriage date a month off.)

Apr. 1857 #55 Dauphin Co., Pa. Appearance Docket filed Mar. 9, 1857. Matilda Carbury, plaintiff in divorce vs. William Carbury, defendant. Feb. 30, 1857 petition of Matilda Carbury by her next friend D.J. Boynton. She stated that she married William Carbury Jun. 9, 1853 and he deserted her without any just or reasonable cause Jun. 15, 1853. Subpoena issued Mar. 9, 1857.

Apr. 1857 #66 Dauphin Co., Pa. Appearance Docket filed Mar. 20, 1857. Henry Lehman, defendant in divorce vs. Mary Lehman, plaintiff. Original papers are now missing.

Apr. 1857 #91 Dauphin Co., Pa. Appearance Docket filed Apr. 7, 1857. Joel Koppenhaffer, defendant in divorce vs. Susanna Koppenhaffer, plaintiff. Original papers are now missing.

Aug. 1857 #1 Dauphin Co., Pa. Appearance Docket filed Apr. 27, 1857. David Bair, plaintiff in divorce vs. Catharine Bair, defendant. Petition of David Bair claimed he married Catharine Roke in Feb. of 1852 and she deserted him without any just or reasonable cause that same month. Apr. 27, 1857 Catharine Bair's answer to his libel was filed in which she stated that they were indeed married Feb. 6, 1852 but it was not her that deserted him but it was he who deserted her and their child Amanda Jane now over five years old. Subpoena issued to David Bair to show cause why he should not pay for maintenance of Catharine Bair for first Monday of Jan. of 1859. Another subpoena issued Feb. 3, 1859 for David Bair to show cause why he should not pay maintenance to Catharine Bair.

Aug. 1857 #10 Dauphin Co., Pa. Appearance Docket filed May 4, 1857. Alfred G. Quinlin, plaintiff in divorce vs. Catharine T. Quinlin, defendant. Apr. 13, 1857 petition of Alfred G. Quinlin stated that he married at Heartleton, Union Co., Pa. Catharine T. Madden Dec. 24, 1844. She deserted him without any just or reasonable cause Nov. 10, 1850. He accused her of adultery and of having two children born to her since her desertion of him, one in 1852 and the other in 1854. Subpoena issued May 4, 1857.

Aug. 1857 #16 Dauphin Co., Pa. Appearance Docket filed May 6, 1857. Catharine Shoop, plaintiff in divorce vs. John Shoop, plaintiff. Apr. 11, 1857 petition of Catharine Shoop by her next friend John Myers in which she stated that she married John Shoop Apr. 11, 1857. (Note: The year of this marriage is obviously in error but this is what the petition actually said.) Her husband deserted her without any just or reasonable cause Mar. 20, 1857.

Aug. 1857 #22 Dauphin Co., Pa. Appearance Docket filed May 12, 1857. Christianna Woertz, defendant in divorce vs. Jacob Woertz, plaintiff. Aug. 29, 1857 Dauphin Co., Pa. sheriff reports that the defendant could not be found in Dauphin Co., Pa. He ordered that proclamations be made in the *American Sentinel* newspaper for four weeks prior to the first day of Nov. 1857 term of court.

Aug. 1857 #98 Dauphin Co., Pa. Appearance Docket filed Jun. 30, 1857. Matilda Carberry, plaintiff in divorce vs. William Carberry, defendant. Original papers are now missing.

Nov. 1857 #3 Dauphin Co., Pa. Appearance Docket filed Aug. 25, 1857. Angeline Foster, plaintiff in divorce vs. George W. Foster, defendant. Aug. 20, 1857 petition of Angeline Foster by her next friend Anthony Lechler stated that she married Mar. 31, 1853 George W. Foster who later deserted her and her child without any just or reasonable cause. "Also the said George by his drunken and quarrelsome habits and disposition, rendered the life of your libellant unhappy and miserable, so much as to make her life burdensome."

Nov. 1857 #4 Dauphin Co., Pa. Appearance Docket filed Aug. 26, 1857. Ellen Brown, plaintiff in divorce vs. George H. Brown, defendant. Jul. 6, 1857 petition of Ellen Brown by her next friend E.T. Pinkerton stated that she married George H. Brown May 24, 1855 and he deserted her without any just or reasonable cause over two years ago. Nov. 24, 1857 Dauphin Co., Pa. sheriff reported that he could not locate George H. Brown in his bailiwick. Alias subpoena issued for Jan. term of 1858.

Nov. 1857 #5 Dauphin Co., Pa. Appearance Docket filed Aug. 25, 1857. Rachel Swab, plaintiff in divorce vs. Jonas Swab, defendant. Aug. 25, 1857 petition of Rachel Swab of Dauphin Co., Pa. by her next friend Daniel Undegrove for a divorce stated that she married Jonas Swab May 17, 1853 and he deserted her without any just or reasonable cause May 1, 1854. On Nov. 25, 1857 the sheriff reported that he couldn't locate Jonas Swab in Dauphin Co., Pa. and an alias subpoena was issued.

Nov. 1857 #25 Dauphin Co., Pa. Appearance Docket filed Sept. 2, 1857. Julia Ann Grimwood, plaintiff in divorce vs. William Grimwood, defendant. Sept. 3, 1857 petition of Julia Ann Grimwood by her next friend Frederick Hake stated that she married William Grimwood Dec. 25, 1851 and he deserted her without any just reason or cause three years ago. Subpoena issued Sept. 3, 1857.

Nov. 1857 #89 Dauphin Co., Pa. Appearance Docket filed Oct. 15, 1857. Frances Antes, defendant in divorce vs. J. Emory Antes. Oct. 1, 1857 petition of J. Emory Antes of Harrisburg, Pa. stated that he married Frances McDonald Feb. 28, 1857. He accused her of adultery. Subpoena issued Oct. 14, 1857. Sheriff reported that defendant could not be found in his bailiwick. Alias subpoena issued for Jan. 7, 1858.

Jan. 1858 #14 Dauphin Co., Pa. Appearance Docket filed Nov. 24, 1857. Ellen Brown, plaintiff in divorce vs. George H. Brown, defendant. Feb. 13, 1858 sheriff reported that George H. Brown could not be found in Dauphin Co., Pa. Feb. 13, 1858 court ordered that notice be place in the *Farmers and Miners Journal* at Lykenstown for four weeks for George H. Brown to appear in court to answer his wife's libel for a divorce.

Jan. 1858 #15 Dauphin Co., Pa. Appearance Docket filed Nov. 24, 1857. Julia Ann Grimwood, plaintiff in divorce vs. William Grimwood, defendant. Original papers are now missing.

Jan. 1858 #25 Dauphin Co., Pa. Appearance Docket filed Nov. 26, 1857. Jonas Swab, defendant in divorce vs. Rachel Swab, plaintiff. Original papers are now missing.

Jan. 1858 #26 Dauphin Co., Pa. Appearance Docket filed Nov. 26, 1857. Frances Antes, defendant in divorce vs. J. Emory Antes, plaintiff. Original papers are now missing.

Jan. 1858 #66 Dauphin Co., Pa. Appearance Docket filed Dec. 18, 1857. Joel Koppenhaffer, defendant in divorce vs. Susanna Koppenhaffer, plaintiff. Dec. 10, 1857 petition of Susanna Koppenhaffer by her father and next friend William Lenker stated that she married Joel Koppenhaffer May 13, 1853. He deserted her without any just or reasonable cause Aug. 26, 1855 and he gave her no support. Feb. 20, 1858 deposition of William E. Lenker brother of Susanna Koppenhaffer stated that he was present at his sister's wedding and knew of her husband's desertion. Feb. 20, 1858 deposition of Lovina Lenker, sister of Susanna Koppenhaffer, stated that she was present at her sister's wedding of knew of her husband's desertion. Mar. 22, 1858 the court granted Susanna Koppenhaffer a divorce from her husband Joel Koppenhaffer.

Apr. 1858 #5 Dauphin Co., Pa. Appearance Docket filed Jan. 21, 1858. John Lochert, defendant in divorce vs. Rosanna Lochert, plaintiff. Jan. 16, 1856 petition of Rosanna Lochert by her next friend Alexander Rogers stated that she married John Lochert in Nov. of 1850. He deserted her without any just or reasonable cause in Sept. of 1852. Rosanna Lochert signed her petition "by mark." Subpoena issued Jan. 21, 1858.

Apr. 1858 #26 Dauphin Co., Pa. Appearance Docket filed Jan. 28, 1858. Jerome Hite, defendant in divorce vs. Lydia Hite, plaintiff. Jan. 15, 1858 petition of Lydia Hite by her next friend Benjamin Zuker stated that she married Jerome Hite Jun. 3, 1855 who deserted her that same day without any just or reasonable cause. Subpoena issued Jan. 28, 1858.

Apr. 1858 #51 Dauphin Co., Pa. Appearance Docket filed Feb. 12, 1858. Mary Ann Hutchinson, plaintiff in divorce vs. Samuel Hutchinson, defendant. Feb. 11, 1858 petition of Mary Ann Hutchinson by her next friend Rodger Shickly stated that she married Samuel Hutchinson Jun. 25, 1854. He deserted her without any just or reasonable cause Dec. 27, 1854. Subpoena issued Feb. 12, 1858.

Apr. 1858 #109 Dauphin Co., Pa. Appearance Docket filed Mar. 22, 1858. Anthony Black, plaintiff in divorce vs. Rosanna Black, defendant. Feb. 24, 1858 petition of Anthony Black (still a minor) by his mother Sarah Black stated that he married Rosanna Ledwith Sept. 29, 1857. He accused his wife of being quarrelsome and abusive.

Apr. 1858 #110 Dauphin Co., Pa. Appearance Docket filed Mar. 22, 1858. Adda Maria Briscoe, plaintiff in divorce vs. Henry Briscoe, defendant. Mar. 19, 1858 petition of Adda Maria Briscoe by her next friend Charles J. Dorris stated that she married Henry Briscoe Nov. 13, 1856 in Harrisburg, Pa. She accused her husband of adultery with Emily Smith of the city of Baltimore, Md.

Apr. 1858 #129 Dauphin Co., Pa. Appearance Docket filed Mar. 26, 1858. Adam Moffat, defendant in divorce vs. Mary E. Moffat, plaintiff. Mar. 11, 1858 petition of Mary E. Moffat by her brother and next friend George W. Starry stated that she married Adam Moffat Nov. 14, 1852. Her husband deserted her without any just or reasonable cause Jun. 30, 1853. Subpoena issued Mar. 26, 1858.

Apr. 1858 #135 Dauphin Co., Pa. Appearance Docket filed Mar. 27, 1858. Jesse Moltz, defendant in divorce vs. Louisa Moltz, plaintiff. Undated petition of Louisa Moltz by her next friend Alexander Phillips stated that she married Jesse Moltz Aug. 1, (1852?). Her husband deserted her without any just or reasonable cause Jan. 1, 1855. Louisa Moltz signed her petition "by mark." Subpoena issued Mar. 27, 1858.

Apr. 1858 #143 Dauphin Co., Pa. Appearance Docket filed Mar. 30, 1858. Abby Umholtz, defendant in divorce vs. Samuel Umholtz, plaintiff. Mar. 11, 1858 petition of Samuel Umholtz of Lykens Twp., Dauphin Co., Pa. stated that he married Abby Mourer Apr. 5, 1857 and she deserted him without any just or reasonable cause May 15, 1857. Subpoena issued Mar. 30, 1858.

Apr. 1858 #153 Dauphin Co., Pa. Appearance Docket filed Apr. 7, 1858. Catharine Hamwood, plaintiff in divorce vs. William Hamwood, defendant. Apr. 6, 1858 petition of Catharine Hamwood by her next friend William Small stated that she married William Hamwood Jul. 1, 1851. "The said William Hamwood hath utterly refused and neglected to provide the common and ordinary necessities of life for his said wife and children and hath also by a continous course of abusive, threatening and violent conduct and language rendered the situation of your libellant painful and dangerous in the extreme as well as made her life burdensome, so as to impair and serious jepardize her health and hapiness. Your libellant further showeth, that the said William Hamwood is a common and habitual drunkard refusing to work or to supply his family with necessities of life." Catharine Hamwood signed her petition "by mark." Subpoena issued Apr. 7, 1858.

Aug. 1858 #6 Dauphin Co., Pa. Appearance Docket filed Apr. 30, 1858. Lydia Ann Moyer, plaintiff in divorce vs. George Moyer, defendant. Apr. 27, 1858 petition of Lydia Ann Moyer by her next friend Daniel Swartz stated that she married George Moyer Oct. 18, 1855. Her husband abused her causing her to leave him Mar. 3, 1858. She petitioned for a divorce and alimony. Subpoena issued Apr. 29, 1858.

Aug. 1858 #12 Dauphin Co., Pa. Appearance Docket filed May 3, 1858. Mary Ann Hutchinson, plaintiff in divorce vs. Samuel Hutchinson, defendant. Aug. 28, 1858 court ordered sheriff to make proclamation. Nov. 13, 1858 Sheriff J.M. Eyster reported that he had made proclamation. Nov. 30, 1858 court appointed Henry Beader, Esq. to take depositions in this case. Dec. 11, 1858 deposition of William Garratt before Henry Beader, J.P. at his office in Harrisburg, Pa. stated he was well acquainted with Mary Ann Hutchinson whose maiden name was Mary Ann Shecky and that she was married about four years ago to Samuel Hutchinson who deserted her about three and a half years ago. "I advanced her money to assist her to bury her child." He knew of no reason for her husband to desert her.
Dec. 11, 1858 deposition of Roger Shecky who testified that he was a brother of Mary Ann Hutchinson. She was married about four years ago and about six months later her husband deserted her. He has not lived with her or provided for her since his desertion. He knew of no reason for his desertion and he did not know where he went to. Dec. 13, 1858 the court granted Mary Ann Hutchinson a divorce from Samuel Hutchinson.

Aug. 1858 #13 Dauphin Co., Pa. Appearance Docket filed Nov. 15, 1858. Adda Maria Briscoe, plaintiff in divorce vs. Henry Briscoe, defendant. Aug. 28, 1858 court ordered the sheriff to make proclamation of divorce.

Aug. 1858 #72 Dauphin Co., Pa. Appearance Docket filed May 13, 1858. Daniel F. Hemperly, defendant in divorce vs. Margaret E. Hemperly, plaintiff. Aug. 23, 1858 answer of Daniel F. Hemperly to the libel of his wife Margaret E. Hemperly by her next friend Benjamin F. Umberger. His wife's petition was dated May 13, 1858 and she accused her husband of adultery and abuse. His answer was that he admitted they were indeed married Jan. 22, 1858 but he denied any abuse or adultery and he signed his answer "by mark."

Aug. 1858 #73 Dauphin Co., Pa. Appearance Docket filed May 13, 1858. Anthony Black, plaintiff in divorce vs. Rosanna Black, defendant. Original papers are now missing.

Aug. 1858 #74 Dauphin Co., Pa. Appearance Docket filed May 13, 1858. Jesse Moltz, defendant in divorce vs. Louisa Moltz, plaintiff. May 2, 1859 court appointed Henry Beader to take depositions in this case. May 2, 1859 D.A.S. Eyster, deputy sheriff reported that he made proper publication of this case for four successive weeks in one newspaper.

Aug. 1858 #107 Dauphin Co., Pa. Appearance Docket filed May 29, 1858. John Lochart, defendant in divorce vs. Rosanna Lochart, plaintiff. Sept. 1, 1858 court ordered sheriff to make proclamation according to law of this divorce action.

Aug. 1858 #108 Dauphin Co., Pa. Appearance Docket filed May 29, 1858. Adam Moffat, defendant in divorce vs. Mary E. Moffat, plaintiff. Sept. 1, 1858 court ordered the sheriff to make proclamation according to law of this divorce action.

Nov. 1858 #20 Dauphin Co., Pa. Appearance Docket filed Sept. 1, 1858. Samuel Reimart, plaintiff in divorce vs. Susanna Reimart, defendant. Aug. 20, 1858 petition of Samuel Reimart of Lower Paxton Twp., Dauphin Co., Pa. stated that he married Susanna Spahn Aug. 23, 1834. He accused her of adultery with John Chambers. He left her in the first week of Jun. 1858. Subpoena issued Sept. 1, 1858.

Jan. 1859 #4 Dauphin Co., Pa. Appearance Docket filed Nov. 17, 1858. William Black, defendant in divorce vs. Rosanna Black, plaintiff. Oct. 7, 1858 petition of Rosanna Black of Harrisburg, Pa. by her next friend Samuel Stehley stated that she married William Black Apr. 3, 1856 and that he left her without any just or reasonable cause more than two years ago.

Jan. 1859 #8 Dauphin Co., Pa. Appearance Docket filed Nov. 23, 1858. Abby Umholtz, defendant in divorce vs. Samuel Umholtz, plaintiff. Feb. 28, 1859 court ordered sheriff to make proclamation according to law. Aug. 22, 1859 court granted Samuel Umholtz a divorce from Abby Umholtz.

Jan. 1859 #14 Dauphin Co., Pa. Appearance Docket filed Nov. 24, 1858. Jonathan B. Snader, defendant in divorce vs. Sarah Snader, plaintiff. Sept. 21, 1858 petition of Sarah Snader of the borough of Harrisburg, Pa. by her next friend Henry Brubaker stated that she married Jonathan B. Snader Mar. 14, 1850. Her husband deserted her without any just or reasonable cause Mar. 22, 1856. Subpoena issued Nov. 24, 1858. Dec. 7, 1859 the court ordered sheriff to make proclamation according to law. Jan. 16, 1860 Sheriff J.M. Eyster reported that he had made proclamation according to law.

Apr. 1859 #2 Dauphin Co., Pa. Appearance Docket filed Jan. 17, 1859. Frederick Parer, defendant in divorce vs. Mary U. Parer, plaintiff. Nov. 16, 1858 petition of Mary U. Parer by her next friend Frances Aldermot stated that she married Frederick Parer Jan. 15, 1849. Her husband abused her and she was forced to leave him Apr. 1, 1857. Subpoena issued Jan. 17, 1859. Aug. 9, 1859 court appointed C.A. Snyder to take depositions in this case.

Apr. 1859 #32 Dauphin Co., Pa. Appearance Docket filed Feb. 2, 1859. George Houser, defendant in divorce vs. Margaret Houser, plaintiff. Feb. 1, 1859 petition of Margaret Houser by her next friend Jacob Ellis stated that she married George Houser Nov. 2, 1851 and he deserted her without any just or reasonable cause that same day. Subpoena issued Feb. 2, 1859.

Apr. 1859 #33 Dauphin Co., Pa. Appearance Docket filed Feb. 2, 1859 Eliza Casey, defendant in divorce vs. John Casey, plaintiff. Undated petition of John Casey stated that he married Eliza McAnil- by Dec. 10, 1857. He accused his wife of adultery with a certain James Carson. In Feb. of 1859 Eliza Casey signed a document which denied she committed adultery and it was witnessed by an alderman in the city of Philadelphia, Pa. John Casey and his wife Eliza Casey separated Jun. 15, 1858.

Apr. 1859 #41 Dauphin Co., Pa. Appearance Docket filed Feb. 3, 1859. Elizabeth Seiders, defendant in divorce vs. Henry Seiders, plaintiff. Feb. 4, 1859 petition of Henry Seiders of Swatara Twp., Dauphin Co., Pa. stated that he married Elizabeth Antrem in 1844. She deserted him without any just or reasonable cause some six months later. Henry Seiders signed his petition "by mark." Subpoena issued Feb. 4, 1859.

Apr. 1859 #75 Dauphin Co., Pa. Appearance Docket filed Feb. 28, 1859. Cecelia C. Houghton, plaintiff in divorce vs. James Houghton, defendant. Feb. 26, 1859 petition of Cecelia C. Houghton of Harrisburg, Pa. by her next friend George Eicholtz stated that she married James Houghton Oct. 13, 1857. She accused her husband of "indignities to her person." Subpoena issued Feb. 28, 1857.

Apr. 1859 #101 Dauphin Co., Pa. Appearance Docket filed Mar. 14, 1859. Otis W. Whittier, defendant in divorce vs. Susan D. Whittier, plaintiff. Feb. 12, 1859 petition of Susan D. Whittier by her next friend Catharine Dubbs stated that she married Otis W. Whittier Jun. 8, 1852. Her husband abused her and thereby forced her to leave him May 11, 1858. Subpoena issued Mar. 14, 1859.

Apr. 1859 #111 Dauphin Co., Pa. Appearance Docket filed Mar. 23, 1859. Adam Bender, defendant in divorce vs. Elizabeth Bender, plaintiff. Mar. 21, 1859 petition of Elizabeth Bender by her next friend Christopher Yeager stated that she married Adam Bender in 1847. She accused him of adultery with Elizabeth Wetzler and she left him in 1848. Nov. 11, 1859 the court ordered Adam Bender to pay wife's court costs through Christopher Yeager. On Jan. 5, 1860 Christopher Yeager testified that Adam Bender had not yet paid him.

Aug. 1859 #12 Dauphin Co., Pa. Appearance Docket filed May 2, 1859. Eleanor Lackey, plaintiff in divorce vs. William Lackey, defendant. Jan. 26, 1859 petition of Eleanor Lackey by her next friend Isaac G. Updynn stated that she married William Lackey about fifteen years ago. He deserted her without any just or reasonable cause about four years ago. Also in this file was Aug. term #12 dated Mar. 12, 1860 in which the court granted Eleanor Lackey a divorce from William Lackey.

Aug. 1859 #13 Dauphin Co., Pa. Appearance Docket filed May 2, 1859. Benjamin Bowman, plaintiff in divorce vs. Mary Bowman, defendant. Undated petition of Mary Bowman for her husband to show cause why he should not pay her alimony.

Aug. 1859 #26 Dauphin Co., Pa. Appearance Docket filed May 10, 1859. Alfred G. Quinlin, defendant in divorce vs. Catharine T. Quinlin, plaintiff in divorce. Apr. 30, 1859 petition of Catharine T. Quinlin by her next friend Samuel H. Madden stated that she married Alfred G. Quinlin Dec. 25, 1844 and he deserted her without any just or reasonable cause Nov. 10, 1850. Subpoena issued May 10, 1859.

Aug. 1859 #49 Dauphin Co., Pa. Appearance Docket filed Jun. 4, 1859. Levi Heim, plaintiff in divorce vs. Mary Heim, defendant. May 23, 1859 petition of Levi Heim stated that he married Mary Reamer Oct. 27, 1846 and he accused her of adultery with William Black. They separated Sept. 27, 1858. Subpoena issued Jun. 4, 1859.

Aug. 1859 #59 Dauphin Co., Pa. Appearance Docket filed Jun. 15, 1859. Catharine Knox, plaintiff in divorce vs. William Knox, defendant. Jun. 15, 1859 petition of Catharine Knox by her mother and next friend Sarah Black. She was living in Harrisburg, Pa. at the time of her petition. She stated that she married William Knox May 2, 1854. "The said William Knox on divers days and times during the last two years has struck me and abused her" etc. Subpoena issued Jun. 15, 1859.

Aug. 1859 #64 Dauphin Co., Pa. Appearance Docket filed Jun. 20, 1859. Caroline Wright, plaintiff in divorce vs. George Wright, defendant. Oct. 14, 1861 court appointed Henry Peffer, Esq. of Harrisburg, Pa. to take depositions in this case
Oct. 19, 1861 between 3 and 5 P.M. Oct. 19, 1861 - "Depositions of witnesses produced, sworn or affirmed and examined by me the 19th day of October A.D. 1861, at my office in the City of Harrisburg, Penna., between the hours of 3 & 5 o'clock P.M., by virtue of the annexed rule of Court of Common Pleas of the County of Dauphin, No. 64, Aug. T. 1859, and notice hereto attached for the examination of witnesses in the case of Caroline Wright by her next friend Henry Lyne vs. George Wright and H.C. Alleman, Esq. appeared for the Plaintiff George Wright defendant appeared in person. John Myers sworn - I am acquainted with Mr. & Mrs. Wright the Plaintiff & Defendant in this case. I have know the Defendant in this case at least ten years, and the Plaintiff in this case Mrs. Wright at least four years. I know them to live together as husband and wife for at least one year, during the year 1857 and a portion of 1858, they separated in Jul. 1858. She left him in consequence of: continued abuse by her husband and refusal to maintain her. I knew him to come home intoxicated repeatedly and abuse her. I saw him a short time before their seperation strike his wife with his fist, and her brother John McCleaster seperated them, he is now in the army. I have often seen him push her, and curse and swear at her. The abuse was often of an outrageous character. I considered it insufferable to bear, the time he struck her, she cried. I was often at the house with George the plaintiff in this case. Sometimes I went there with her brother, he was an associate of mine. Just before they parted George was drunk all the time, and the abuse he gave her and the refusal to maintain her, caused her to leave. him. Examined by Plaintiff - I went to your house with your consent and in your company. I lived in 4th Street at the time. I became acquainted with your wife in

your house. The first time I went to the house was with her brother John, when you was about the house you abused your wife. Sworn, examined and subscribed before me October 19th 1861." (signed Henry Peffer commissioner)

"The plaintiff acknowledged before me that he was married to Caroline McCleaster his present wife the Plaintiff in this case on the 23d of February 1854, Henry Beader, Esq. married us." (signed Henry Peffer commissioner)

"Henry Beader Esq. affirmed. I am an acting Justice of the Peace in this city. I was so in 1854. On the 22d day of February 1854 I married George Wright and Caroline his present wife, the Plaintiff in this case." (signed Henry Beader) "Affirmed, Examined and Subscribed October 19th 1861" (signed Henry Peffer, Commissioner)

Oct. 19, 1861 "I Hereby certify that the above or within witnesses, were duly qualifed and examined at the time and placed stated in the aforegoing caption and subscribed their depositions in my presence." (signed Henry Peffer, commissioner)

Nov. 1, 1861 - "Henry Lyne sworn November 1st, 1861 - I know George Wright and Caroline Wright the parties in this case. I have known George since he was a boy, and have known her since the time they were married. They seperated in July 1858, about one year before they seperated I was Borough Constable, and complaint was lodged to me of bad treatment given by George Wright to his wife. She had a black eye were (*sic*) she was struck by her husband. She made information against him and I arrested him and took him to prison." (signed Henry Lyne)

Nov. 18, 1861 - "Nov. 18, 1861, on hearing the within evidence the court decrees a divorce from the bond of matrimony between Caroline and George Wright, and that they be from henceforth forever seperated from each other - the said defendant to pay the costs of the proceedings." (signed Js. J. Pearson Prest., judge) "Alleman"

Aug. 1859 #78 Dauphin Co., Pa. Appearance Docket filed Jun. 27, 1859. Elizabeth Seiders, defendant in divorce vs. Henry Seiders, plaintiff. Jun. 27, 1859 court issued an alias subpoena.

Aug. 1859 #95 Dauphin Co., Pa. Appearance Docket filed Jul. 11, 1859. Jonathan B. Snader, defendant in divorce vs. Sarah Snader, plaintiff. Original papers are now missing.

Aug. 1859 #101 Dauphin Co., Pa. Appearance Docket filed Jul. 18, 1859. Michael Clarkin, defendant in divorce vs. Mary Clarkin, plaintiff. Jul. 13, 1859 petition of Mary Clarkin of Harrisburg, Pa. by her next friend Josiah Light stated that she married Michael Clarkin Sept. 12, 1857. Her husband deserted her without any just or reasonable cause Sept. 20, 1857. Subpoena issued Jul. 18, 1859.

Nov. 1859 #4 Dauphin Co., Pa. Appearance Docket filed Aug. 24, 1859. Michael Machen, defendant in divorce vs. Mary Machen, plaintiff. Jan. 29, 1859 agreement between the two parties that Michael Machen is to pay all costs of his witnesses and court costs and attorney costs plus $75.00 a year to his wife during their seperation.

Nov. 1859 #17 Dauphin Co., Pa. Appearance Docket filed Sept. 1, 1859. Cornelius Croley, defendant in divorce vs. Hannah Croley, plaintiff. Aug. 31, 1859 petition of Hannah Croley by her next friend B.R. Steinruel stated that she married Cornelius Croley Dec. 23, 1854. Cornelius Croley deserted his wife without any just or reasonable cause May 30, 1857.

Nov. 1859 #32 Dauphin Co., Pa. Appearance Docket filed Sept. 12, 1859. Eleanor Lackey, plaintiff in divorce vs. William Lackey, defendant. Original papers are now missing.

Nov. 1859 #35 Dauphin Co., Pa. Appearance Docket filed Sept. 12, 1859. Alfred G. Quinlin, defendant in divorce vs. Catharine T. Quinlin, plaintiff. Original papers are now missing.

Nov. 1859 #61 Dauphin Co., Pa. Appearance Docket filed Oct. 10, 1859. Cecelia C. Houghton, plaintiff in divorce vs. James Houghton, defendant. Nov. 21, 1859 court issued an order for proclamations to be made. Jan. 16, 1860 sheriff returned that proclamation were made.

Nov. 1859 #62 Dauphin Co., Pa. Appearance Docket filed Oct. 10, 1859. Levi Heim, plaintiff in divorce vs. Mary Heim, defendant. Original papers are now missing.

Jan. 1860 #3 Dauphin Co., Pa. Appearance Docket filed Nov. 21, 1859. John A. Hyers, defendant in divorce vs. Rebecca Jane Hyers, plaintiff. Nov. 14, 1859 petition of Rebecca Jane Hyers by her next friend George S. Allen stated that she married (by the Rev. Joseph Ross of Middletown, Pa.) John A. Hyers Jul. 20, 1849. She accused her husband of adultery with Caroline Wright for which she was sentenced by the Aug. 1858 Sessions of Dauphin Co., Pa. Subpoena issued Nov. 21, 1859.

Jan. 1860 #6 Dauphin Co., Pa. Appearance Docket filed Nov. 22, 1859. Mary Robinson, plaintiff in divorce vs. William Robinson. Undated petition of Mary Robinson by her next friend Washington Barr stated that she married William Robinson Feb. 1, 1847 and he deserted her May 1, 1847. Subpoena issued Nov. 22, 1859.

Jan. 1860 #35 Dauphin Co., Pa. Appearance Docket filed Dec. 6, 1859. Emily Bennett, defendant in divorce vs. Thomas Bennett, plaintiff. Dec. 6, 1859 petition of Thomas Bennett stated that he married his present wife Emily Bennett Nov. 13, 1852. She deserted him without any just or reasonable cause in Aug. of 1858. Subpoena issued Dec. 6, 1859.

Jan. 1860 #65 Dauphin Co., Pa. Appearance Docket filed Dec. 19, 1859. Cornelius Croley, defendant in divorce vs. Hannah Croley, plaintiff. Original papers are now missing.

Apr. 1860 #1 Dauphin Co., Pa. Appearance Docket filed Jan. 16, 1860. Elizabeth Preston, plaintiff in divorce vs. John Preston, defendant. Jan. 13, 1860 petition of Elizabeth Preston by her next friend Polly Patton stated that she married John Preston Jan. 1, 1856 and he "refused to maintain her the said Elizabeth Preston and hath abused her by striking her so as to render her life burdensome and her home unhappy." Therefore she left her husband Jan. 1, 1858. Subpoena issued Jan. 16, 1860.

Apr. 1860 #5 Dauphin Co., Pa. Appearance Docket filed Jan. 17, 1860. Anthony Black, defendant in divorce vs. Rosanna Black, plaintiff. Jan. 3, 1860 petition of Rosanna Black by her next friend Michael Ledwith stated that she married Anthony Black of Harrisburg, Pa. Sept. 29, 1857. She suffered both physical and verbal abuse from her husband causing her to leave him over nine months ago.

Apr. 1860 #7 Dauphin Co., Pa. Appearance Docket filed Jan. 18, 1860. Emily Bennett, defendant in divorce vs. Thomas Bennett, plaintiff. Original papers are now missing.

Apr. 1860 #10 Dauphin Co., Pa. Appearance Docket filed Jan. 19, 1860. Mary Imshoffstall, plaintiff in divorce vs. John Imshoffstall defendant. Jan. 18, 1860 petition of Mary Imshoffstall by her next friend John Snyder stated that she married John Imshoffstall May 30, 1854. "The said John Imshoffstall during the period of three years last past has abused and ill-treated your petitioner by kicking and striking her and threatened to cut and stab her and take her life with dangerous weapons and instraments and has offered such indignities to the person of your petitioners by reason of his kicking and striking her and threatening to cut and stab her as to make her life intolerable and her life burdensome and thereby force her to withdraw from his house and family." She left him Dec. 22, 1859. Subpoena issued Jan. 19, 1860.

Apr. 1860 #49 Dauphin Co., Pa. Appearance Docket filed Feb. 6, 1860. Barbara Denny, plaintiff in divorce vs. Edward Denny, defendant. Jan. 27, 1860 petition of Barbara Denny by her next friend John Q. Adams stated that she married Edward Denny Aug. 21, 1855. She accused him of threatening to throw her down the stairs, break her neck, strike her and - to kick her out of the house.

Apr. 1860 #133 Dauphin Co., Pa. Appearance Docket filed Mar. 12, 1860. Mary Robinson, plaintiff in divorce vs. William Robinson, defendant. Original papers are now missing.

Aug. 1860 #4 Dauphin Co., Pa. Appearance Docket filed Apr. 24, 1860. Conrad Hurd, defendant in divorce vs. Mary L. Hurd, plaintiff. Mar. 13, 1860 petition of Mary L. Hurd by her next friend Alexander Poist stated that she married Conrad Hurd Oct. 14, 1859. He abused her and she left him Nov. 14, 1860. She requested divorce from his bed and board and alimony not to exceed a third of his income and she signed her petition "by mark." Subpoena issued Apr. 23, 1860.

Aug. 1860 #5 Dauphin Co., Pa. Appearance Docket filed Apr. 24, 1860. Eliza Miller, defendant in divorce vs. John J. Miller, plaintiff. Apr. 20, 1860 petition of John J. Miller of Harrisburg, Pa., barber, stated that he married Eliza Lowry Jan. 8, 1842. She abused him and he therefore left her Jul. 15, 1858. Subpoena issued Apr. 23, 1860.

Aug. 1860 #17 Dauphin Co., Pa. Appearance Docket filed Apr. 27, 1860. Catharine Williamson, plaintiff in divorce vs. Silas Williamson, defendant. Apr. 27, 1860 petition of Catharine Williamson by her next friend Simon Eberly stated that she married Silas Williamson Aug. 6, 1857. Her husband abused her and she therefore left him Feb. 20, 1860. Subpoena issued Apr. 26, 1860.

Aug. 1860 #145 Dauphin Co., Pa. Appearance Docket filed Jul. 27, 1860. Margaret Bolen, plaintiff in divorce vs. John Bolen, defendant. Jul. 27, 1860 petition of Margaret Bolen late Margaret Berrier by her next friend Joseph Berrier stated that she married John Bolen Feb. 7, 1850. However, unknown to her new husband was still married to a Mary Gallagher who she believes is still alive. Her husband deserted her without any just or reasonable cause more than two years ago.

Aug. 1860 #180 Dauphin Co., Pa. Appearance Docket filed Jun. 29, 1860 is according to the indexes Frances West, plaintiff in divorce vs. Robert West, defendant. Actually, this file is of an entirely different case.

Nov. 1860 #3 Dauphin Co., Pa. Appearance Docket filed Aug. 28, 1860. Herman Sauppe, plaintiff in divorce vs. Salina Sauppe, defendant. Jul. 14, 1860 petition of Herman Sauppe stated that he married Salina Ely, Aug. 15, 1859. He accused her of adultery with a certain man, name unknown, who was with her in Philadelphia, Pa., Jul. 4, 1860 and there committed adultery with her. Subpoena issued Aug. 27, 1864.

Nov. 1860 #5 Dauphin Co., Pa. Appearance Docket filed Aug. 28, 1860. Eliza Miller, defendant in divorce vs. John J. Miller, plaintiff. Original papers are now missing.

Nov. 1860 #12 Dauphin Co., Pa. Appearance Docket filed Aug. 31, 1860. Margaret Bolen, plaintiff in divorce vs. John Bolen, defendant. Dec. 5, 1860 Dauphin Co., Pa. sheriff reported that the defendant John Bolen was not to be found in his bailiwick. He also said he had published notice for him to appear in court in *The Patriot and Union* newspaper for four successive weeks.

Nov. 1860 #80 Dauphin Co., Pa. Appearance Docket filed Oct. 15, 1860. Catharine G. Balmer, plaintiff in divorce vs. Benjamin Franklin Balmer, defendant. Oct. 11, 1860 petition of Catharine G. Balmer, a minor now in her 19th year, by her next friend Ezekial R. Kindig. She married Mar. 1, 1860 Benjamin Franklin Balmer. Shortly before her miscarriage in Aug. of 1860, her husband abused her and threatened to kick her. Because of this abuse and a lack of food, she was forced to leave her husband Sept. 18, 1860.

Nov. 1860 #96 Dauphin Co., Pa. Appearance Docket filed Oct. 30, 1860. Amelia Romberger, defendant in divorce vs. Jonas Romberger, plaintiff. Oct. 6, 1860 petition of Jonas Romberger of Mifflin Twp., Dauphin Co., Pa. stated he married Amelia Pontius Mar. 6, 1856 and she deserted him without any just or reasonable cause Sept. 11, 1858. Subpoena issued Oct. 29, 1860.

Jan. 1861 #24 Dauphin Co., Pa. Appearance Docket filed Dec. 4, 1860. Amelia Romberger, defendant in divorce vs. Jonas Romberger, plaintiff. Dec. 4, 1860 subpoena issued to Amelia Romberger for the third Monday of Jan. 1861. Dec. 11, 1860 sheriff reported that he had served subpoena on Amelia Romberger. Feb. 6, 1861 Jonas Romberger was ordered to pay Amelia Romberger $45.00 for her expense in preparing and taking care of her defense. Feb. 27, 1861 order served on Jonas Romberger by sheriff.

Jan. 1861 #25 Dauphin Co., Pa. Appearance Docket. Amelia Romberger, defendant in divorce vs. Jonas Romberger, plaintiff.

Dec. 27, 1860 petition of Amelia Romberger denies she deserted her husband "but that from sickness and bodily infirmity and the cruel conduct of her husband she was obliged to leave him in the year 1858 when she was in a family way and go to her mother's in the neighborhood and that her said husband has been to see her but twice since the birth of her last child in 1858 and has evinced no wish or desire to have her live with him and treat her becomeingly. That her said husband has a reasonable amount of personal property that her said husband is a young, energetic capable man abundantly able to earn a living for himself and his wife and children and that his father is a man of considerable wealth. That your petitioner is a young woman with two children, one about four years of age, the other about two years of age and both helpless and that she has no means in her own right to pay the expences of his proceedings against her or to support herself and children during the time said proceedings are pending and has not received a penny from her said husband for her own or their children's support for more than two years past and has refused to contribute to their support." Defendant's bill Nov. term 1861 was $64.22 included: Henry Martin 74 miles 6 days, John Lehman 80 miles 6 days, Peter Deibler 76 miles 6 days, Mary Taylor 66 miles 6 days, A.J. Pontius 74 miles 6 days, Sarah Pontius 74 miles 6 days, J.D. Pontius 74 miles 6 days, B. Rumberger 80 miles 5 days, Joseph Enterline 78 miles 6 days. Jan. 1862 Term Mary Martin 74 miles 1 day, John Lehman 80 miles 1 day, B. Rumberger 80 miles 1 day, J.D.Pontius 74 miles 1 day, B. Buffington 76 miles 1 day, Dr. Stroup 76 miles 1 day Total Bill $89.70 1/2. Dr. Stroup sentenced to twenty days in Dauphin Co., Pa. Jail for contempt of court by not appearing in court as subpoenaed in this case.

Jan. 15, 1861 - "Jonas Romberger vs. Amelia Romberger: In Dauphin Comm. Pleas No. 24 Jan. T. 1861 In the matter of the Rule to show case etc. - Jonas Romberger in answer saiths, that he is possessed of or owns no property whatsoever except a few articles of personal property and these being chiefly pieces of furniture still kept by him since he was compelled to break up housekeeping by the causeless desertion of him by his wife, all of said property not being worth more than two hundred dollars. That he is dependent solely upon his own exertions for a livelihood and since his wife deserted him has not received any help from his father. That he has no trade or occupation save that of a farmer, and after his marriage he farmed a part of his father's farm on the shares and it took all he made to keep himself and his wife. That he has no work now and has had none for some time. That last spring and summer he assisted a painter and paper-hanger in his work and that for such assistance he received his boarding, and his wages or earnings amounted to between $30. and $40. according to the best of his recollection. That because of the wilful (*sic*) and malicious desertion of him by his wife he was compelled in the spring of 1859 to give up farming on the shares as herin before mentioned, and since that time except in the summer of 1859 when he was well he has worked when he could find work ans has difficulty to earn enough for his own livelihood. That to so much of the allegations in the petition upon which the Rule in this case is found as charge him with neglect or improper conduct to his wife or family he now interposes his solemn denial." (signed Jonas Romberger) "Sworn and Subscribed before me this 15 Jan. 1861" (signed Wm. Mitchell Prothy.)

Jan. 1861 #49 Dauphin Co., Pa. Appearance Docket filed Dec. 19, 1860. David W. Goodfellow, defendant in divorce vs. Henrietta Anderson Goodfellow, plaintiff. Dec. 19, 1860 petition of Henrietta Anderson Goodfellow by her next friend William K. Verbeke stated that she married David W. Goodfellow Apr. 27, 1857 in the borough of Harrisburg, Pa. David W. Goodfellow deserted his wife without any just or reasonable cause Jun. 5, 1857. He had been married before and his first wife was still married to him at the time he married Henrietta Anderson without telling her he was still married. Subpoena issued Dec. 19, 1860.

Apr. 1861 #21 Dauphin Co., Pa. Appearance Docket. Jan. 26, 1861 petition of John H. Jones stated that he had married Martha Updegrove May 27, 1852. He accused her of adultery with Benjamin Hartshorne. Subpoena issued Jan. 29, 1861. In an undated petition Martha Jones denies adultery.

Apr. 1861 #65 Dauphin Co., Pa. Appearance Docket filed Feb. 25, 1861. Herman Suppe, plaintiff in divorce vs. Salina Sauppe, defendant. Original papers are now missing.

Apr. 1862 #4 Dauphin Co., Pa. Appearance Docket filed Jan. 20, 1862. Levi Heim, defendant in divorce vs. Mary Heim, plaintiff. Sept. 26, 1861 petition of Mary Hime (sic) by her next friend Henry Lyon stated that she married Levi Hime (sic) Oct. 1, 1853. She accused him of adultery with Kate Spazn and of abusing her and forcing her to leave him. She signed her petition "by mark." Subpoena issued Jan. 20, 1862. Oct. 30, 1863 court appointed John McClaughlin, Esq., alderman and justice of the peace to take depositions in this case on Nov. 9, 1863 between the hours of 10 A.M. and 3 P.M.

Nov. 1863 #20 Dauphin Co., Pa. Appearance Docket filed Sept. 5, 1863. Levi Heim, defendant in divorce vs. Mary Heim, plaintiff. Sept. 2, 1863 petition of Mary Hime (sic) by her next friend Henry Lyon stated that she married Oct. 31, 1853 Levi Hime (sic). She accused him of adultery with Elizabeth Stetzel since Jan. 1, 1863 and also mentioned that she had left her husband Jun. 1, 1861 because of his abuse to her. Supboena issued Sept. 2, 1863.

Nov. 16, 1863 - "Depositions of Witnesses produced, sworn and examined by me the 16th day of Novr. A.D. 1863 at my office at Harrisburg between the hours of 6 o'clock A.M. and 9 P.M. by virtue of the Enexed (sic) rule of Court of (word left blank) and notice hereto attached for the examination of witnesses, in a certain case depending in said Court, wherein Mary Hime (sic) is plaintiff, and Levi Hime, (sic) is defendant. Ann Pugh aged twenty four residence Harrisburg being produced, sworn and examined on the part of the plaintiff, deposeth and saith I have known Levi Himes (sic) to come to the part of the house formerly occupied by me, and knocked and was admited (sic) and passed through my appartment (sic) into that part occupide (sic) by Elizabeth Zitzel and went upstares (sic) and there remained untill 4 or 5 o'clock in the morning with said Zitzel, thare (sic) being but one bed in that part of the house occupide (sic) by said Zitzel. I have known him to come and remain as much as three nights in one weak (sic) untill Four o'clock in the morning with said Zitzel above mentioned. Said Levi Himes (sic) visited said Zitzel in this manner in the months of Jul. Aug. and Sept. 1863. Said Levi Himes (sic) is the husband of Mary Hime (sic) the plaintiff, and further saith not." (signed Ann Pugh)

Anna Emanuel, aged twenty, residing in Harrisburg, being produced (and sworn), and examined on the part of the plaintiff as a witnesses deposeth and saith, that in the month of Aug. 1863 I lived next door to Elizabeth Zitzel and often seen Levi Hime (sic) come to said Zitzel's house and take said Zitzel out walking, and once they went together to the Circus. I have seen him, said Hime (sic) gow (sic) into said Zitzel's house several times from nine to ten o'clock at night and further saith not." (signed by mark Anna Emanuel)

Edward Poist aged sixteen years residence Harrisburg being sworn and examnined on the part of the plaintiff as a witness deposeth and saith - that in the month of Aug. 1863, I was in the neighbourhood of Elizabeth Zitzel and I saw Levi Hime (sic) coming out of the house of Elizabeth Zitzel about five o'clock in the morning. I saw said Hime there once before that, said Zitzel invited him, said Himes (sic) to take supper with her, he refused. I have a knoledge (sic) of all the peopel (sic) in that neighbourhood, Hime (sic) did not live in that part of the city, further saith not." (signed by mark Edward Poist)
Court granted divorce Dec. 1, 1863.

Apr. 1867 #129 Dauphin Co., Pa. Appearance Docket filed Feb. 9, 1867. Samuel Glassbrenner, defendant in divorce vs. Susanna Glassbrenner, plaintiff. Feb. 2, 1864 petition of Susanna Glassbrenner by her next friend and father Samuel Handshue stated that she married Samuel Glassbrenner Jan. 25, 1855. Her husband abused her and she therefore left him Jul. 8, 1855. She had been granted a divorce and now wants $40.00 a year alimony. Subpoena issued Feb. 5, 1867.

York County, Pennsylvania
Divorces, 1790-1860

◆　　　◆　　　◆

Mar. 27, 1790 - Petition of John Brugh before W. Scott. John Brugh of Franklin Twp., York Co., Pa. married about twenty-four years ago Catharine Sweigart by a German clergyman in the borough of York, Pa. At that time he lived in a rented house in Paradise Twp., York Co., Pa. About two years later he purchased a small farm in Warrington Twp., York Co., Pa. and soon after that they moved onto it. The farm was too small to maintain his family, so about six years later he sold it. He leased a valuable farm near Hagerstown, Md. but his wife would not accompany him. Seven months later he returned to York Co., Pa. because all his efforts to persuade her to join him had failed. He bought a mill and farm in Strabine Twp., York Co., Pa. but still his wife would not live with him. She moved to Baltimore, Md. where she still is living. He testified that he treated his wife very well. Since her removal to Baltimore, Md. she has been repeatedly guilty of adultery and has had two children born to her there.

Jan. 21, 1792 - Subpoena from the Commonwealth of Pennsylvania to Catharine Brugh formerly Catharine Swigert of York Co., Pa. to appear in court in Philadelphia, Pa. Apr. 2, 1792.

Feb. 23, 1792 - Petition of John Brugh before John Edie, justice of the peace of York Co., Pa. He had married Catharine Swigert about eighteen years ago and lived together nine years and upwards bearing three children. He has been a resident of Pa. over a year. Catharine Brugh left her husband and children almost nine years ago and moved to Baltimore, Md. She has had two bastard children born in Baltimore, the last one is from a married man with whom she lives. John Brugh signed his petition in German script.

Sept. 3, 1793 - Commonwealth of Pennsylvania to Catharine Brugh wife of John Brugh late of York Co., Pa. subpoena to appear in court in Philadelphia, Pa. on the second Monday of Dec. 1793.

Mar. 31, 1798 - Commonwealth of Pennsylvania subpoena to Catherine Brugh the wife of John Brugh late of York Co., Pa. to appear in court in Philadelphia, Pa. the first Monday of Sept. 1798.

Sept. 1798 - William McClellan, sheriff, testified that he left a copy of subpoena Aug. 10, 1798, at the house of Abraham Swigart of Berwick Twp., York Co., Pa. the last place of residence in Pa. of Catherine Brugh.

Apr. 27, 1790 - Petition of John Etter of Lancaster Co., Pa., yeoman, before Henry Flagle next friend of Barbara Selser wife of Michael Selser of York Co., Pa. She married Michael Selser Sept. 1, 1789 in Hopewell Twp., York Co., Pa. He abused her and was found guilty of assault and battery by the Court of General Quarter Sessions of York Co., Pa. Earlier he had shot and wounded her "in a most dangerous manner." His threats forced her to leave "and hath thrown her into the greatest distress and misery." Barbara Selser signed her petition "by mark."

May 4, 1790 - William Atlee ordered a subpoena to Michael Selser to answer to his wife's libel for a divorce.

Apr. 15, 1791 - Subpoena to Michael Selser of York Co., Pa. for him to appear in court to answer his wife's libel for a divorce in July of 1791 at Philadelphia, Pa. Conrad Laub, sheriff, reported that he had served the subpoena.

Jun. 23, 1791 - Petition before Thomas McKean, Esq., chief justice of the Supreme Court of Pennsylvania, of Matthew Martin of Hamilton Bann Twp., York Co., Pa., farmer. He married in Apr. of 1783 Elizabeth Matthias. In Aug. of 1785 she deserted him without any just cause and never returned. She has frequently committed adultery with Neil O'Donnel and on Aug. 10, 1790, she was married to him by Daniel Griffith, Esq. justice of the peace in Chester Co., Pa. In Oct. of 1790, she had a child by Neil O'Donnel and she declared that Neil O'Donnel was its father.

May 20, 1793 - Petition of Frederick Lawber of York Co., Pa. who had married Barbara Ebersole. She committed adultery with a married man, Henry Bowman, of Washington Co., Md. and had confessed to doing so. Despite repeated admonishing, she left him and "continues to live a prostitute and seperate from the petitioner." Frederick Lawber swore his petition before Samuel Edie, associate judge of York Co., Pa. and signed his petition "by mark."

May 25, 1793 - Subpoena issued to Barbara Lawber to appear in court at Philadelphia, Pa. Sept. 9, 1793, to answer her husband's libel for a divorce.

Feb. 1, 1786 - Marriage license for Philip Adam Shreiner of Manheim Twp., Lancaster Co., Pa., yeoman, to marry Elizabeth Singhaas of Donegal Twp., Lancaster Co., Pa.

Jun. 10, 1793 - Petition of Philip Shriner of Newberry Twp., York Co., Pa. that he married, Jan. 31, 1786, Elizabeth Singhaas the daughter of Casper Singhaas of Mount Joy Twp., Lancaster Co., Pa. They had three children Catharine, Michael and Elizabeth all since dead. Over a year ago she abandoned him without any reasonable cause. She has since committed adultery with Joseph Watkins and married him in May 1794. They now live in Northumberland Co., Pa.

Oct. 20, 1794 - John Hubley, Esq., clerk of the Court of Quarter Sessions of Lancaster Co., Pa. testified that Philip Adam Shreiner took out a license to marry Elizabeth Singhaas Feb. 1, 1786.

Oct. 21, 1794 - Deposition of David Hammond, Esq., that he married in May or Jun. of 1793, a woman calling herself Elizabeth Singhorse (sic) to a man calling himself Joseph Watkins.

Jul. 26, 1795 - Favel Roan, Esq., late sheriff of Northumberland Co., Pa., testified he served a subpoena on Elizabeth Shreiner by leaving her a copy more than fifteen days before she was due to appear in court.

Sept. 13, 1795 - Court appointed William Wilson, John Thornburg and Walter Clark to take depositions in this case.

Oct. 25, 1795 - Henry Muhlenberg, minister at Lancaster, Pa. testified that he married Philip Adam Shreiner of Manheim Twp., Lancaster Co., Pa., yeoman, to Elizabeth Singhaas of Donegal Twp., Lancaster Co., Pa. Feb. 1, 1786.

Oct. 25, 1795 - Deposition of Abel Person that a woman known as Elizabeth Singhaas was married to Joseph Watkins in Turbot Twp., Northumberland Co., Pa. by David Hammond, Esq., last May or Jun. He also said that they have continued to live together as man and wife in Turbot Twp., Northumberland Co., Pa. He has also heard Elizabeth say that she was formerly married to a Philip Shreiner and that they had lived together as man and wife in Newberry Twp., York Co., Pa.

Oct. 25, 1795 - Robert Chambers gave a deposition stated that he knew Philip and Elizabeth Schreiner (sic) when they lived together as man and wife in Newbury Twp., York Co., Pa. He knows that she left her husband in Apr. of 1794. He has often heard Elizabeth say that she is the daughter of Casper Singhaas of Lancaster Co., Pa. Robert Chambers signed his deposition "by mark."

Apr. 9, 1796 - Court granted Philip Shriner a divorce from his wife Elizabeth Shriner.

Dec. 3, 1799 - Petition of Jacob Hantz before Jacob Rudisell, judge of the Court of Common Pleas of York Co., Pa. testified that he married Elizabeth Sheaffer about four years ago. At the time of the marriage she was pregnant by a certain George Spone but he did not know that fact until after they were married. After their marriage his wife often committed adultery with George Spone.

Dec. 28, 1799 - Subpoena to Elizabeth Hantz, late of York Co., Pa. for her to appear in court at Philadelphia, Pa. the third Monday of Mar. 1800, to answer her husband's libel for a divorce (Mar. 28, 1800).

Mar. 28, 1800 - Nicholas Gelovick, sheriff, reported that he served the subpoena on Elizabeth Hantz Mar. 13, 1800.

Dec. 27, 1800 - Court appointed Jacob Eddy, Esq., and Conrad Laub, Esq., to be commissioners to take testimony in this case.

Dec. 28, 1800 - Subpoena to Elizabeth Hantz, wife of Jacob Hantz of York Co., Pa., to appear in court to answer his libel for a divorce in Philadelphia, Pa. the third Monday of Mar. 1801.

Feb. 19, 1801 - Subpoena to Elizabeth Hantz notifying her that depositions concerning her husband's libel for a divorce will be taken at the house of Philip Gossler, innkeeper, in the borough of York, Pa. Mar. 5, 1801.

Mar. 5, 1801 - Deposition of John Kniseley, aged 47 years, who said he served a copy of the subpoena on Elizabeth Hantz or Spahr, Feb. 23, 1801. He knew both parties since they were about ten or twelve years old. He knew they went to Church together and were regarded as man and wife. He had noticed she was pregnant shortly before her marriage. She now lives with George Spahr as his wife. They have had two children since she separated from Hantz and it is reported they are married. He has heard Elizabeth say that the child she had after her marriage to Hantz was actually a child of George Spahr.

Mar. 5, 1801 - Deposition of Catharine Hantz of Dover Twp., York Co., Pa. widow, aged fifty years and upwards. She is the mother of Jacob Hantz and has known his present wife Elizabeth Hantz since her infancy and was present with Rev. Gaub married them over four years ago. Her son discovered his wife's pregnancy about four weeks after his marriage. About four and a half months after that she had a male child and a few days later she went to see her daughter-in-law and the new child. At that time her daughter-in-law told her that the child's father was George Spahr. About four or five weeks after the birth, Elizabeth went home to her parents. Her husband went away to Spain and returned about a year later. After his return his wife went to live with George Spahr and has continued there having two more children by him. The three children are with their mother at the house of George Spahr and are supported by him. Catharine Hantz signed her deposition "by mark."

Mar. 5, 1801 - Deposition of John Hantz of Dover Twp., York Co., Pa., farmer, aged about thirty years and a brother of the libellant Jacob Hantz, who he has known since he was seven years old. He was present at his brother's wedding about four years and upwards ago. He has heard that Jacob Hantz's wife Elizabeth said that the child born four or five months after their marriage was really fathered by George Spahr. He has heard that she has had two more children by George Spahr.

Mar. 26, 1801 - Supreme Court of Pennsylvania granted a divorce to Jacob Hantz from his wife Elizabeth Hantz.

May 2, 1800 - Petition of Catharine Bernhart of the borough of York, Pa. by her next friend Conrad Laub stated she was married by William Kuntz, German clergyman, in the borough of York, Pa. Jacob Bernhart lived in York, Pa. and vicinity until 1792 at which time he sold all the family's provisions and deserted her. He continued to live in York Co., Pa. but separated from her until Jan. 1795 when he left the area entirely and she has not seen or heard of him since. Catharine Bernhart testified these facts before Andrew Billmeyer and signed her petition "by mark."

Jul. 21, 1800 - Ludwick Shrive testified before John Forsyth, justice of the peace of York Co., Pa. that he made diligent inquiry to find Jacob Bernhart in York Co., Pa. and could not find him. He left a copy of the subpoena at his last known residence, the home of James Murray in the borough of York, Pa.

Sept. 13, 1800 - Subpoena from the Commonwealth of Pennsylvania to Jacob Bernhart late of the borough of York to appear in court the second Monday of Dec. 1800 in Philadelphia, Pa.

Nov. 22, 1800 - Nicholas Gelovick, sheriff of York Co., Pa., testified that he made proclamation at the York Co., Pa. courthouse Nov. 19th, 20th, and 21st of 1800 for the appearance in court of Jacob Bernhart to answer his wife's libel for a divorce.

Mar. 20, 1801 - Commonwealth of Pennsylvania issued a subpoena to Jacob Bernhart late of the borough of York, Pa. to appear in court in Philadelphia, Pa. the first Monday of Sept. 1801.

Mar. 28, 1801 - (No. 154 Sept. 1800 term) Subpoena from the Commonwealth of Pennsylvania to John Edie and Jacob Hay both of York Co., Pa. to take testimony in the case of Catherine Bernhart vs. Jacob Bernhart a libel in divorce.

Sept. 14, 1801 - Deposition of Ignatius Lightner, aged about 40 years, of the borough of York, Pa. before John Edie and Jacob Hay taken at the house of George Hay in the borough of York, Pa. He testified that Jacob Bernhart and his wife Catharine were married about 1783 by Rev. Nicholas Kuntz, Lutheran minister in the borough of York, Pa. and that they had several children and lived in the borough of York, Pa. several years. Sometime in 1795, Jacob Bernhart deserted his family and never returned. Catharine Bernhart has continued to live in the borough of York, Pa. ever since. Rumor has it that Jacob went to Va. Jacob Bernhart was "a worthless man" and he was "very much addicted to strong drink."

Sept. 14, 1801 - Deposition of John Glessner of the borough of York, Pa., cordwainer, aged about 33 years before John Edie and Jacob Hay taken at the home of George Hay in the borough of York, Pa. He testified that Jacob and Catharine Bernhart lived several years in the borough of York, Pa. prior to Jacob's desertion of his family in 1795. Immediately after he left, Jacob Bernhart went to Shepherstown, Va. Jacob Bernhart never came back to Pa. and he doesn't know where he is now. Jacob Bernhart "was a drunken worthless man" who left no provision for his wife and children.

Sept. 18, 1801 - The Supreme Court of Pennsylvania granted Catharine Bernhart a divorce from her husband Jacob Bernhart.

Jan. 21, 1786 - Subpoena from the Commonwealth of Pennsylvania to John Shultz of York Town, York Co., Pa. to appear in court Apr. 10, 1786, in Philadelphia, Pa. to show cause why his wife Barbara should not have a divorce from him.

Apr. 5, 1786 - William McClelland, deputy sheriff of York Co., Pa., testified before William Scott, justice of the peace of York Co., Pa., that he served subpoena on John Shultz, Mar. 25, 1786, by leaving him a copy at York Town for him to appear in court Apr. 10, 1786.

Apr. 21, 1801 - Petition of Barbara Shultz (formerly Barbara Milhoof) by her next friend Frederick Younce, of the borough of York, Pa. She said that about twenty years ago she was married to John Shultz, a stocking weaver of the borough of York, Pa. by Rev. Kurtz a German clergyman in the borough of York, Pa. They lived together about four years, then her husband left her and went to his step-father's house in Freys-Town, York Co., Pa. "removing with him all the property she had received from her father." He stayed there about a year then went to Abbottstown then in York Co., Pa. now in Adams Co., Pa. where he has resided ever for the past fifteen years. Barbara Shultz testified her petition before Jacob Rudisell, associate judge of the Court of Common Pleas, York Co., Pa. and signed her petition "by mark."

Apr. 28, 1801 - Subpoena from the Commonwealth of Pennsylvania to John Shultz, late of York Co., Pa., stocking weaver, to appear in court in Philadelphia, Pa. the first Monday of Sept. 1801. Summons was served Jun. 28, 1801, on John Shultz by Nicholas Gelovick, sheriff, who charged mileage 103 miles to Philadelphia, Pa.

Sept. 19, 1801 - Subpoena from the Commonwealth of Pennsylvania to John Shultz, late of York Co., Pa., stocking weaver, to appear in court in Philadelphia, Pa. the second Monday of Dec., 1801. Copy of subpoena left at his residence Oct. 12, 1801, by Nicholas Gelovick, sheriff of York Co., Pa., who charged mileage of 103 miles to Philadelphia, Pa.

Dec. 14, 1801 - Supreme Court of Pennsylvania appointed Conrad Laub and John Forsyth to take depositions in the divorce action of Barbara Shultz vs. John Shultz.

Dec. 18, 1801 - Deposition of Martin Brenisen of the borough of York, Pa., aged about 70 years, taken at the house lately of Balser Spangler, deceased. Martin Brenisen had known John Shultz thirty years and his wife Barbara Shultz about twenty years. They lived together in the same house as man and wife three or four years. John Shultz without any just cause left his wife about sixteen or seventeen years ago taking with him the goods she received from her father.

Dec. 18, 1801 - Deposition of Captain John Brenisen, aged about forty years, of the borough of York, Pa. He had known John Shultz about thirty years and Barbara Shultz about twenty years. They lived together as man and wife three or four years. John Shultz deserted his wife in 1783 or 1784 and never returned. John Shultz had no reason to complain about his wife yet still was determined to leave her.

Dec. 18, 1801 - Deposition of Margaret Brenisen, aged about sixty-six years, of the borough of York, Pa. She had known John Shultz nearly thirty-five years and had known Barbara Shultz about twenty years. About twenty years ago, Barbara Shultz and John Shultz were accompanied by several persons who had been at their marriage to York Town. The marriage took place at the home of Barbara's father in the county. John and Barbara Shultz came to York Town and rented in the house of Jacob Reedisole and from there came and lived with her (Margaret Brenisen). They lived together as man and wife about four years. John Shultz deserted his wife without any reasonable cause. Barbara Shultz behaved kindly to him but John Shultz would not live with her. When he left he took nearly all the property his wife had received from her father. He left her about sixteen years ago. John Shultz was extremely cruel to his wife. When they lived in her house "John Shultz beat and severely used the said Barbara Shultz without the least provocation." Margaret Brenisen signed her deposition "by mark."

Sept. 19, 1801 - Subpoena from the Commonwealth of Pennsylvania to Barbara Mayer to appear in court in Philadelphia, Pa. the second Monday of Dec. 1801, to answer her husband's libel for a divorce.

Oct. 13, 1801 - Petition of Rudolph Myer of Somerset Co., Pa. that he married his present wife in May of 1776, Barbara, and they lived together fourteen years and she has "for a considerable time past given herself up to adulterous practices." He therefore wanted a divorce.

Dec. 14, 1801 - John Mayer testified that he served the subpoena on Barbara Mayer on or before Nov. 23, 1801, and he signed his name as "Johannes Mayer."

Dec. 14, 1801 - Subpoena from the Commonwealth of Pennsylvania to Barbara Mayer to appear in court in Philadelphia, Pa. the third Monday of Mar. 1802, to answer her husband's libel for a divorce.

Dec. 15, 1801 - Court appointed John Tome and John Gloniger to take depositions in the divorce action of Rudolph Mayer vs. Barbara Mayer.

Dec. 23, 1801 - Deposition of Jacob Mayer of Dauphin Co., Pa. who testified that he knew John Mayer since infancy and became acquainted with Barbara Mayer at her father's house in Heidleburg Twp., Lancaster Co., Pa. and at her brother-in-law John Mayer's house in Heidleburg Twp., Lancaster Co., Pa. about two years before the marriage of John and Barbara Mayer. He was present at their wedding about twenty-six years ago in the Mennonite meetinghouse in Lebanon Twp. then in Lancaster Co., Pa. which was preformed by Frederick Kauffman a Mennonite minister, since deceased. They lived as man and wife about fourteen or fifteen years. It was "common report" and was "generally believed" that Barbara Mayer committed adultery with Benjamin Young of Heidleburg Twp. now in Dauphin Co., Pa. Barbara Mayer deserted her husband about eleven or twelve years ago when they lived in York Co., Pa. and eloped without any just cause.

Dec. 23, 1801 - Deposition of Henry Mayer of Lebanon Twp., Dauphin Co., Pa., farmer. He had known John Mayer since infancy and had known Barbara Mayer about two years before her marriage while she lived in her father's house. They were married about twenty-six years ago by Frederick Kauffman, since deceased, in Mennonite meetinghouse and lived as man and wife about fifteen years. It was commonly believed that Barbara Mayer had committed adultery with Benjamin Young "as she herself had made oath thereof before a Justice of the Peace as he this affirmant is informed." About eight or nine years ago, Barbara Mayer told him she was married to Frederick Fuhrman. About two months later he was at Frederick Fuhrman's house and noted that they did indeed live together. She had left John Mayer about eleven years ago while they lived in York Co., Pa.

Dec. 23, 1801 - Deposition of John Shenk of Heidleburg Twp., Dauphin Co., Pa., miller. He had known John Mayer since infancy and had known Barbara Mayer shortly before her marriage to John Mayer. He was present at their wedding about twenty-five or twenty-six years ago in Mennonite meeting house in Lebanon Twp. by Frederick Kauffman. They lived together fourteen or fifteen years. After Barbara Mayer left her husband she had a child and Benjamin Young was reported to be the father of this child.

Dec. 24, 1801 - Deposition of George Hoke of Warwick Twp., York Co., Pa., farmer. He "is little acquainted with the Libellant, that he has been acquainted with the defendant about seven or eight years." Barbara Mayer told him that her daughter living with her was the daughter of Benjamin Young. He knows this girl and she is about eleven or twelve years old. He also knows Frederick Fuhrman and he "further told this affirmant that he Fuhrman did sleep with her the Defendant and he would sleep with her if Rudolph Mayer was present." Frederick Fuhrman and Barbara Mayer have lived together in his neighborhood about three years just as if they were man and wife.

Dec. 24, 1801 - Deposition of Henry Sheffer, Esq., of Heidleburg Twp., Dauphin Co., Pa. He knew John Mayer about twenty years and he knew Barbara Mayer since she was a child and lived with her father who was a near neighbor of his. John and Barbara Mayer lived together as man and wife about fourteen or fifteen years. About ten or eleven years ago Barbara Mayer made oath before him that she had a bastard child and the father of the child was Benjamin Young of Heidleburg Twp. He issued a warrant and as he understood the affair was settled. At the time she pressed charges against Benjamin Young, her husband lived in York Co., Pa. He knows that Frederick Fuhrman and Barbara Mayer have lived together for seven or eight years now.

Mar. 15, 1802 - Court granted John Mayer a divorce from his wife, Barbara Mayer.

Mar. 25, 1802 - Abraham Mayer, farmer, of Dauphin Co, Pa. testified that he served a subpoena on Barbara Mayer Feb. 20, 1802, for her to appear in court to answer her husband's libel for a divorce.

Jan. 2, 1802 - Commonwealth of Pennsylvania issued a subpoena to Anthony Black to appear in court in Philadelphia, Pa. the third Monday of Mar. 1802 to answer his wife's libel for a divorce.

Jan. 14, 1802 - Petition of Mary Black by her next friend Henry Lechler, Jr. before Jacob Crever, justice of the peace. She testified that she married Anthony Black Feb. 16, 1789, and he deserted her without any just reason or cause Dec. 4, 1794. She therefore wanted a divorce.

Mar. 9, 1802 - Robert Grayson, sheriff, testified that he could not find Anthony Black in his bailiwick and left a copy of the subpoena at his last residence in Carlisle, Pa.

Mar. 15, 1802 - Commonwealth of Pennsylvania issued a subpoena to Anthony Black to appear in court in Philadelphia, Pa. the first Monday of Sept. 1802 to answer his wife's libel for a divorce.

Mar. 15, 1802 - Supreme Court of Pennsylvania appointed George Logue, Esq. and James McCormick, Esq. of Carlisle, Pa. to take testimony in the case of Mary Black, libellant, vs. Anthony Black, respondent.

Sept. 4, 1802 - Deposition of Abraham Loughridge, merchant, of Carlisle, Pa. He was present at their wedding in York Co., Pa. about ten or eleven years ago. They lived together over four years and had three children. Anthony Black left his family in the fall of 1794 and went to Va., where he is now he doesn't know. Catherine Black then went to live with her mother in the borough of Carlisle, Pa. Anthony Black visited his wife at her mother's house about fifteen months after he left but only stayed one or two hours. He abandoned his wife "at night with all the property he could take with him and defrauded his creditors and it was reported he took a woman with him from one Fergerson near Mount (Cook?) about six miles west of Carlisle."

Sept. 6, 1802 - Israel Israel, Esq., high sheriff of the city and county of Philadelphia, testified he made public proclamation at the old courthouse as well as in market place three successive days for the appearance of Anthony Black to answer his wife's libel for a divorce.

Feb. 20, 1806 - Feb. Term, 1806, Common Pleas Docket Book B, York Co., Pa., page 352 - petition of Elizabeth Chesney by her next friend Jacob Grove for a divorce from Thomas Chesney. Court subpoenaed Thomas Chesney to appear at the next court of common pleas the third Monday of May 1806.

Aug. Term 1806 #14 - Joshua Cooper vs. Isabella Cooper - Note: The Common Pleas Docket didn't specify if this was a divorce action or not, but I included this because it might possibly be a divorce action.

Nov. Term 1813 - Nov. 5, 1813 - Proof of the service or the subpoena in the case of John Lauck for a divorce being made in open court. An Alias subpoena awarded returnable at next term.

Apr. Term 1816 - Apr. 1, 1816, Andrew Zimmerman failed to appear in court to answer his wife Lydia's libel for a divorce. Apr. 2, 1816, the court declared them divorced.

Aug. Term 1816 - (between cases 232 and 233) Aug. 7, 1816, court issued a divorce in the case of Christian Rokohl vs. Mary Rokohl.

Jan. Term 1817 - (between cases 98 and 99) John Baugher petitioned for a divorce from his wife Elizabeth Baugher. Subpoena issued for the first Monday of Apr. 1817.

Jan. Term 1817 #206 - John Baugher vs. Elizabeth Baugher. York Co. sheriff served subpoena on defendant Apr. 7, 1817. Court appointed Jacob Ernst, Esq. commissioner to hold an interrogation at Little Winchester, Baltimore Co., Md. May 12, 1818, Court of Common Pleas of York Co., Pa. declines to grant a divorce because "he has not proved a residence in Pennsylvania sufficient to entitle him to a Divorce."

Apr. Term 1817 - (between cases 167 and 168) Petition of Susanna Grove by her next friend John Flory, Sr. for a divorce from her husband Jacob Grove. Subpoena issued for the first Monday of Aug. 1817.

Aug. Term 1817 - (between cases 284 and 285) Aug. 15, 1817, petition of John Walter for a divorce. Case to he heard on the first Monday of Nov. 1817.

Aug. Term 1817 - Petition of Rachel Dare by her next friend Joseph Hutton for alimony. Subpoena issued to Michael Dare. Continued Aug. Term 1818 #226.

Dec. Term 1817 - (between cases 128 and 129) Petition of Mary Aston by her next friend Hugh Morthland for a divorce from her husband James Aston. See divorce Aug. Term 1818 #221. Subpoena issued Nov. 3, 1817. Defendant not found in the county by sheriff. Alias subpoena issued and sheriff reported again that defendant could not be found in his bailiwick Apr. 9, 1818. Depositions taken Aug. 6, 1818, and the court gave Mary Aston her divorce Aug. 6, 1818.

Nov. Term 1817 - Petition of Elizabeth Welsh by her next friend John Brennshols for a divorce from her husband Frederick Welsh. Continued Aug. 1818 Term #222. Subpoena issued Nov. 4, 1817. Defendant not in sheriff's bailiwick. Alias subpoena issued for the first Monday of Jan. 1818. Sheriff reported that defendant was still not to be found in his bailiwick. Nov. 2, 1818 depositions taken and the court granted Elizabeth Welsh a divorce from her husband Frederick Welsh.

Nov. Term 1817 - Nov. 13, 1817, petition of Elizabeth Walters by her next friend George Trump for a divorce from Frederick Walters. Subpoena issued for an inquisition the first Monday of Jan. 1818.

Nov. Term 1817 - Nov. 14, 1817, petition of Anthony Stewart for a divorce from his wife Susanna Stewart. Subpoena issued for the first Monday of Jan. 1818.

Nov. Term 1817 - Dec. 16, 1817, in the case of John Walter against Elizabeth Walter for a divorce. Court appointed George Haller and Daniel Heckert to investigate.

Jan. Term 1818 - Jan. 5, 1818, petition of Susanna Noon by her next friend Samuel Miller for a divorce from her husband Samuel Noon. Subpoena issued returnable the first Monday of Apr. 1818.

Apr. Term 1818 - Apr. 7, 1818, petition of Catharine Palmer for a divorce from her husband Godfrey Palmer. Subpoena issued for the first Monday of Aug. 1818.

Apr. Term 1818 - Apr. 9, 1818, three divorces granted in the cases of Susanna Grove vs. Jacob Grove, Elizabeth Walters vs. Frederick Walters, and John Walter vs. Elizabeth Walter.

Aug. Term 1818 - Aug. 3, 1818, petition of Jacob Sides for a divorce from his wife Susanna Sides. Subpoena issued returnable the first Monday of Nov. 1818.

Aug. Term 1818 #223 - Christina Burk by her next friend Frederick Stein vs. Thomas Burk. Subpoena issued returnable the first Monday of Aug. 1818. Sheriff says Thomas Burk was not to be found in his bailiwick. Alias subpoena issued and sheriff again stated that Thomas Burk was not to be found in his bailiwick. Jan. 7, 1819, depositions were taken and divorce was granted.

Aug. Term 1818 #224 - Hannah Getz by her next friend Joseph Smith vs. John Getz. Subpoena issued to John Getz returnable the first Monday of Aug. 1818. Sheriff reported that John Getz was not to be found in his bailiwick. Alias subpoena issued returnable the first Monday of Nov. 1818. Sheriff again reported that John Getz was not to be found in his bailiwick. Jan. 4, 1819, the sheriff reported that he had duly published the notices required by law in two area newspapers. Depositions were taken Apr. 5, 1819, and the court granted Hannah Getz her divorce Aug. 2, 1819.

Aug. Term 1818 #225 - Mary Wolf by her next friend George Wolf vs. Anthony Wolf. Aug. 6, 1818, Mary Wolf petitioned for a divorce from her husband Anthony Wolf. Subpoena issued Nov. 2, 1818. Sheriff reported that Anthony Wolf was not to be found in his bailiwick. Alias subpoena issued returnable the first Monday of Jan. 1819 (Jan. 4, 1819). Sheriff again reported that Anthony Wolf was not to be found in his bailiwick. May 5, 1819, sheriff reported that he had published the notices required by law in the York Recorder but had received no response. Depositions were taken Aug. 2, 1819, and the court then granted Mary Wolf a divorce from her husband Anthony Wolf.

Aug. Term 1818 #226 - Rachel Dare by her next friend Joseph Hutton vs. Michael Dare. Rachel Dare petitioned for alimony Sept. 16, 1817. Subpoena returnable Nov. 3, 1817, was served on oath Nov. 6, 1817. Depositions taken Jan. 8, 1818. Continued 1818 through Jan. 1824.

Aug. Term 1818 #227 - Petition of Anthony Stewart for a divorce from his wife Susanna Stewart. Subpoena returnable the first Monday of Jan. 1818 was served on defendant Jan. 8, 1818. Continued 1818 through Jan. 1824.

Aug. Term 1818 #228 - Jacob Sides vs. Susanna Sides petition for a divorce. Subpoena returnable the first Monday of Nov. 1818. Subpoena issued and returned by the sheriff not served. Alias subpoena issued returnable the first Monday of Jan. 1819 (Jan. 4, 1819). Sheriff reported that defendant was not to be found in his bailiwick. Apr. 5, 1819, sheriff reported that he published notice in the *York Recorder* without response. Aug. 2, 1819, depositions were taken and divorce was granted.

Apr. Term 1819 #179 - Rachel Dare by her next friend John Hart vs. Michael Dare. Apr. 7, 1819, petition for a divorce. Subpoena returnable the first Monday of Aug. 1819. Sheriff returned that he had served the subpoena. Ruled for trial to be held Oct. 26, 1819. Oct. 26, 1819, the jury ruled for Rachel Dare and granted her a divorce from her husband Michael Dare.

Apr. Term 1819 #316 - Catharine Miller by her next friend Jacob Shuk vs. Christian Miller petition for a divorce. Subpoena issued was returnable the first Monday of Aug. 1819. Alias subpoena issued returnable for the first Monday of Nov. 1819. Sheriff reported that Christian Miller was not in his bailiwick. Jan. 4, 1820, sheriff reported that notice was served in several newspapers without a response. Case continued through Jan. 1824.

Apr. Term 1819 #317 - William Kline vs. Catherine Kline petition for a divorce. Subpoena issued returnable first of Nov. 1819. Summons was served. Continued Jan. 3, 1821, but neither party appeared. Court then appointed Daniel Heckert, Esq. to take depositions of witnesses in this case. Continued through Jan. Term 1824.

Aug. Term 1820 #333 - John Sherman vs. Sarah Sherman petition for a divorce. Subpoena returnable the first Monday of Apr. 1820, was returned by sheriff not served. Alias subpoena returnable the first Monday of Aug. 1820 served on Sarah Sherman Aug. 8, 1820. Jan. 12, 1821, the libellant files for commission to Manchester, Baltimore Co., MD. Jan. 3, 1822, divorce granted by the court.

Aug. Term 1820 #334 - Joseph Eck vs. Susanna Eck petition for a divorce. Subpoena returnable the first Monday of Apr. 1820, also not found. Nov. 6, 1820, sheriff reported that he had placed notice in the *York Recorder* but no response for four successive weeks. Court then appointed Daniel Stechert, Esq. to take depositions in this case.

Aug. Term 1820 #334 - Mary Ann Desours vs. Ernest Desours petition for a divorce. Subpoena returnable the first Monday of Apr. 1820. Sheriff reported it was not served because defendant could not be found in his bailiwick. Alias subpoena issued that was returnable the first Monday of Aug. 1820 but was returned unserved. Nov. 6, 1820, the sheriff reported that he had advertised in the *York Recorder* for four successive weeks without a response. Court appointed Daniel Steckert, Esq. to take depositions of witnesses in this case. Jan. 1, 1821, depositions were taken and the court granted Mary Ann Desours a divorce from her husband Ernest Desours.

Aug. Term 1820 #335 - Magdalena Richmond by her next friend Isaac Depew vs. John Richmond petition for a divorce. Subpoena issued returnable the first Monday of Aug. 1820 was returned not served. Aug. 7, 1820, alias subpoena issued for first Monday of Nov. 1820. Sheriff served this subpoena. Several continuations. On July 29, 1822, the court granted Magdalena Richmond a divorce from her husband John Richmond.

Aug. Term 1820 #336 - Michael Beard vs. Elizabeth Beard petition for a divorce. Aug. 8, 1820, subpoena for the first Monday of Nov. 1820 (Nov. 6, 1820). Nov. 17, 1820, answer of respondent filed. Continuation through Jan. Term 1824.

Aug. Term 1821 #307 - Paul Illins vs. Salome Illins petition for a divorce. Aug. 6, 1821, subpoena served on respondent. Jan. 3, 1822, the court granted Paul Illins a divorce from his wife Salome Illins.

Aug. Term 1821 #308 - John Leas vs. Sarah Leas petition for a divorce. Aug. 6, 1821, subpoena not served. Alias subpoena issued returnable Nov. 6, 1821, was served on Sarah Leas but she failed to appear or file any answer to the petition. Depositions of witnesses in this case were to be taken by William Squibb, Esq. Continued through Aug. Term 1829.

Aug. Term 1821 #309 - George Stahli vs. Elizabeth Stahli petition for a divorce. Aug. 8, 1821, subpoena issued returnable Nov. 6, 1821. Sheriff said Elizabeth Stahli was not in his bailiwick. Alias subpoena issued returnable Jan. 7, 1822, and the sheriff again reported that Elizabeth Stahli was not to be found in his bailiwick. Apr. 1, 1822, sheriff reported that notice was placed in the *York Gazette* for four successive weeks. Aug. 6, 1822, depositions were given and the court granted George Stahli a divorce from his wife Elizabeth Stahli.

Aug. Term 1821 #310 - Elizabeth Mullin vs. John Mullin petition for a divorce. Aug. 8, 1821, subpoena issued returnable Nov. 6, 1821. Sheriff reported that John Mullin was not to be found in his bailiwick. Alias subpoena issued returnable Jan. 7, 1822. Again the sheriff reported that John Mullin was not to be found in his bailiwick. Apr. 1, 1822, sheriff reported that noticed was published in the *York Gazette* for four successive weeks without respond. Aug. 6, 1822, depositions were taken and the court granted Elizabeth Mullin a divorce from her husband John Mullin.

Aug. Term 1821 #311 - Margaret Workman by her next friend Nicholas Pyle vs. Samuel Workman petition for a divorce. Aug. 8, 1821, subpoena returnable Nov. 6, 1821 was issued. Nov. 6, 1821, sheriff reported that Samuel Workman was not to be found in his bailiwick. Alias subpoena issued returnable Jan. 7, 1822, also returned because the sheriff could not find Samuel Workman in his bailiwick. Apr. 1, 1822, sheriff reported that notice had been placed in the *York Gazette* for four successive weeks without any response. Court appointed Daniel Steckert, Esq. to take depositions in this case. Case continued through Aug. Term 1829.

Jan. Term 1822 #150 - John Stouffer vs. Mary Stouffer petition for a divorce and subpoena issued for Apr. 1, 1822. Sheriff returned that libellent could not be found in his bailiwick. Alias subpoena issued for Aug. 5, 1822. Sheriff again reported that Mary Stouffer could not be found in his bailiwick. He advertised in York newspapers for four successive weeks but Mary Stouffer failed to respond. Apr. 5, 1823, the court granted John Stouffer a divorce from his wife Mary Stouffer.

Jan. Term 1822 #151 - Catharine Hoover by her next friend John Song vs. John Hoover petition for a divorce. Subpoena issued for Apr. 1, 1822. Sheriff said libellant was not to be found in his bailiwick. Alias subpoena issued for Aug. 5, 1822. Sheriff again said John Hoover was not to be found in his bailiwick. He placed notice in the *York Gazette* for four consecutive weeks but John Hoover failed to appear. The court granted Catharine Hoover a divorce from her husband John Hoover Jan. 6, 1823.

Jan. Term 1822 #152 - Sarah Adams by her next friend George Leitner vs. Peter Adams petition for a divorce. Subpoena issued for Apr. 1, 1822. Sheriff reported that Peter Adams was not to be found in his bailiwick. Alias subpoena for Aug. 5, 1822, was issued but results were the same. The sheriff placed notice for Peter Adams to appear in court for four successive weeks in the *York Gazette* but Peter Adams failed to appear. The court granted Sarah Adams a divorce from her husband Peter Adams Jan. 6, 1823.

Jan. Term 1822 #213 - Magdalena Thomas by her next friend George Walters vs. Isaac Thomas petition for a divorce. Subpoena issued for Apr. 1, 1822, but libellent was not to be found in sheriff's bailiwick. Alias subpoena issued for Aug. 5, 1822, but again Isaac Thomas was not to be found in the sheriff's bailiwick. The sheriff placed four weeks notice for him to appear in York, Pa. newspapers Nov. 4, 1822, but he failed to appear on that date. Court granted Magdalena Thomas a divorce from her husband Isaac Thomas Aug. 4, 1823.

Aug. Term 1822 #273 - Eve Hummer by her next friend Jacob Zeigler vs. John Hummer petition for a divorce dated Aug. 5, 1822. Subpoena issued for the first Monday of Nov. 1822. Sheriff served the subpoena. Continued to Apr. 14, 1823. Court granted Eve Hummer a divorce from her husband John Hummer Apr. 18, 1823.

Aug. Term 1822 #274 - Margaret Larew by her next friend Jacob Fissell vs. William Larew petition for a divorce dated Aug. 5, 1822. Subpoena issued for the first Monday of Nov. 1822. Sheriff said that William Larew was not to be found in his bailiwick. Alias subpoena was issued for Jan. 6, 1823, and the sheriff again said that William Larew was not to be found in his bailiwick. Four weeks notice to appear was placed by the sheriff in York, Pa. newspaper but there was no response. On Nov. 3, 1823, depositions were taken and the court granted Margaret Larew a divorce from her husband William Larew.

Aug. Term 1822 #287 - Isabel Skully by her next friend William John vs. Stephen Skully petition for divorce dated May 28, 1822. Subpoena issued for Aug. 5, 1822. Sheriff returned that Stephen Skully was not to be found in his bailiwick. Alias subpoena was issued for Nov. Term 1822, but still the sheriff reported that Stephen Skully was not to he found in his bailiwick. The sheriff placed four weeks of successive notice for Stephen Skully's appearance in court in York, Pa. newspaper but he received no response. Jan. 8, 1823, the court appointed Daniel Steckert, Esq. to take depositions in this case. Continued through Jan. Term 1824.

Nov. Term 1822 #170 - Mary Eichholtz by her next friend George Aughinbach vs. Jacob Eichholtz petition for a divorce. Subpoena issued for first Monday of Jan. 1823. Feb. 6, 1823, settled and ended by the parties in person and all costs were then paid.

Nov. Term 1822 #171 - Elizabeth Iser by her next friend Samuel Hill vs. Joshua Iser petition for a divorce dated Nov. 13, 1822. Subpoena issued for Jan. 6, 1823. Sheriff reported that respondent was not to be found in his bailiwick. Alias subpoena issued for Apr. 8, 1823, but the respondent or libellee was still not to be found. Four successive weeks notice was placed in the York Gazette, a York, Pa. newspaper, by the sheriff without any response. Aug. 4, 1823, the court appointed Daniel Steckert, Esq. to take depositions. Continued through Jan. Term 1824.

Jan. Term 1823 #107 - Rosanna Crowl by her next friend Jacob Gitier vs. William Crowl petition for a divorce. Subpoena issued for the first Monday of Apr. 1823. Continued through Aug. Term 1829.

Apr. Term 1823 #317 - John Nelson vs. Polly Nelson petition for a divorce dated Mar. 1, 1823. Subpoena issued but sheriff returned that libellee is not to be found in his bailiwick. Alias subpoena issued for Aug. 4, 1823. Sheriff again returned that libellee is not to be found in his bailiwick. Notice was published by the sheriff in the newspaper for her to appear in court Nov. 3, 1823, to answer her husband's libel for a divorce. Nov. 3, 1823, the court appointed Isaac Kirk, Esq. to take depositions in this case. Continued through Jan. Term 1824.

Apr. Term 1823 #318 - Phebe Bayly by her next friend Joseph Taylor vs. James Bayly petition for a divorce. Subpoena issued for the first Monday of Aug. 1823. Sheriff returned that libellee was not to be found in his bailiwick. Alias subpoena was issued for the first Monday of Nov. 1823. Sheriff again returned that libellee was not to be found in his bailiwick. Sheriff placed notice in the *York Gazette* for four successive weeks for the appearance of James Bayly but he failed to appear. Jan. 5, 1824, the court appointed George Hoober, Esq. to take depositions in this case. The court granted Phebe Bayly a divorce from her husband James Bayly Apr. 7, 1824.

Apr. Term 1823 #319 - William Flinn vs. Julian Flinn petition for a divorce. Subpoena issued returnable the first Monday of Aug. 1823. Sheriff reported that libellee Julian Flinn was not to he found in his bailiwick "and now 8th August 1823 James Lewis, Esq. attorney for the libellee (Julian Flinn) appears for the said Julian Flinn and states he is not interested to gainsay the facts stated in the libel and confesses the same. Whereupon proclamation being made, and the Court Decree (*sic*) a Divorce and separation between the parties above named and that the marriage between them is null and void."

Aug. Term 1823 #265 - John Keller vs. Susanna Keller petition for a divorce dated Aug. 4, 1823. Subpoena returnable Nov. 3, 1823. Sheriff returns that libellee is not to be found in his bailiwick. Alias subpoena was issued for Jan. 5, 1824. Libellee was not to be found in his bailiwick the sheriff again reported. Court ordered the sheriff to place notice in York newspaper for libellee to appear to be published for four successive weeks.

Aug. Term 1824 #11 - Catherine Hammer by her next friend Andrew Perky vs. George Hammer petition for a divorce. Alias subpoena issued Aug. 3, 1824, returnable. Aug. 3, 1824, the court appointed Jacob Ruthuck, Esq. to take depositions in this case.

Nov. Term 1825 #80 - William Young vs. Eliza Young petition for a divorce. Subpoena issued returnable the first Monday of Nov. 1825.

Apr. Term 1826 #28 - William Young vs. Eliza Young petition for a divorce. Apr. 3, 1826, court appointed George Klinefelter, Esq. to take depositions in this case. Apr. 5, 1826, the court gave William Young a divorce from his wife Eliza Young and ordered the libellant to pay all the court costs.

Apr. Term 1826 #34 - Letitia Marshall by her next friend Charles Bailey vs. James Marshall petition for a divorce. Subpoena issued that was returnable Feb. 6, 1826. Apr. 5, 1826, the court appointed George Hoober, Esq. to take depositions in this case. On May 9, 1826, the court granted Letitia Marshall a divorce from her husband James Marshall.

Aug. Term 1826 #14 - Charlotte Bushman by her next friend John Demath vs. Abraham Bushman petition for a divorce. Subpoena issued returnable Apr. 10, 1826. Apr. 10, 1826, alias subpoena issued. See Nov. Term 1826 #4.

Aug. Term 1826 #15 - Mary Bair by her next friend Jacob Krone vs. George Bair. Subpoena on divorce issued returnable Apr. 10, 1826. Alias subpoena issued Apr. 10, 1826. See Nov. Term 1826 #3.

Aug. Term 1826 #48 - Frances Mary Fattnal by her next friend Michael Sour vs. Samuel Alexander Fattnal petition for a divorce. Subpoena issued returnable Oct. 16, 1826. Alias subpoena issued Oct. 16, 1826. Continued Jan. Term 1827 #19.

Aug. Term 1826 #49 - Ebenezer Bell vs. Rebecca Bell petition for a divorce. Subpoena issued returnable Oct. 16, 1826. Alias subpoena issued Oct. 16, 1826. Continued Apr. Term 1827 #51.

Nov. Term 1826 #3 - Mary Bair by her next friend Jacob Trone vs. George Bair petition for a divorce. Alias subpoena issued. Court appointed D. Shultz, Esq. to take depositions Nov. 7, 1826. Continued to Aug. Term 1830 #2.

Nov. Term 1826 #4 - Charlotte Bushman by her next friend John Demuth vs. Abraham Bushman petition for a divorce. Alias subpoena issued. Nov. 7, 1826, the court appointed Ignatius Leitner, Esq. to take depositions in this case. Jan. 1, 1827, the court granted Charlotte Bushman a divorce from her husband Abraham Bushman and ordered the libellant to pay the costs.

Jan. Term 1827 #19 - Francis Mary Fatnall by her next friend Michael Sower vs. Samuel Alexander Fatnall petition for a divorce.

Apr. 5, 1827, the court appointed Daniel Heckert, Esq. of the borough of York, Pa. to take depositions and on the same day the court replaced him with John Darraugh of the City of Pittsburgh, Pa.

Jan. Term 1827 #36 - Hannah Schnell by her next friend Thomas Metzler vs. Phillip Schnell petition for a divorce. Alias subpoena issued Dec. 19, 1827. Original subpoena was issued Feb. Term, 1826, #24. Apr. 5, 1827, the court appointed Daniel Heckert, Esq. to take depositions and also appointed James Hughes, Esq. of Mifflin Co., Pa. to take depositions on behalf of the plaintiff.

Jan. Term 1827 #37 - Frederick Morganthal vs. Lydia Morganthal petition for a divorce. Alias subpoena issued Dec. 19, 1826. Original was Nov. Term 1826 #8. Apr. 2, 1827, Daniel Heckert, Esq. was appointed by the court to take depositions. Apr. 4, 1827, the court granted Frederick Morganthal a divorce from his wife Lydia Morganthal and ordered the libellant to pay costs of $11.80. Apr. 26, 1827, the plaintiff paid the costs in full.

Apr. Term 1827 #48 - Mary Machlin by her next friend William Ramsey vs. John Machlin petition for a divorce. Subpoena issued Feb. 23, 1827. Alias subpoena continued to Aug. Term 1827 #13.

Apr. Term 1827 #50 - Susan Clark by her next friend Michael Welsh vs. Harman Clark petition for a divorce. Alias subpoena issued Feb. 23, 1827, "issued in mistake" original Nov. Term 1825 #97. (Note: I'm not sure whether "issued in mistake" was referring to the first or the second subpoena - E.T.)

Apr. Term 1827 #51 - Ebenezer Bell vs. Rebecca Bell subpoena in divorce. Original Nov. Term 1826 #49. Subpoena was issued Feb. 23, 1827. Case was continued through Apr. Term 1836.

Apr. Term 1827 #55 - Samuel Winter vs. Eve Winter. Subpoena in divorce issued Feb. 28, 1827. Alias subpoena continued to Aug. Term 1827 #14.

Aug. Term 1827 #13 - Mary Machlin by her next friend William Ramsey vs. John Machlin. Original Apr. Term 1827 #48. Alias subpoena issued. On Aug. 6, 1827, the court appointed Robert Hammersly, Esq. to take depositions in this case. Publication of hearing in the Oct. 16, 23, and 30th, 1827, issued of the *York Gazette* was made. On Nov. 8, 1827, the court granted Mary Machlin a divorce from her husband John Machlin.

Aug. Term 1827 #14 - Samuel Winter vs. Eve Winter. Alias subpoena in divorce issued Aug. 4, 1829. On Nov. 6, 1827, the court appointed Joseph Welshons, Esq. to take depositions in this case.

Jan. Term 1828 #5 - Mary Siechrist by her next friend Philip Sheffor vs. Daniel Siechrist. Subpoena in divorce issued. Alias subpoena continued to Apr. Term 1828 #17.

Jan. Term 1828 #6 - Eva Fissel vs. John Fissel original Jun. Term 1827 #189. Alias subpoena issued. On Aug. 4, 1824, the court appointed Charles F. Fisher, Esq. to take depositions in this case. On Nov. 4, 1828, the court granted Eva Fissel a divorce from her husband John Fissel and ordered the libellant to pay the costs.

Jan. Term 1828 #7 - George S. Nichols vs. Hannah Nichols. Original Nov. Term 1827 #187. Alias subpoena issued. On Apr. 7, 1828, the court appointed Daniel Heckert, Esq. to take depositions in this case. On Apr. 8, 1828, the court granted George S. Nichols a divorce from his wife Hannah Nichols and ordered the libellant to pay all costs.

Apr. Term 1828 #4 - Elizabeth Martin, alias Norbec, by her next friend John Hughenbaugh vs. Henry Martin, alias Norbec. Subpoena in divorce issued.

Apr. Term 1828 #5 - Elizabeth Schweitzer by her next friend Philip Waggoner vs. David Schweitzer. Subpoena in divorce issued. Alias subpoena continued to Aug. Term 1828 #25.

Aug. Term 1828 #16 - Sarah Koch by her next friend Elizabeth Buehler vs. Daniel Koch. Subpoena in divorce issued. On Aug. 4, 1828, the court appointed Charles F. Fisher, Esq. to take depositions in this case. On Aug. 6, 1828, the court granted Sarah Koch a divorce from her husband Daniel Koch and ordered the respondent to pay all the costs.

Aug. Term 1828 #25 - Elizabeth Schweitzer by her next friend Philip Waggoner vs. David Schweitzer. Alias subpoena in divorce issued. The original was Apr. Term 1828 #5. On Jan. 5, 1829, the court appointed Larkwith Spangler, Esq. to take depositions in this case. On Jan. 5, 1829, the court granted Elizabeth Schweitzer a divorce from her husband David Schweitzer and ordered the libellant to pay the costs.

Apr. Term 1829 #11 - Mary Alderice by her next friend John Woyer vs. David Alderice subpoena in divorce.

Aug. Term 1829 #9 - Sally Worley by her next friend William

Worley vs. Jacob Worley subpoena in divorce. Alias subpoena continued to Nov. Term 1829 #68.

Aug. Term 1829 #10 - Jacob Smyser vs. Nancy Smyser subpoena in divorce.

Nov. Term 1829 #4 - Maria Haines by her next friend Joseph B. Archer vs. Henry Haines subpoena in divorce. Alias subpoena continued to Jan. Term 1830 #48.

Nov. Term 1829 #14 - Elizabeth Morx by her next friend Henry Grass vs. John Morx alias subpoena in divorce. Original was Aug. Term 1829 #61. Jan. 5, 1830, court appointed Z. Spangler to take depositions in this case. Feb. 9, 1830, the court granted Elizabeth Morx a divorce from her husband John Morx.

Nov. Term 1829 #55 - Barbara Mickey by her next friend Samuel Stouch vs. John Mickey subpoena in divorce. Alias subpoena continued to Jan. Term 1830 #14.

Nov. Term 1829 #68 - Sally Worley by her next friend William Worley vs. Jacob Worley alias subpoena in divorce. Original was Aug. Term 1829 #9. Nov. 4, 1829, court appointed Charles F. Fisher, Esq. to take depositions in this case. Jan. 7, 1830, court granted Sally Worley a divorce from her husband Jacob Worley. Jan. 30, 1830, all costs paid.

Nov. Term 1829 #69 - Elizabeth Baugher by her next friend Peter Sontay vs. John Baugher alias subpoena in divorce. Original was Apr. Term 1829 #68. Jan. 6, 1830, court appointed Penrose Robinson, Esq. to take depositions in this case. May 4, 1830, depositions were read to the court and the court granted Elizabeth Baugher a divorce from her husband John Baugher.

Jan. Term 1830 #3 - Nancy Miller vs. John Miller subpoena in divorce. Alias subpoena in divorce continued to Apr. Term 1830 #14.

Jan. Term 1830 #12 - Elizabeth Sheffer by her next friend Rudolph Forry vs. Jacob Sheffer alias subpoena in divorce. Original was Nov. Term 1829 #27.

Jan. Term 1830 #14 - Barbara Mickey by her next friend Samuel Stouch vs. John Mickey alias subpoena in divorce. Original was Nov. Term 1829 #55. Apr. 6, 1830, court appointed Penrose Robinson, Esq., to take depositions in this case. May 4, 1830, depositions were read to the court and the court granted Barbara Mickey a divorce from her husband John Mickey.

Jan. Term 1830 #48 - Maria Haines by her next friend Joseph B. Archer vs. Henry Haines alias subpoena in divorce. Original was Nov. Term 1829 #4. Jan. 4, 1830, court appointed Penrose Robinson, Esq. to take depositions in this case. Apr. 5, 1830, depositions were filed and the court granted Maria Haines a divorce from her husband Henry Haines.

Jan. Term 1830 #14 - Nancy Miller vs. John Miller alias subpoena in divorce. Original was Jan. Term 1830 #3. Apr. 5, 1830, the court appointed Zachariah Spangler, Esq. to take depositions in this case.

Aug. Term 1830 #2 - Mary Bair (sic) by her next friend Jacob Trone vs. George Bear (sic) subpoena in divorce issued Apr. 13, 1830. Original was Nov. Term 1826 #3. Nov. 7, 1826, D. Shults, Esq. was appointed by the court to take depositions. Aug. 2, 1830, depositions filed and the court granted Mary Bair a divorce from her husband George Bear.

Aug. Term 1830 #54 - Jane Dougherty by her next friend Emmanuel Bullet vs. Henry Dougherty subpoena in divorce issued June 28, 1830. Alias subpoena in divorce continued to Nov. Term 1830.

Nov. Term 1830 #9 - Jane Dougherty by her next friend Emmanuel Bullet vs. Henry Dougherty. Original was Aug. Term 1830 #54. Alias subpoena issued Aug. 16, 1830. On Jan. 1, 1831, the court appointed Robert Cunningham, Esq. of Peachbottom Twp., York Co., Pa., to take depositions in this case. Apr. 4, 1831, depositions were filed and the court granted Jane Dougherty a divorce from her husband Henry Dougherty. Total costs of this case were $13.12 1/2.

Nov. Term 1830 #40 - Daniel Fry vs. Lydia Fry subpoena in divorce issued Sept. 14, 1830. Alias subpoena continued to Apr. Term 1831 #26.

Apr. Term 1831 #4 - Elizabeth Kimmell by her next friend Peter Dinkle vs. Joseph Kimmell subpoena in divorce issued Jan. 8, 1831. Alias subpoena in divorce continued to Aug. Term 1831 #6.

Apr. Term 1831 #26 - Daniel Fry vs. Lydia Frey alias subpoena issued Mar. 4, 1831. Original was Nov. Term 1830 #40.

Aug. Term 1831 #4 - Elizabeth Eisenhart by her next friend Peter Moul vs. Samuel Eisenhart subpoena in divorce served. On Aug. 2, 1831, the court appointed Jacob Ernst, Esq. to take depositions in this case. On Aug. 22, 1831, the depositions were filed. On Jan. 2, 1832, the court granted Elizabeth Eisenhart a divorce from her husband Samuel Eisenhart. The costs of this case were $10.01.

Aug. Term 1831 #5 - John P. Lechrone vs. Catharine Lechrone subpoena in divorce served. On Aug. 2, 1831, the court appointed Penrose Robinson, Esq. to take depositions in this case. On July 29, 1831, "the Libellant appears and denies the several matters and things alleged in the libel except as to the marriage and prays an issue be found to inquire of a publication filed." On Aug. 17, 1835, the jury finds for the defendant. Fees for this case were $16.00.

Aug. Term 1831 #6 - Elizabeth Kimmell by her next friend Peter Dinkle vs. Joseph Kimmell alias subpoena in divorce. Original to Apr. Term 1831 #4. On Aug. 2, 1831, the court appointed Esquire Ross of Rosstown to take depositions in this case. On Sept. 6, 1831, the depositions were filed and read to the court and the court granted Elizabeth Kimmell a divorce from her husband Joseph Kimmell. Fees in this case were $14.84.

Aug. Term 1831 #16 - Catharine Ingles by her next friend Adam N. Zopus vs. Thomas Ingles subpoena in divorce served. On Aug. 2, 1831, the court appointed George Klinefelter, Esq. to take depositions in this case. On Sept. 6, 1831, the depositions were filed and read to the court and the court granted Catharine Ingles a divorce from her husband Thomas Ingles. On Nov. 8, 1831, the defendant was ordered to pay the costs of these proceedings which was $8.37 1/2.

Aug. Term 1831 #39 - Jacob Koch vs. Eve Koch subpoena in divorce served. On Aug. 2, 1831, the court appointed William Caldwell, Esq. to take depositions in this case. On Sept. 1, 1831, the defendant by his attorney John Evans appears and makes a defense.

Aug. Term 1831 #60 - Sarah Wolf by her next friend Daniel Moore vs. Jacob Wolf subpoena in divorce. On Aug. 2, 1831, the court appointed William Caldwell, Esq. to take depositions in this case. On Sept. 6, 1831, the depositions were filed and read to the court. On Nov. 8, 1831, the court granted Sarah Wolf a divorce from her husband Jacob Wolf and decreed that the defendant should pay the costs which were $8.25.

Nov. Term 1831 #36 - Catharine Bear by her next friend David Kimmell, Esq. vs. John B. Bear subpoena in divorce served. On Nov.

8, 1831, the court appointed Z. Spangler, Esq. to take depositions in this case. On Jan. 23, 1831 the depositions were filed. On Feb. 14, 1832, rule to take depositions on ten days notice to adverse counsel. On Apr. 6, 1832, case was argued. On May 1, 1832, the court decreed a divorce for Catharine Bear from her husband John B. Bear. On May 21, 1832, the respondent by his attorney Daniel Durkee appealed the court's decree to the supreme court. On May 29, 1834, the supreme court upheld the decree issued by the Court of Common Pleas of York, Pa.

Jan. Term 1832 #2 - John Burger vs. Catharine Burger subpoena in divorce "served by copy."

Apr. Term 1832 #3 - Nancy Geitz by her next friend John Geitz vs. Jacob Geitz subpoena in divorce served. Defendant pleads that the facts contained in the petition are not true. Plaintiff replies that the facts are indeed true. Apr. 2, 1832, the court appointed Daniel Bailey, Esq. to take depositions in this case between 10 o'clock A.M. and 5 P.M. on May 12, 1832. On Aug. 7, 1832, the court appointed Penrose Robinson, Esq. to take depositions that same day. On Aug. 8, 1832, the court decreed a divorce for Nancy Geitz from her husband Jacob Geitz. Costs were $12.06 in this case.

Apr. Term 1832 #10 - Catharine Reiley by her next friend John Reiman vs. John Reiley subpoena in divorce. Alias subpoena continued to Aug. Term 1832 #22.

Apr. Term 1832 #21 - Peter Dinkle, Jr. vs. Catharine Dinkle subpoena in divorce "served by copy." On Apr. 4, 1832, the court decreed a divorce for Peter Dinkle, Jr. from his wife Catharine Dinkle. Costs were $10.20 in this case

Apr. Term 1832 #26 - Matthias Bollinger vs. Elizabeth Bollinger subpoena in divorce. Alias subpoena in divorce continued to Aug. Term 1832 #108.

Aug. Term 1832 #4 - George Winebrener vs. Mary Winebrener subpoena in divorce served. On Aug. 7, 1832, the court ordered Mary Winebrener to reply to her husband's libel by three o'clock this afternoon which she did. Court granted George Winebrener a divorce from his wife Mary Winebrener Aug. 7, 1832. Costs were $10.00

Aug. Term 1832 #22 - Catharine Reiley by her next friend John Reiman vs. John Reiley alias subpoena in divorce. Original to Apr. Term 1832 #10. On Nov. 8, 1832, the court appointed George Klinefelter, Esq. to take depositions in this case. On Nov. 8, 1832, because a subpoena and alias subpoena revealed that respondent could not be found in York Co., Pa. and notice was placed four successive weeks in *York Republican* and *York Democrat* prior to the first day of Aug. Term 1832 the court appointed George Klinefelter, Esq. to take depositions. On Dec. 11, 1832, the depositions were filed and the court granted Catharine Reiley a divorce from her husband John Reiley.

Aug. Term 1832 #108 - Matthias Bollinger vs. Elizabeth Bollinger alias subpoena in divorce. On Nov. 6, 1832, the court appointed David Shultz, Esq. to take depositions in this case. On Dec. 11, 1832, the depositions were filed and the court granted Matthias Bollinger a divorce from his wife Elizabeth Bollinger.

Nov. Term 1832 #2 - Charles F. Wagner vs. Julianna E. Wagner subpoena in divorce. Alias subpoena continued to Jan. Term 1833 #29.

Nov. Term 1832 #3 - John Throne vs. Christina Throne subpoena in divorce served. On Jan. 10, 1832, the court decreed a divorce for John Throne from his wife Christina Throne. Costs were $5.62 1/2.

Nov. Term 1832 #4 - Conrad Koutz vs. Hellen Koutz subpoena in divorce served.

Nov. Term 1832 #8 - Barbara Himmens by her next friend Philip Sheffer vs. John Himmens subpoena in divorce served.

Nov. Term 1832 #33 - Catharine White by her next friend Hugh C. Ramsay vs. William White, Esq. subpoena in divorce served. On May 7, 1833, court appointed John Kauffelt, Esq. to take depositions in this case.

Jan. Term 1833 #3 - John Kolb, Jr. vs. Mary Kolb subpoena in divorce served. On Jan. 10, 1823, rule to file an answer in two weeks' from time of notice served on defendant. Case transferred to district court Mar. Term 1833 #33.

Apr. Term 1833 #61 - Samuel G. Coble vs. Mary Goble subpoena in divorce served. Alias subpoena continued to Aug. Term 1833 #49.

Aug. Term 1833 #1 - Samuel G. Coble vs. Mary Coble alias subpoena in divorce served. Original from Apr. Term 1833 #61.

Aug. Term 1833 #45 - Mary Grove by her next friend Joseph Gardner vs. Henry Grove subpoena in divorce served. On June 24, 1833, special pleas filed. On Sept. 28, 1833 transferred to district court Aug. Term 1833 #27. On Jan. 21, 1835 remanded to court of common pleas by district dourt. On Mar. 12, 1836, the plea and answer on the part of defendant were withdrawn and the facts set forth in the libel admitted. Court granted Mary Gove a divorce from her husband Henry Grove.

Aug. Term 1833 #49 - Samuel G. Coble vs. Mary Coble alias subpoena in divorce served. Original from Apr. Term 1833 #61. On Sept. 17, 1833, the court appointed Jacob Smith, Esq. to take depositions. On Nov. 7, 1833, the depositions were filed and the court granted Samuel G. Coble a divorce from his wife Mary Coble.

Aug. Term 1833 #62 - Mary Dare by her next friend John Machlin vs. Michael Dare subpoena in divorce served. Sept. 11, 1833, "Defendant pleads that the facts put forth by Libellant are not true. Mary Dare replies that the facts set forth in her libel and petition are true." Transferred to district court Aug. Term 1833 #28 on Sept. 28, 1833.

Nov. Term 1833 #23 - John Kolb vs. Mary Kolb subpoena in divorce. On Jan. 6, 1834 the court ordered Mary Kolb to answer the charges of her husband's petition. On Jan. 18, 1834, the case was transferred to district court Nov. Term 1833 #23. On Jan. 24, 1834, Mary Kolb's answer to her husband's petition was filed. On Jan. 19, 1835, "Rule to show cause why this case should not be remanded to Court of Common Pleas. Jan. 21, 1835 rule made absolute." On Apr. 26, 1835, a jury of twelve good and lawful men found Mary Kolb willfully and maliciously had left her husband John Kolb without a cause more than two years ago. The charges against Mary Kolb of adultery and the charges against John Kolb for adultery were both found not guilty. On Apr. 26, 1835, rule to show cause why a new trial should not be granted. Reasons were filed. On Nov. 1, 1836, the court granted John Kolb a divorce from his wife Mary Kolb.

Jan. Term 1834 #6 - Catharine Bollinger by her next friend Michael Klinefelter vs. Peter Bollinger subpoena in divorced served. On Jan. 7, 1834, the court appointed Charles F. Fisher, Esq. to take depositions in this case. On Feb. 14, 1834, the depositions were filed. On Feb. 18, 1834, the court granted Catharine Bollinger a divorce from her husband Peter Bollinger. Costs were $10.26 and they were paid by George Klinefelter.

Jan. Term 1834 #7 - Samuel Dierdorff vs. Catharine Dierdorff subpoena in divorce served. Alias subpoena continued to Apr. Term 1834 #9.

Apr. Term 1834 #3 - Mary Wilhelm by her next friends John

Bortner and Jacob Nunnemaker vs. Jacob Wilhelm subpoena in divorce. Alias subpoena continued to Aug. Term 1834 #50.

Apr. Term 1834 #4 - Mary Smith by her next friend Penrose Robinson. Esq. vs. Andrew Smith subpoena in divorce. Alias subpoena continued to Nov. Term 1834 #4.

Apr. Term 1834 #5 - Mary Eicholtz by her next friend George Aughenbach vs. Jacob Eicholtz subpoena in divorce served.

Apr. Term 1834 #9 - Samuel Dierdorff vs. Catharine Dierdorff alias subpoena in divorce. Original in Jan. Term 1834 #7. On Aug. 5, 1834, the court appointed Charles F. Fisher, Esq. to take depositions in this case. On Sept. 16, 1834, depositions were filed and the court granted Samuel Dierdorff a divorce from his wife Catharine Dierdorff. Costs were $9.87 3/4.

Aug. Term 1834 #4 - Anna Maria Fink by her next friend John Gardner, Esq. vs. Sebastian Fink subpoena in divorce. On Apr. 10, 1834, the defendant appears and pleads that the facts set forth in the petition are true. On Apr. 11, 1834, the court grants Anna Maria Fink a divorce from her husband Sebastian Fink.

Aug. Term 1834 #5 - Julianna Allen by her next friend Michael Graybill vs. James Allen subpoena in divorce. Alias subpoena continued to Nov. Term 1834 #25.

Aug. Term 1834 #26 - Margaret Parker by her next friend William Diven, Esq. vs. Samuel Parker subpoena in divorce "made known to Sarah Parker." On Sept. 16, 1834, the court appointed James O'Hail of Monoghan Twp., York Co., Pa. to take depositions in this case. On Apr. 9, 1835, the court ruled Samuel Parker was to answer his wife's libel within ten days' time.

Aug. Term 1834 #32 - John Boak vs. Mary Boak subpoena in divorce. The defendant acknowledged service of subpoena. On Aug. 5, 1834, the court appointed John B. Klein, Esq. of New Cumberland, Pa. to take the depositions in this case. On Oct. 25, 1834, depositions were filed. On Apr. 13, 1835, the court granted John Boak a divorce from his wife Mary Boak. Costs were $9.00.

Aug. Term 1834 #50 - Mary Wilhelm by her next friends John Bortner and Jacob Nunnemaker vs. Jacob Wilhelm alias subpoena in divorce. Original Apr. Term 1834 #3. On Nov. 3, 1834, the court appointed Benjamin Lannis, Esq. to take depositions in this case. On Nov. 3, 1834, the depositions were filed. On Nov. 4, 1834, the court granted Mary Wilhelm a divorce from her husband Jacob Wilhelm. Costs were $11.90.

Nov. Term 1834 #2 - Ann A. Dorman by her next friend John Gardner, Esq. vs. Samuel C. Dorman subpoena in divorce. Alias subpoena continued to Jan. Term #9.

Nov. Term 1834 #3 - Mary Berger by her next friend John Rouse, Sr. vs. William Berger subpoena in divorce. Alias subpoena continued to Jan. Term 1835 #18.

Nov. Term 1834 #4 - Mary Smith by her next friend Penrose Robinson, Esq. vs. Andrew Smith alias subpoena in divorce. Original Apr. Term 1834 #4. "Made known personally to Andrew Smith."

Nov. Term 1834 #25 - Julianna Allen by her next friend Michael Graybill vs. James Allen alias subpoena in divorce. Original Aug. Term 1834 #5. On Nov. 3, 1834, court appointed Zachariah Spangler, Esq. to take depositions in this case. On Nov. 7, 1834, the depositions were filed and the court granted Julianna Allen a divorce from her husband James Allen. Costs were $13.62 1/2.

Jan. Term 1835 #9 - Ann A. Dorman by her next friend John Gardner, Esq. vs. Samuel C. Dorman alias subpoena in divorce. Original Nov. Term 1834 #2. On Jan. 5, 1835, the court appointed Zachariah Spangler, Esq. to take depositions. On Apr. 7, 1835, the depositions were filed and the court granted Ann A. Dorman a divorce from her husband Samuel C. Dorman. Costs were $17.30.

Jan. Term 1835 #18 - Mary Berger by her next friend John Rouse vs. William Berger alias subpoena in divorce. Original was Nov. Term 1834 #3. On Apr. 7, 1835, the court appointed Charles F. Fisher, Esq. to take depositions in this case. On Apr. 21, 1835, the court granted Mary Berger a divorce from her husband William Berger. Costs were $10.53 3/4.

Apr. Term 1835 #3 - Elizabeth Cookes by her next friend Samuel Platts vs. John Cookes subpoena in divorce. "R(obert) J. Fisher appeared for the defendant and pleaded that the facts set forth by Plaintiff in the libel are not true and asks issue to try the same."

Apr. Term 1835 #7 - Lavinia Conner by her next friend Leonard Stough vs. Robert Conner subpoena in divorce. Alias subpoena continued to Nov. Term 1835 #27.

Apr. Term 1835 #21 - Catharine Devinney by her next friend John Hildebrand vs. Daniel Devinney. Robert J. Fisher appears for defendant and desires the allegations set out by libellant in his libel and asks that the same may be inquired of by the county. On Apr. 17, 1837, depositions were filed. On Apr. 17, 1837, respondent withdraws pleas and case submitted to the court and depositions filed "wherewith the court decreed a divorce a vinculo matrimonii by proclamation." Costs were $9.52 1/2.

Apr. Term 1835 #22 - Nancy Raffelsperger by her next friend John Rentzell vs. Jeremiah Raffelsperger subpoena in divorce Apr. 7, 1835, requiring respondent to appear in court May 5, 1835 to answer the allegations contained in the libel of the libelent. On Apr. 7, 1835, the court appointed Jacob Ernst, Esq., to take depositions in this case. On Aug. 3, 1835, the court granted Nancy Raffelsperger a divorce from her husband Jeremiah Raffelsperger. Costs were $7.96.

Apr. Term 1835 #24 - Christiana Christine by her next friend Jacob Kraft vs. Benjamin Christine "subpoena of divorce served Discontinued vide Day Book."

Apr. Term 1835 #29 - Conrad Koutz vs. Helena Koutz subpoena in divorce. Alias subpoena continued to Aug. Term 1835 #4.

Apr. Term 1835 #66 - Catharine Bachman by her next friend Soloman Rudisell vs. Michael Bachman subpoena in divorce. Alias subpoena continued to Aug. Term 1835 #3.

Aug. Term 1835 #3 - Catharine Bachman (sic) by her next friend Soloman Rudisell vs. Michael Baughman (sic) alias subpoena in divorce. Original Apr. Term 1835 #66. On Apr. 13, 1835, the court appointed William D. Gobrecht, Esq., to take depositions in this case.

Aug. Term 1835 #4 - Conrad Koutz vs. Helena Koutz alias subpoena in divorce. Original Apr. Term 1835 #29. On Jun. 20, 1835, the libellant enters a rule to take depositions on five days notice (two rules). On Aug. 4, 1835, depositions were filed and the court on motion of Thomas C. Hambly, Esq. decreed a divorce a vinculo matrimonii.

Nov. Term 1835 #7 - Elizabeth Shue by her next friend William H. Kurtz, Esq. vs. Isaac Shue subpoena in divorce. On Nov. 6, 1835, the court appointed John A. Wilson, Esq. to take depositions in this case. On Dec. 8, 1835, the court granted Elizabeth Shue a divorce from her husband Isaac Shue.

Jan. Term 1836 #5 - Elizabeth Kochenour by her next friend Samuel Meishelter vs. Samuel Kochenour subpoena in divorce. Alias subpoena continued to Apr. Term 1836 #20.

Jan. Term 1836 #25 - Hannah W. Hannawalt by her next friend Isaac Koller vs. Levi Hannawalt subpoena in divorce.

Jan. Term 1836 #36 - Elizabeth Clerk by her next friend Daniel Eichelberger vs. John Clerk subpoena in divorce. Alias subpoena continued to Apr. Term 1836 #3.

Jan. Term 1836 #74 - Mary McVannon by her next friend George Wolf vs. Joseph McVannon subpoena in divorce. Alias subpoena continued to Apr. Term 1836 #12.

Apr. Term 1836 #3 - Elizabeth Clerk by her next friend Daniel Eichelberger vs. John Clerk subpoena in divorce. Original Jan. Term, 1836, #36. On May 2, 1836, the court appointed Frederick Bahn, Esq and Adam Ebaugh, Esq. to take depositions in this case. Interrogatories filed July 20, 1836. On Aug. 2, 1836, the court granted Elizabeth Clerk a divorce from her husband John Clerk.

Apr. Term 1836 #12 - Mary McVannon by her next friend George Wolf vs. Joseph McVannon alias subpoena in divorce. Original Jan. Term 1836 #74. On Aug. 3, 1836, the court appointed George Klinefelter, Esq. to take depositions in this case and ordered notice to be given in the papers. On Sept. 15, 1836, the court granted Mary McVannon a divorce from her husband Joseph McVannon.

Apr. Term 1836 #20 - Elizabeth Kochenour by her next friend Samuel Meisenhelter vs. Samuel Kochenour alias subpoena in divorce. Original Jan. Term 1836 #5. On Aug. 2, 1836, the court appointed John A. Wilson, Esq. to take depositions in this case. On Aug. 3, 1836, depositions were filed and the court granted Elizabeth Kochenour a divorce from her husband Samuel Kochenour.

Apr. Term 1836 #22 - Hannah W. Hannawalt by her next friend Isaac Koller vs. Levi Hannawalt alias subpoena issued. Original Jan. Term 1836 #25. On May 17, 1836, the court appointed John A. Wilson, Esq. to take depositions in this case. On Aug. 1, 1836, the court replaced him with Frederick Bahn, Esq. On Sept. 6, 1836, the Commission was returned. On Nov. 11, 1836, the court granted Hannah W. Hannawalt a divorce from her husband Levi Hannawalt. Total costs were $14.62.

Nov. Term 1836 #1 - Abraham Wolf vs. Catharine Wolf alias subpoena in divorce. Original Aug. Term 1836 #34. On Nov. 9,

1836, libellee appears and answers that the facts set forth in petition are true. On Nov. 9, 1836, the court grants Abraham Wolf a divorce from his wife Catharine Wolf.

Nov. Term 1836 #37 - Mary Cunningham by her next friend Samuel Morrison vs. Joseph Cunningham subpoena in divorce from bed and board and alimony. Jan. 4, 1837, rule on the defendant to reply. Mar. 8, 1837, respondent's answer filed. On Apr. 7, 1837, the court directed an issue in this case.

Jan. Term 1837 #1 - Mary Dougherty by her next friend Joseph Weitzell vs. Anthony Dougherty subpoena in divorce. Alias subpoena continued to Apr. Term 1837 #7.

Apr. Term 1837 #2 - John Watt vs. Sarah Watt subpoena in divorce. On Aug. 9, 1837 the court appointed Zachariah Spangler, Esq. to take depositions in this case. On Aug. 24, 1837, the respondent pleads that the facts contained in the petition are not true. On Sept. 12, 1837, the depositions were filed.

Apr. Term 1837 #7 - Mary Dougherty by her next friend Jacob Weitzell vs. Anthony Dougherty alias subpoena in divorce. Original Jan. Term 1837 #1. On Apr. 7, 1837, the court appointed Jesse Bryan, Esq. and Daniel Yeager, Esq. to take depositions. On Aug. 22, 1837, the depositions were filed and the court granted Mary Dougherty a divorce from her husband Anthony Dougherty.

Aug. Term 1837 #59 - Eve Beidleman by her next friend Jacob Fissel vs. Samuel Beidleman subpoena in divorce. Alias subpoena continued to Nov. Term 1837 #9.

Nov. Term #8 - Henriet Mossie by her next friend Joseph Donaldson vs. John C. Mossie subpoena in divorce. Alias subpoena continued to Jan. Term 1838 #3.

Nov. Term 1837 #9 - Eve Beidleman by her next friend Jacob Fissel vs. Samuel Beidleman alias subpoena in divorce. Original Aug. Term 1837 #59. On Jan. 20, 1838, the court appointed John A. Wilson, Esq. to take depositions in this case. On Feb. 1, 1838, the depositions were filed. On Feb. 13, 1838, the court granted Eve Beidleman a divorce from her husband Samuel Beidleman.

Nov. Term 1837 #11 - Daniel Neff vs. Margaret Neff subpoena in divorce. "Feb. 13, 1838 Mr. Gardner appears for Respondent and pleads that the facts set forth in this libel in this case are untrue and asks the court to direct an issue to try the same." On Apr. 16,

1838, a trial by jury finds for the plaintiff. On Apr. 20, 1838, the court granted Daniel Neff a divorce from his wife Margaret Neff.

Jan. Term 1838 #3 - Henrietta Mossie by her next friend Joseph Donaldson vs. John C. Mossie alias subpoena in divorce. Original Nov. Term 1837 #8. On Jan. 20, 1838, the court appointed John A. Wilson, Esq. to take depositions in this case. On Mar. 27, 1838, the depositions were filed. On Apr. 2, 1838, the court granted Henrietta Mossie a divorce from her husband John C. Mossie.

Jan. Term 1838 #4 - Barbara Hershy by her next friend John Strickhouser vs. John Hershy subpoena in divorce. Alias subpoena continued to Apr. Term 1838 #5.

Aug. Term 1838 #9 - Maria Hostler by her next friend George Hetrick vs. John Hostler subpoena in divorce. Alias subpoena continued to Apr. Term 1839 #12.

Aug. Term 1838 #31 - Elizabeth Finfrock by her next friend Michael B. Hoff vs. John Finfrock subpoena in divorce served personally Jul. 18, 1838. On Nov. 10, 1838, the court appointed John A. Wilson, Esq. to take depositions in this case. On Dec. 12, 1838, the depositions were filed and the court granted Elizabeth Finfrock a divorce from her husband John Finfrock. Costs were $11.92.

Nov. Term 1838 #1 - Samuel Shaffer vs. Elizabeth Shaffer subpoena in divorce "served by copy." On Dec. 8, 1838, the respondent's answer was filed. On Feb. 11, 1839, replication was filed and libellant prays an issue. On Apr. 16, 1839, interrogations were filed. On Apr. 20, 1839, rule by plaintiff to take depositions on ten days notice in common force. On Jan. 9, 1840, the court subpoenaed William Hamilton, John Barr, John Park and James Heuss as witnesses in this case. On Jan. 21, 1840, trial ordered and jury was called. Libellent's counsel requested the court "to require Respondent to elect one of the pleas relied on and to strike off the rest of the pleas, on the ground that only one plea and issue is admissible in this case. Motion overruled per Curiam. Same day Libellant's counsel moved the court to strike out the second and third pleas in this case on the ground that more than one plea and issue is not admissible. Motion overruled per Ciriam." On Jan. 21, 1840, trial was held. On Jan. 22, 1820, the court granted Samuel Shaffer a divorce from his wife Elizabeth Shaffer. On Jan. 23, 1840, the court required the respondent to pay costs of proceedings.

Apr. Term 1839 #12 - Maria Hostler by her next friend George Hetrick vs. John Hostler alias subpoena in divorce. Original Aug.

Term 1838 #9. "Non Est Inventus" Costs were sheriff $.27, Clerk $1.25.

Jan. Term 1840 #30 - Mahala McCauley by her next friend John Kauffelt vs. Thomas McCauley, libel of divorce. Subpoena awarded "Non Est Investus". Alias subpoena continued to Apr. Term 1840 #37. Mahala McCauley's attorneys were Kurtz and Campbell. Costs were $.27 for the sheriff.

Apr. Term 1840 #37 - Mahala McCauley by her next friend John Kaufelt vs. Thomas McCauley alias subpoena in divorce "Non Est Investus." Mahala McCauley's attorneys were Kurtz and Campbell. On Aug. 7, 1840, the court appointed John W. Hetrick, Esq. commissioner to take testimony in this case. Costs were $.27 to the sheriff and $3.75 to the proth.

Aug. Term 1840 #38 - Sarah Hammond by her next friend Joseph Stiles vs. William Talbot Hammond. On Jun. 10, 1848, libel of divorce was presented to Hon. Samuel C. Bonham, Esq. and subpoena issued Jun. 10, 1840 "Non Est Inventus." On Aug. 5, 1840, on motion of her attorney Robert J. Fisher, Esq. the court appointed John W. Hetrick, Esq. to take depositions of witnesses. Notice given to Mr. Hambly at bar. On Aug. 6, 1840, the depositions of witnesses was filed and the court granted Sarah Hammond a divorce from her husband William Talbot Hammond Aug. 6, 1840. Costs were $.18 to the high sheriff; $.18 to the sheriff; $1.50 for the proclamation; $3.00 to the attorney and $4.50 to the proth., making a total of $9.36 plus an additional cost of $2.00 for a copy of the divorce decree making a grand total of $11.36.

Apr. Term 1840 #79 - Dorcas Sumwalt by her next friend Runyen Sumwalt vs. Jacob Sumwalt. On Mar. 17, 1840, petition for divorce presented to the court and on motion of her attorney Robert J. Fisher, Esq. the court awarded a subpoena Mar. 17, 1840, "Non Est Inventus." On Apr. 8, 1840, on motion of Mr. Fisher, the court awarded an alias subpoena returnable the first Monday of Aug. 1840. On Jun. 15, 1840, exit alias subpoena. Costs were $.27 to the sheriff.

Aug. Term 1840 #42 - Dorcas Sumwalt by her next friend Runyen Sumwalt vs. Jacob Sumwalt alias subpoena in divorce. Original Apr. Term 1840 #79, "Non Est Inventus". Nov. Term 1840 continued and Jan. Term 1841 continued. On Jan. 8, 1841, the court appointed Robert Richie, Esq., commissioner, to take testimony. On Jun. 21, 1842, depositions were filed. On Dec. 8, 1842, the court decreed a divorce "a vinculo matrimonia". Costs were $.18 to the sheriff; $.27 to the sheriff; $3.00 to the attorney; $1.50 for advertising;

$1.50 for the proclamation; and $5.25 to the proth., making a total of $11.70 taking off the $3.00 paid to the attorney making a new total of $8.70. On Sept. 26, 1846 Received of Robert J. Fisher eight dollars and seventy cents. Signed by J.R. Donnell.

Nov. Term 1840 #7 - Dinah Hageman by her next friend Bernard Decker vs. Henry Hageman. On Jan. 8, 1841, the court appointed John A. Wilson, Esq. commissioner to take testimony in this case. Costs were $.19 to the sheriff and $4.82 to the proth.

Aug. Term 1841 #32 - Charlotte Wolf by her next friend Jeremiah Cullison vs. Spangler Wolf. On May 11, 1841, libel of divorce presented to the court and subpoena was issued. "N.E.I. so answers M. Hoke, Shff." Alias subpoena continued to Nov. Term 1841 #14. Charlotte Wolf had a Mr. Ramsey as an attorney. Costs was $.18 3/4 to the sheriff.

Nov. Term 1841 #14 - Charlotte Wolf by her next friend Jeremiah Cullison vs. Spangler Wolf alias subpoena in divorce. On Nov. 2, 1841, the court appointed John A. Wilson, Esq. to take testimony in this case. Nov. 18, 1841, exit copy of commissioner appointment. On Jan. 4, 1842, depositions were filed. On Jan. 4, 1840, on motion of Mr. Ramsey the court decreed Charlotte Wolf a divorce from her husband Spangler Wolf. Costs were $.18 3/4 to the sheriff; $.18 3/4 to the sheriff for the original subpoena; $1.50 for the proclamation; and $4.50 to the proth., making a total of $6.37 1/2 plus an additional cost of $2.00 for advertising making a new total of $8.37 1/2.

Jan. Term 1842 #10 - Michael Dunn vs. Hetty Dunn. On Nov. 17, 1841 libel of divorce presented to the Honorable Daniel Durkee. Subpoena issued Nov. 17, 1841 returned "N.E.I." On Jan. 5, 1842, on motion of Mr. Morris alias subpoena awarded to Apr. Term 1841 #29. Costs were $.18 3/4 to the sheriff.

Apr. Term 1842 #4 - Mary Ann Warner by her next friend William Matson vs. Rinehart Warner. On Jan. 5, 1842, libel in divorce presented to the court and subpoena awarded. On Jan. 6, 1842, subpoena was issued. On Feb. 4, 1842, rule on defendant to plead in ten day's notice to Mr. Morris at bar. On Feb. 28, 1842, "summoned defendant by reading writ to him so answers M. Hoke, Sheriff." Mr. Shelly was the attorney for Mary Ann Warner and a Mr. Morris was the attorney for Rinehart Warner. Costs were $1.00 to the sheriff and $2.75 to the proth.

Apr. Term 1842 #5 - Ann Maria Foster by her next friend Michael Beokel vs. Samuel Foster. On Jan. 4, 1812, libel in divorce presented to the court. Subpoena issued Jan. 4, 1842. "N.E.I. so answers N. Hoke, Sheriff." Alias subpoena continued to Aug. Term 1842 #99. Mr. C.A. Barnitz was the attorney for Ann Maria Foster. Costs were $.18 3/4 to the sheriff.

Apr. Term 1842 #14 - Charlotte Christiana Lange by her next friend Frederick Stark vs. Daniel P. Lange. On Jan. 18, 1842, her libel in divorce was presented to the Honorable Daniel Durkee. Subpoena was awarded Jan. 18, 1842 and issued on Jan. 18, 1842. The subpoena was served on the defendant by reading the same to him so answers M. Hoke, sheriff on Jan. 22, 1842. On Apr. 7, 1842, rule to take depositions of witnesses before Jesse Frysinger, Esq., in the borough of Hanover, Pa. on ten days notice. On Jul. 13, 1842, the depositions were filed. Costs were $1.94 to the sheriff and $4.25 to the proth.

Apr. Term 1842 #23 - Susanna Arnold by her next friend Jacob Wolf vs. Joseph Arnold. On Aug. 8, 1842, on motion of John Shelly, Esq., (Susanna Arnold's attorney) the court appointed Joseph McCreary, Esq. to be a commissioner to take testimony in this case. On Jul. 16, 1842, the depositions were filed. On Aug. 6, 1842, the court granted Susanna Arnold a divorce from her husband Joseph Arnold. Costs were $.18 3/4 to the sheriff; another $.18 3/4 to the sheriff; $4.50 to the proth.; $3.00 to the attorney; and $1.50 for the proclamation making a total cost of $9.37 1/2 plus additional cost of $1.50 for prints and a $.75 cost which was not specified who it was for making a new total cost of $11.62 1/2.

Apr. Term 1842 #29 - Michael Dunn vs. Hetty Dunn alias subpoena in Divorce. "N.E.I. so answers M. Hoke, Shff." Michael Dunn's attorney was a Mr. Morris. Costs were $.18 3/4 to the sheriff and $3.50 to the proth.

Apr. Term 1842 #52 - Ann Maria Stoutzenberger by her next friend Levi McCormick vs. Andrew Stoutzenberger. On Feb. 9, 1841, her libel in divorce was presented to the court. Subpoena was awarded and it was issued Feb. 16, 1842. "N.E.I. so answers M. Hoke, Shff." On Aug. 8, 1842, on motion of Mr. Ramsey, Anna Maria Stoutzenberger's attorney, the court awarded an alias subpoena continued to Aug. Term 1842 #37. Cost was $.18 3/4 to the sheriff.

Aug. Term 1842 #2 - Mary Simmons by her next friend Thomas Owens vs. Henry Simmons. Libel in divorce presented to the court. Subpoena issued "N.E.I. so answers M. Hoke Sheriff." Alias subpoena continued to Nov. Term 1842 #6. Mary Simmon's attorney was a Mr. Stahle. Cost was $.18 3/4 to the sheriff.

Aug. Term 1842 #37 - Ann Maria Stoutzenberger by her next friend Levi McCormick vs. Andrew Stoutzenberger. On Nov. 11, 1842, on motion of Mr. Ramsey, Ann Maria Stoutzenberger's attorney, the court appointed John A. Wilson, Esq. a commissioner to take testimony in this case. Exit commission. On Jan. 5, 1843, the depositions were filed. On Jan. 12, 1843, the court granted Ann Maria Stoutzenberger a divorce from her husband Andrew Stoutzenberger. Costs were $.18 3/4 to the sheriff and $4.50 to the proth.

Aug. Term 1842 #99 - Anna Maria Foster by her next friend Michael Beokel vs. Samuel Foster. On Aug. 6, 1842, on motion of Mr. C.A. Barnitz, Anna Maria Foster's attorney, the court appointed John A. Wilson, Esq. a commissioner to take testimony in this case. On Nov. 9, 1842, the commission was issued and depositions were filed that same date. On Nov. 10, 1842, the court noted that on two successive subpoena the respondent could not be found in York Co., Pa. and after the last subpoena the sheriff had put notice in the *York Republican*, a York, Pa. newspaper, for four successive weeks requesting the respondent to appear and he did not. Therefore the court granted the divorce and directed the libellant to pay the costs of the proceedings. The Costs were $.18 3/4 to the sheriff; another $.18 3/4 to the sheriff; $3.00 to the attorney; $1.50 for the proclamation; $1.00 for the Commission; $5.25 to the proth.; and $1.00 for advertising making a total cost of $12.62 1/2. Received all above cost except $3.00 for attorney. Signed by W. Ilg.

Nov. Term 1842 #6 - Mary Simmons by her next friend Thomas Owens vs. Henry Simmons. On Nov. 10, 1842, on motion of Mary Simmons' attorney Mr. Stahle the court appointed John A. Wilson, Esq. a commissioner to take testimony in this case. On Jan. 12, 1843, the depositions were filed and the court granted Mary Simmons a divorce from her husband Henry Simmons. Costs were $.18 3/4 to the sheriff and $4.50 to the proth.

Nov. Term 1842 #30 - Leah Price by her next friend John B. Kister vs. Thomas Price. On Sept. 13, 1842, her libel in divorce was presented to the court and a subpoena issued. Subpoena was returned "N.E.I. so answers J. Hantz, Shff." On Nov. 10, 1842, on motion of Mr. Shelly, Leah Price's attorney, the court awarded an alias subpoena continued to Jan. Term 1843 #9. Costs were $.18 3/4 to the sheriff.

Nov. Term 1842 #31 - Mary Stough by her next friend William Lenhart vs. Englehart Stough. On Sept. 13, 1842, her libel in divorce was presented to the court and subpoena was issued. It was returned "N.E.I. so answers J. Hantz, Shff." On Nov. 10, 1842 on motion of D.G. Barnitz, Esq., Mary Stough's attorney, the court awarded an alias subpoena continued to Jan. Term 1843 #10. Costs were $.18 3/4 to the sheriff.

Jan. Term 1843 #8 - Mary Ann Quinn by her next friend John Sinclair vs. Thomas Quinn. On Nov. 10, 1842, her libel in divorce was presented to the court and subpoena issued. It was returned "N.E.I. so answers J. Hantz, Shff." On motion of Mr. Campbell the court awarded an alias subpoena Jan. 21, 1842, continued to Apr. Term 1843 #29. Mr. Kurtz was the attorney for Mary Ann Quinn. Costs were $.18 3/4 to the sheriff.

Jan. Term 1843 #9 - Leah Price by her next friend John B. Kister vs. Thomas Price. Alias subpoena in Divorce returned "N.E.I. so answers J. Hantz, Shff." On Jan. 6, 1843, on motion of Mr. Shelly, Leah Price's attorney, the court appointed Jacob Kirk, Esq. to be the commissioner to take testimony in this case. Costs were $.18 3/4 to the sheriff; another $.18 3/4 to the sheriff; $1.50 for advertising; $3.00 to the attorney; $4.50 to the proth. and $1.50 for the proclamation making a total cost of $10.77 1/2.

Jan. Term 1843 #10 - Mary Strough by her next friend William Lenhart vs. Englehart Strough. Original was Nov. Term 1842 #31. Alias subpoena in divorce returned "N.E.I. so answers, J. Hantz, Shff." On Jan. 12, 1843, on motion of Mr. Barnitz, Mary Strough's attorney, the court appointed Mr. John A. Wilson, Esq. to be commissioner to take testimony in this case. On Apr. 6, 1843, depositions were filed and the court granted Mary Strough a divorce from her husband Englehart Strough. Costs were $.18 3/4 to the sheriff; an additional $.18 3/4 to the sheriff; $3.00 to the attorney; $1.50 to the proth.; $1.00 to the commissioner; $1.00 for advertising; and $5.25 for the proclamation, making a total cost of $12.12 1/2. Received above costs except attorney and commissioner fee. Signed W. Ilg.

Apr. Term 1843 #29 - Mary Ann Quinn by her next friend John Sinclair vs. Thomas Quinn. Alias subpoena in Divorce. Original was Jan. Term, 1843, #8. "N.E.I. so answers J. Hantz, Shff." On Aug. 12, 1843, the court appointed John W. Hetrick a commissioner to take depositions in this case. Costs were $.18 3/4 to the sheriff and $3.75 to the proth.

Aug. Term 1843 #21 - Elizabeth Sechrist by her next friend Frederick Bahn, Esq. vs. Daniel Sechrist. On Apr. 21, 1843, her libel in divorce was presented to Hon. Daniel Durkee and a subpoena awarded and issued by him. It was returned "N.E.I. so answers J(acob) Hantz, Shff." Alias subpoena continued Nov. Term 1843

#22. Elizabeth Sechrist's attorneys were Evans and Mayer. Cost was $.18 3/4 to the sheriff.

Aug. Term 1843 #26 - Susan Krone by her next friend George Minnich vs. Philip Krone. Petition or libel in divorce was presented to the Hon. Daniel Durkee and subpoena awarded by him. Subpoena was issued Apr. 28, 1843. "Summoned defendant by reading writ to him - so answers, J(acob) Hantz, Shff." On Aug. 22, 1843, the court appointed John A. Wilson, Esq. a commissioner to take testimony of witnesses in this case. On Sept. 10, 1843, depositions were filed and read to the court. On motion of Mr. Chapin, Susan Krone's attorney, the court granted Susan Krone a divorce from her husband Philip Krone on Sept. 10, 1843. Costs were $1.00 to the sheriff; $3.00 to the attorney; $4.50 to the proth.; and $1.50 for the proclamation, making a total cost of $10.00. Received my own and Sheriff's fee of E. Chapin, Esq. Signed by W. Ilg.

Nov. Term 1843 #6 - Elizabeth Rinehart by her next friend Jacob Gilmon vs. Jonathan or Jonas Rinehart. On Aug. 8, 1843, her libel in divorce was presented to the court and a subpoena awarded. On Aug. 11, 1843, a subpoena was issued which was returned "N.E.I. so answers J. Hantz, Shff." On Nov. 11, 1843 alias subpoena was awarded by the court to Jan. Term 1844 #13. Elizabeth Rinehart's attorney was a Mr. Stahle. Costs were $1.00 to the sheriff.

Nov. Term 1843 #22 - Elizabeth Sechrist by her next friend Frederick Bahn, Esq. vs. Daniel Sechrist. Original Aug. Term 1843 #21. Alias subpoena in divorce returned "N.E.I. so answers Jacob Hantz, Shff." On Nov. 11, 1843, the court, on motion of plaintiff's counsel, ordered a publication on this case according to law. On Jan. 6, 1844, on motion of Messrs. Evans and Mayer (Elizabeth Sechrist's attorneys), the court appointed Robert Richie, Esq., a commissioner to take testimony in this case. On Feb. 13, 1844, depositions were filed. On Feb. 13, 1844, on motion of Mr. Evans the court granted Elizabeth Sechrist a divorce from her husband Daniel Sechrist. Costs were $1.87 1/2 to the sheriff; an additional $.18 3/4 to the sheriff; $3.00 to the attorney; $1.00 for advertising; $1.50 for the proclamation and $5.00 to the proth., making a total cost of $12.56 1/4.

Nov. Term 1844 #2 - Catharine Newhaus by her next friend Frederick Bahn vs. Conrad Newhaus. On Aug. 6, 1844, her libel in divorce was presented to the court and subpoena issued. "Oct. 18, 1844 served on Conrad Newhause by reading writ of subpoena to him so answers J. Hantz, Shff." Attorney for Catharine Neuhaus was Mr. C.A. Barnitz. Costs were $2.20 to the sheriff; $3.00 to the attorney; $.75 for the writ; and $2.25 for the proclamation, making a total cost of $8.20 which was paid by the defendant. Acknowledgement of payment was signed by W. Ilg.

Nov. Term 1844 #3 - Barbara Roser by her next friend John Albright vs. John Roser. On Aug. 6, 1844, her libel in divorce was presented to the court and subpoena issued. It was returned "N.E.I. so answers J. Hantz, Shff." On Nov. 5, 1844, an alias subpoena in divorce was awarded issued to Jan. Term 1845 #3. Barbara Roser's attorney was Mr. Stahle. Costs were $.75 to the sheriff.

Nov. Term 1844 #4 - Andrew Brubacher vs. Susanna Brubacher. On Aug. 6, 1844, his libel in divorce was presented to the court and a subpoena issued. It was returned "N.E.I. so answers J. Hantz, Shff." On Nov. 5, 1844, an alias subpoena in divorce was awarded by the court continued to Jan. Term 1845 #4. Andrew Brubacher's attorney was a Mr. Barnitz. Costs were $.18 3/4 to the sheriff.

Nov. Term 1844 #31 - George Creily vs. Catharine Creily. On Sept. 17, 1844, his libel in divorce was presented to the court and a subpoena was awarded. It was returned "N.E.I. so answers J. Hantz, Shff." On Nov. 5, 1844, an alias subpoena in divorce was awarded by the court continued to Jan. Term 1845 #5. George Creily's attorney was a Mr. Ramsey. Costs were $.18 3/4 to the sheriff.

Jan. Term 1845 #3 - Barbara Roser by her next friend John Albright vs. John Roser alias subpoena in divorce. Original was Nov. Term 1844 #3. It was returned "N.E.I. so answers J. Hantz, Shff." Barbara Roser's attorney was a Mr. Stahle. Costs were $.18 3/4 to the sheriff and $2.97 to the proth.

Jan. Term 1845 #4 - Andrew Brubaker vs. Susanna Brubaker an alias subpoena in divorce. Original was Nov. Term 1844 #4. It was returned "N.E.I. so answers J. Hantz, Shff." On Jan. 8, 1845, Sheriff Hantz made proof in open court that respondent could not be found in his bailiwick whereupon the court, on motion, appointed John A. Wilson, commissioner to take testimony of witnesses in this case. On Apr. 8, 1845, the depositions were filed and that same day on motion of D.G. Barnitz, Esq. the court decreed a divorce a vinculo matrimonii between the parties. Andrew Brubaker's attorney was Mr. D.G. Barnitz, Esq. Costs were $.18 3/4 to the sheriff; an additional $.18 3/4 to the sheriff; $4.06 to the proth.; $3.00 to the attorney and $1.50 for the proclamation, making a total cost of $8.95 1/2. Recd. costs signed by W. Ilg.

Jan. Term 1845 #5 - George Creily vs. Catharine Creily an alias subpoena in divorce. Original was Nov. Term 1844 #31. It was returned "N.E.I. so answers J. Hantz, Shff." On Jan. 8, 1845, proof was made in open court by Sheriff Hantz that respondent cannot be found in his bailiwick. On Apr. 8, 1845, on motion of Mr. Ramsey the court appointed Jacob Glessner, Esq., commissioner to take testimony of witnesses in this case. On Apr. 21, 1845, depositions were filed and that same day on motion of Mr. Ramsey the court decreed a divorce between George Creily and his wife Catharine Creily. Mr. Ramsey was the attorney for George Creily. Costs were $.18 3/4 to the sheriff; $1.50 for the proclamation; $3.00 to the attorney and $4.37 1/2 to the proth., making a total cost of $9.06 1/4.

Aug. Term 1845 #1 - Samuel Through vs. Elizabeth Through. On Apr. 7, 1845, libel in divorce was presented to the court and subpoena awarded. On Jul. 26, 1845, the subpoena was served on defendant by reading writ to her so answers J. Hantz, shff. On Aug. 6, 1845, rule on defendant to plead in twenty-two days after notice to her on judgment. On Nov. 4, 1845, on proof being made that the rule on respondent was duly served on her on the second day of Oct., 1845, the court appointed James Adams, Esq., commissioner to take testimony in this case. On Nov. 4, 1845, depositions were filed and read to the court. Whereupon the court, on motion of David G. Barnitz, Esq., decreed a divorce between Samuel Through and his wife Elizabeth Through. Samuel Through's attorney was David G. Barnitz, Esq. Costs were $2.00 to the sheriff; $1.90 to the sheriff on rule; $1.50 for the proclamation and $4.25 to the proth., making a total cost of $9.65 with an additional cost of $3.00 for the attorney changing the total cost to $12.65.

Aug. Term 1845 #2 - Catharine Newhouse by her next friend Frederick Bahn, Esq. vs. Conrad Newhouse. On Apr. 7, 1845, a libel in divorce was presented to the court and a subpoena awarded and issued. "May 26, 1845, served on defendant by reading the within writ to him so answers J. Hantz, Shff." On Aug. 5, 1845, rule was made on the defendant to plead in ten days on judgment. Notice to Mr. Campbell at bar. Aug. 15, 1845, the respondent admits the marriage and says that other matters set forth in the libel are not true. Whereupon, on motion of libellant's counsel the court directed an issue in this case-and rule for trial. Oct. 2, 1845, libellant enters a rule to take depositions of witnesses, Ex parte on ten days notice. Oct. 24, 1845, depositions filed. Nov. Term, 1845 continued Jan. Term, 1846 Continued. Jan. 7, 1846, Cause continued by order of court on proof of sickness of respondent who is directed by the court to pay costs hitherto incurred by the libellant in making preparations for trial for Jan. Term 1846. Respondent ordered to give notice of continuance of cause to libellant's witnesses Feb., 1846. Adjd. court, Feb. 9, 1846, continued on payment of costs of term by defendant. Mar., 1846, Adjd. Court Apr. Term 1846, continued Aug. Term 1846 continued Oct. Term 1846 Adjd. Court Nov. Term 1846 continued. Dec. 15, 1846, trial ordered whereupon a jury of the county being called, came, to wit, Jacob Bahn, Charles Phahler, Henry Leber, John Flinchbach, Michael Shenherger, Daniel Leese, Esq., David Cochlin, Thomas McAleer, Thomas Reese, David Williams, Esq., Barnhart Myers and George Rinehart, twelve good and lawful men of the county of York who being all duly sworn and affirmed well and truly to try the issue joined. Dec. 19, 1846, the jury aforesaid, upon their oaths or affirmations aforesaid do respectfully say, that they find for the defendant.

Jan. 4, 1847 - On motion of libellant's counsel for rule to show cause why a new trial should not be granted in this case. Reasons filed. Jan. 12, 1847, on motion refused by the court Jan. 13, 1847, at instance of plaintiff's counsel the president judge is respectfully requested to reduce to writing his opinion, with the reasons therefore given, on decision of plaintiff's motion for rule to show cause why a new trial should not be granted and to file the same of record in this case. See paper filed. Jan. 11, 1847, notes of evidence and charge of court to jury filed. Feb. 19, 1847, defendant moves the court to dismiss the petition of Catharine Newhouse by her next friend Frederick Bohn. Motion granted and petition dismissed by the court. Same day the defendant moves the court for a rule on Frederick Bahn, to show cause why court should not award costs to the defendant in whose favor sentence has been passed. Returnable on Mar. 15, 1847. Rule to show cause granted by the court. Sept. 30, 1847, rule to show cause argued C.A.V. Oct. 6, 1847, rule made absolute and Frederick Bahn ordered by the court to pay defendant's cost. See paper filed. Oct. 28, 1847, opinion of court filed. Jan. 8, 1848, exceptions filed to bill of defendant's costs. See bill. Jan. 31, 1854, this case being called up and no evidence being adduced to sustain the exceptions, they are overruled and the taxation of costs by the proth. confirmed. Oct. 3, 1854, court granted a rule on Frederick Rahn to show cause why he should not pay the costs in this case by the first Monday of Nov., 1854, otherwise an attachment to issue against him. Nov. 10, 1854, Frederick Bahn appears by his counsel, Messrs. Evans and Mayer, and pleads payment and payment with leave Dec. 1857, Adjud. let. (Aug. Term) Dec. 17, 1857, rule to show cause discharged by the court. Evans and Mayer were the attorneys for Catharine Newhouse and Mr. Campbell was the attorney for Conrad Newhouse. Costs were $2.20 to the sheriff, $3.44 to the proth.; $142.50 1/2 to the defendant; $4.00 to the jury; $7.56 for the proclamation; and $3.00 to the attorneys making a total cost of $162.80 1/2 with an additional cost of $2.00 for a subpoena making a grant total cost of $164.80 1/2.

Aug. Term 1845 #4 - Anna Mary Hare by her next friend David Rudy vs. Reuben Hare. Apr. 9, 1845, libel in divorce presented to the court and subpoena awarded. Issued "June 10, 1845 Summonsed defendant by reading writ to him so answers J. Hantz, Shff." Nov. 12, 1845, rule on defendant to plead in ten days on judgement after notice to him. (Two copies). Dec. 20, 1815, on proof of due service of rule to plead on defendant, the court appointed Benjamin Lannis, Esq., commissioner to take testimony in this case. (One copy) Jan. 10, 1846, depositions filed and read to the court. Whereupon the court, on motion of John Shelly, Esq., counsel for the libellant, decree a divorce a vinculo matrimonii between the parties according to the Acts of Assembly in such case made and provided. Anna Mary Hare's attorney was John Shelly, Esq. Costs were $1.96 to the sheriff; $2.75 to Proth. L.; $1.75 to Proth. D.; $1.50 for the proclamation; $3.00 to the attorney and $.50 for the recording. Received of Mr. Shelly $5.00 signed by W. Ilg. Received $2.25 in fees in this case of W. Ilg. Signed by J.R. Donnell.

Nov. Term 1845 #2 - William Grove vs. Ann Maria Grove. On Aug. 5, 1845, libel in divorce was presented to the court and subpoena awarded. Same day subpoena was issued. Sept. 16, 1845, libellant enters a rule to take depositions of witnesses ex parte on ten days notice. (Two copies). Oct. 18, 1845, depositions filed. "August 29, 1845, subpoened defendant by reading subpoena to her. So answers J. Hantz, Shff." Nov. 10, 1845, rule on respondent to plead in ten days after notice to her or her counsel on judgment. Nov. 14, 1845, Respondent by her attorney, J.F. Welsh, Esq. denies the allegations set forth in libel and for plea says that the same are not true. Same day libellant by his attorney comes and says that he is read to verify the matters and things by him as his said libel and prayer set forth and prays that a jury may be called to inquire thereof according to the form of the several Acts of Assembly in this behalf made and provided. Same day court directed an issue etc. Jan. Term 1846; continued Feb. Term 1846, Adjed. Court (J.L.); continued Apr. Term 1846; continued Aug. Term 1816 (J.L.). Aug. 13, 1846, agreement of attorneys filed. Same day trial ordered whereupon a jury of the county being called, came, to wit; Jacob Tyson, Samuel Prowell, Allen Miller, Michael Rutledge, John Earhart, Michael Hademan, Josiah V. Hoshour, Josiah Wilson, Adam Free, Mathew Douglass, Michael Anstine and Philip Krone, twelve good and lawful men of the county of York, who being duly summoned affirmed well and truly to try the issue joined etc. Aug. 4, 1846, the jury aforesaid, upon their oaths or affirmations aforesaid, do respectfully say that they find for the libellant William Grove. Sept. 16, 1846, the court decreed a divorce a vinculo matrimonii between the parties according to Acts of Assembly in such case made and provided and direct the libellant to pay all the costs except those on the part of the respondent. William Grove's attorney was a Mr. Gobrecht. Ann Maria Grove's attorneys were Mr. Morris and Mr. Welsh. Costs for this case were $2.44 to the sheriff; $3.25 to the proth.; $4.00 to the jury; $3.00 to the attorney; and $7.12 1/2 to Proth. D. making a total of $19.81 1/2 with an additional cost of $1.50 to the proth., making a grand total of $21.31 1/2. Deducting the $3.00 paid to the attorney the remainder was $18.31 1/2 which was paid by the plaintiff. Singed by J.R. Donnell and W. Ilg.

Nov. Term 1845 #44 - Elizabeth Smith by her next friend Joseph Stouffer vs. Washington Smith. Libel in divorce presented to the Hon. Samuel C. Bonham and subpoena in divorce was awarded by the court and issued that same day. "October 28, 1845, served the within on defendant by reading writ to him - so answers, Thos. Jameson Shff." Nov. 3, 1845, on motion of Mr. Ramsey the court awarded an alias subpoena in divorce - because the service of the first was not made fifteen days before the return day. Alias subpoena issued to Jan. Term 1846 #7. Elizabeth Smith's attorney was Mr. Ramsey. Costs were $2.60 to the sheriff and $2.50 to the proth., making a total cost of $45.10. March 12, 1849 received of J.R. Donnell my fees in this case. Signed by Thos. Jameson.

Jan. Term 1846 #7 - Elizabeth Smith by her next friend Joseph Stouffer vs. Washington Smith. Alias subpoena in divorce continued from the original Nov. Term 1845 #44. "Dec. 10, 1845 served the within subpoena on Washington Smith by reading the contents to him and also leaving an attested copy with him so answers Thos. Jameson, Shff." Jan. 10, 1846, on motion of Mr. Ramsey the court appointed Daniel Bailey, Esq., commissioner, to take testimony of witnesses in this case. (One copy) Sept. 15, 1846, depositions filed- same day the court on motion of Alfred C. Ramsey, Esq. attorney for libellant (Elizabeth Smith) the court decreed a divorce a vinculo matrimonii between the parties according to Acts of Assembly in such case made and provided. Costs were $2.97 1/2 to the sheriff; $3.00 to the attorney; $1.50 for the proclamation; and $1.75 to Proth. D. making a total cost of $9.22 1/2 to which was added the original $5.10 cost of Nov. Term 1845 #44 making a total cost of $14.37 1/2 along with an additional charge of $.75 making a grand total cost of $15.07 1/2. Received $8.00 signed by R. Donnell. Received the balance of costs same. Signed by W. Ramsy. Received my fees in this case, signed by W. Ilg.

Jan. Term 1846 #14 - Sarah Kuhn by her next friend John Shaeffer vs. John Kuhn. On Nov. 14, 1845, libel in divorce was presented to the court and subpoena awarded by the court. It was returned "N.E.I. so answers Thos. Jameson, Shff." On Apr. 9, 1846, alias subpoena in divorce was awarded per curiam issued to Aug.

Term 1846 #3. Sarah Kuhn's attorney was a Mr. Shaw. Costs were $.18 3/4 to the sheriff and $1.25 to the proth., making a total cost of $1.43 3/4. Received $1.25 my fees, signed by W. Ilg.

Apr. Term 1846 #24 - Polly Strickhouser by her next friend John Behler vs. John Strickhouser (son of John Strickhouser). Libel for divorce presented to the court and subpoena awarded. Subpoena was issued. "March 18, 1846 served the within on John Strickhouser by reading within subpoena to him and leaving him an attached copy of the same so answers Thos. Jameson Shff." Sept. 25, 1846, defendant by his attorney appears and denies all the allegations set forth in the libel and for a plea saith the same are not true. Oct. 28, 1846, at the instance of the petitioner the court appointed John S. Kline, Esq., commissioner to take testimony in this case. (One copy) Dec. 5, 1846, commission and depositions filed. Dec. 19, 1846, depositions filed. Polly Strickhouser had Mr. Evans and Mr. Strayer as her attorneys. John Strickhouser had Mr. Buchanan and Mr. Potts as his attorneys. Costs were $2.60 to the sheriff and $5.50 to Proth. D. Received my fees, signed by J.R. Donnell.

Apr. Term 1846 #35 - Sarah Taylor vs. Isaac Taylor - Certiorari to John Moore, Jr., Esq. - Mar. 4, 1846, Affidavit filed. Same day Daniel Miller sent in $25.00 as bail for the defendant to the plaintiff in this case. J.R. Donnell, proth. Mar. 4, 1846, defendant enters a rule to take depositions ex parte on ten days notice. (2 copies) Mar. 24, 1846, proceedings returned. Mar. 27, 1846, depositions filed. Apr. 6, 1846, exceptions filed. Oct. 29, 1846, proceeding reversed by the court for want of jurisdiction of the justice in the subject matter. Attach. No. 33 Nov. Term 1850. Evans and Mayer were the attorneys for Isaac Taylor. Costs were $3.00 to the attorneys; $1.00 for the proclamation; $2.37 1/2 to the proth.; $2.11 for the Bill; $.37 1/2 for the return; $.84 for the Justice and $.18 3/4 for something I couldn't read making a total cost of $9.88 1/4.

Apr. Term 1846 #51 - Michael B. Hoff vs. Elizabeth Hoff. Mar. 18, 1846, libel in divorce presented to the court and subpoena awarded. Same day subpoena issued. "March 24, 1846, N.E.I. so answers Thos. Jameson Shff." Alias Nov. Term 1846 #7. Mr. Gobrecht was the attorney for Michael B. Hoff. Costs were $2.44 to the sheriff; $1.00 for the writ and $1.75 to the proth., making a total cost of $5.19.

Aug. Term 1846 #3 - Sarah Kuhn by her next friend John Sheaffer vs. John Kuhn - alias subpoena in divorce original to Jan. Term, 1846, #14. "Non Est Inventus so answers Thos. Jameson, Shff." Sept. 16, 1846, proof made in open court that the sheriff could not find respondent in his bailiwick. Nov. 4, 1846, on motion of the plaintiff's counsel, the court appointed William R. Morris, Esq., commissioner, to take testimony in this case. (2 copies) Dec. 18, 1846, depositions filed. Same day Mr. Shaw decreed a divorce a vinculo matrimonii between the parties according to Acts of Assembly in such case made and provided. Mr. Shaw and Mr. Buchanan were the attorneys for Sarah Kuhn. Costs were $.18 3/4 to the sheriff; $1.50 for the proclamation; $3.00 to the attorneys; $3.50 for the writ and $.50 for a copy making a total of $8.68 3/4 with an additional cost of $3.00 for advertising and an additional cost of $1.43 3/4 for the original action making a grand total of $13.12 1/2 for this divorce proceeding.

Nov. Term 1846 #7 - Michael B. Hoff vs. Elizabeth Hoff - alias subpoena in divorce - original to Apr. Term, 1846, #51. "September 23, 1846 N.E.I. so answers Thos. Jameson, Shff." Jan. 6, 1847, on motion of William D. Gobrecht, Esq. the court appointed Jesse Frysinger, Esq., commissioner, to take testimony of witnesses in this case. (1 copy) Mar. 15, 1847, depositions filed. Nov. 5, 1847, it appearing to the court that proof was made that respondent could not be found in the county and that the sheriff gave the notice to respondent required by the Act of Assembly by publication in a newspaper for four successive weeks, whereupon the court decreed a divorce a vinculo matrimonii between the parties according to the Act of Assembly in such case made and provided. Mr. Gobrecht was the attorney for Michael B. Hoff. Costs were $.18 3/4 to the sheriff; $3.00 to the attorney; $4.50 to the proth.; $1.50 for the proclamation; and $2.44 to the sheriff on the original making a total of $11.62 3/4 with additional costs of $1.00 for copy of the record; $1.25 for advertising and $1.75 for the original making a grand total cost of $15.62 3/4.

Nov. Term 1846 #20 - Leah Worley by her next friend Adam Leitner vs. William Worley. Sept. 15, 1846, libel in divorce presented to the court and subpoena awarded. Same day issued. "Oct. 22, 1846 served within subpoena on William Worley by reading the within to him - so answers-Thos. Jameson Shff." Nov. 2, 1846, rule on respondent to appear and plead in ten days after notice to him - otherwise the court will decree a divorce according to Act of Assembly in such case made and provided. (two copies). Mr. S.M. Barnitz was the attorney for Leah Worley. Costs were $2.12 1/2 to the sheriff, $1.00 for the writ and $3.75 to Proth. D., making a grand total cost of $6.87 1/2.

Jan. Term 1847 #20 - Rosanna Knab by her next friend Samuel Kochenour vs. John Knab. Libel in divorce from bed and board and praying allowance of alimony etc. presented to the Hon. Samuel C. Bonham - and subpoena awarded and issued. "Dec. 16, 1846, served the within subpoena on Defendant by reading the same to him and handing him an attested copy of the same. So answers Thos. Jameson, Shff." Jan. 12, 1847, at instance of plaintiff's counsel, rule on defendant to answer and plead in this case in ten days after notice to his counsel on record Mr. Stahle or judgment. (two copies) Feb. 22, 1847, respondent admits marriage and for plea says the other matters set forth in libel are not true, etc. Feb. 26, 1847, all the allegations in the petition being admitted except that the respondent "by cruel and barbarous treatment endangered the petitioner's life and offered such indignities to her person as to render her condition intolerable and life burdensome, and thereby forced her to withdraw from his house and family" which allegations are denied by the respondent. Whereupon the petitioner prays the court to direct issues to be tried by a jury in the following form, to find, first, whether the respondent by cruel and barbarous treatment endangered the petitioner's life. Second, whether respondent offered such indignities to petitioner's person as to render her condition intolerable and life burdensome and thereby forced to withdraw from his house and family. See agreement filed. Whereupon the court direct issue accordingly. Evans and Mayer were the attorneys for Rosanna Knab. Mr. Stahle was the attorney for John Knab. Costs were $1.77 1/2 to the sheriff; $3.00 to the attorneys; and $5.56 1/4 to Proth. D., making a total cost of $10.33 3/4. Recd. of Mr. Mayer seven dollars and 33 3/4 cents my own and shff.'s fees. Recd. seven dollars and thirty three cents of above costs. Signed by J.R. Donnell. Recd. my costs. Signed by Thos. Jameson.

Apr. Term 1847 #5 - Margaret Feeny by her next friend Philip Roser vs. John Feeny. Jan. 8, 1847, libel in divorce presented to the court and subpoena awarded. Same day subpoena issued. "March 20, 1847 N.E.I. so answers Thos. Jameson Shff." Alias subpoena to Aug. Term 1847 #34. Mr. Shelly was the attorney for Margaret Feeny. Costs were $1.60 to the sheriff; $3.00 to the attorney and $2.75 to Proth. J.R. Donnell.

Aug. Term 1847 #34 - Margaret Feeny by her next friend Philip Roser vs. John Feeny: alias subpoena in divorce original Apr. Term, 1847, #5. "July 21, 1847, N.E.I. so answers Thos.Jameson, Shff." Aug. 6, 1847, on motion of Mr. Shelly, the court appointed Richard James, Esq., commissioner to take testimony of witnesses in this case. (one copy). Nov. 3, 1848, depositions filed. Apr, 5, 1848, on motion of John Shelly, Esq., the court decreed divorce a vinculo matrimonii between the parties according to Act of Assembly in such case made and provided. Mr. John Shelly was the attorney for Margaret Feeny. Costs were $.18 3/4 to the sheriff; another $.18 3/4 to the sheriff; $1.50 for copies recd.; $3.00 to the attorney; and $4.62 1/2 to Proth. Donnell, making a total cost of $9.50 to which was added $7.35 the cost of the original court action making a grand total cost of $16.85.

Nov. Term 1847 #8 - Mary Ann Luttman, by her next friend Daniel B. Yeaple vs. Oliver Luttman. Libel in divorce presented to the court and subpoena awarded and issued. "Oct. 18, 1847, N.E.I. so answers Thos. Jameson Shff." Nov. 5, 1847, alias subpoena in divorce awarded by the court in this case. Alias subpoena to Apr. Term 1848 #8. Mr. Stahle was the attorney for Mary Ann Luttman. Cost was $.18 3/4 to the sheriff.

Nov. Term 1847 #9 - Dr. Samuel H. Frazier vs. Jane E. Frazier: Libel in divorce presented to the court and subpoena awarded and issued. "Sept. 25, 1847, served the within writ on Defendant by reading the same to her - so answers, Thos. Jameson, Shff." Nov. 3, 1847, rule on respondent to appear and plead in ten days or judgment notice to be given to respondent. (two copies) Jan. 4, 1848, rule to plead on this case having been returned by the sheriff "N.E.I." the court on motion appointed James Adams, Esq., commissioner, to take testimony in this case and notice of time and place of taking the same to be given by publication for four successive weeks in the *York Gazette* a newspaper printed in the borough of York. And that the rule to plead or a certified copy thereof be posted up in the proth.'s office for four weeks as notice to respondent. Mar. 21, 1848, depositions filed and same day the court decreed a divorce a vinculo matrimonii between the parties according to Act of Assembly in such case made and provided. Mr. Charles A. Barnitz was the attorney for Dr. Samuel H. Frazier. Costs were $1.00 to the sheriff; $3.00 to the attorney; $4.75 to Proth. Donnell; $1.50 for the proclamation; and an amount left blank for advertising.

Nov. Term 1847 #32 - Henry Etter, Jr. vs. Mary Etter: libel in divorce presented to the Hon. Samuel C. Bonham and subpoena awarded by him. Same day subpoena issued. "October 18, 1847, N.E.I. so answers Thos. Jameson, Shff." Nov. 6, 1847, on due proof having been made by the sheriff that defendant could not be found in his bailiwick the court awarded an alias subpoena returnable first Monday of Jan., 1848. Alias subpoena issued to Jan. Term 1848 #7. Mr. Hainbly was the attorney for Henry Etter, Jr.

Jan. Term 1848 #7 - Henry Etter, Jr. vs. Mary Etter: alias subpoena in divorce. Original No. 32 Nov. Term 1847. "N.E.I. so answers Thos. Jameson, Shff." Jan. 4, 1848, the court direct the sheriff of York Co. to give four weeks notice to respondent by advertisement in the *Advocate* and *York Republican* two newspapers printed in the borough of York. Mar. 21, 1848, the court appointed John K. Willis, Esq., commissioner, to take testimony of witnesses in this case. Apr. 24, 1848, depositions filed. May 9, 1848, it appearing to the court that notice was duly given to the respondent to appear and answer, etc., whereupon the court decreed a divorce a vinculo matrimonii between the parties according to Act of Assembly in such case made and provided. Mr. Hanibly was the attorney for Henry Etter, Jr. Costs were $.18 3/4 to the sheriff; an additional $.18 3/4 to the sheriff; $3.00 to the attorney; $1.50 for the proclamation; $1.50 for advertising; and $4.50 to the proth., making a total cost of $10.87 1/2.

Apr. Term 1848 #8 - Mary Ann Luttman by her next friend Daniel B. Yeaple vs. Oliver Luttman: alias subpoena in divorce. Original No. 8 Nov. Term 1847. "March 22, 1848 N.E.I. so answers Thos. Jameson Shff." May 9, 1848, the court appointed James Adams, Esq., commissioner to take testimony in this case, and order the sheriff to publish notice to respondent for four weeks in the York Gazette, a newspaper printed in the borough of York. Mr. Stahle was the attorney for Mary Ann Luttman. Costs were $.18 3/4 to the sheriff.

Aug. Term 1848 #8 - Catharine Gise by her next friend John Albright vs. John Gise: Apr. 4, 1848, libel in divorce presented to the court and subpoena awarded returnable first Monday of Aug. 1848. "N.E.I. so answers Thos. Jameson, Shff." Aug. 8, 1848, alias subpoena awarded in this case returnable to Nov. Term next. Oct. 14, 1848, subpoena issued to Nov. Term 1848 #46. Mr. Shelley was the attorney for Catharine Gise and Mr. Stahle was the attorney for John Gise. Costs were $.18 3/4 to the sheriff.

Aug. Term 1848 #9 - Joseph Stevens vs. Elizabeth Stevens: Apr. 4, 1848, libel in divorce presented to the court and subpoena awarded returnable first Monday of Aug. 1848. "N.E.I. so answers Thos. Jameson, Shff." Aug. 8, 1848, alias subpoena awarded by the court in this case returnable to Nov. Term next. Oct. 14, 1848, alias subpoena issued to Nov. Term 1848 #47. Mr. Stahle was the attorney for Joseph Stevens. Cost was $.18 3/4 to the sheriff.

Nov. Term 1848 #6 - Mary Forster by her next friend Daniel Knaub vs. William Forster: Aug. 14, 1848, libel on divorce presented to Hon. Samuel C. Bonham and subpoena awarded returnable on first Monday of Nov. 1848 - a mensa et thoro - subpoena issued. "Aug. 31, 1848, served the within writ on William Forster by reading the same to him - so answers, Thos. Jameson, Shff." Nov. 11, 1848, rule on respondent to put in his answer to petition or libel in this case by the first Monday of Jan. next - or judgment notice to Messrs. Evans and Mayer at bar Dec. 14, 1848, answer of respondent filed. Jan. 26, 1850, Replication to respondent's answer. See paper filed with statements, Feb. 1850, Adjd. Court (J.L.) Feb. 27, 1850, trial ordered, whereupon a jury of the county being called came, to wit, George Beck, Henry Lehman, John J. Cochran, Daniel Snyder, Henry Shue, Jacob Werner, Carl Forney, Frederick Stover, Joseph Shuman, John Runk, Samuel Berkheimer and Philip Glatfeller twelve good and lawful men of the county of York, who being all duly sworn or affirmed well and truly to try the issue joined etc. and who upon their oaths and affirmations aforesaid do respectively say, that they find for the defendant. - Judgment nisi. Feb. 29, 1850, at the insistance of defendant, rule on Daniel Knaub, next friend of the libellant, to show cause why he should not pay the costs of defendant in this case. Rule returnable fourth Monday of Apr. 1850. Mar. 25, 1851, rule to show cause enlarged until fourth Monday of Apr. 1850. (two copies) May 2, 1851, Mr. Gallagher appears for Knaub. Jul. 16, 1851, rule made absolute by consent of counsel. Mr. Gallagher was the attorney for Mary Forster and Messrs. Evans & Mayer were the attorneys for William Foster. Costs were $2.28 to the sheriff; $15.86 1/2 for the defendant's bill; $4.00 for the jury; $7.25 for the proth.; $3.00 for the attorney and J. Lehmas' original notice $.50 making a total cost of $32.89 1/2.

Nov. Term 1848 #26 - Michael A. Palmer vs. Elizabeth A. Palmer: Sept. 11, 1848, libel in divorce presented to the Hon. Samuel C. Bonham and subpoena awarded by him returnable first Monday of Nov. next. Issued Sept. 25, 1848, served, the within writ on Elizabeth A. Palmer by reading within writ to her - so answers Thos. Jameson Shff." Mr. Buchanan was the attorney for Michael A. Palmer. Cost was $1.00 to the sheriff.

Nov. Term 1848 #28 - Elizabeth Steiner by her next friend John Carman vs. George Steiner: Sept. 12, 1848, libel in divorce presented to the court and subpoena awarded returnable first Monday of Nov. 1848. Issued. Jan. 5, 1849, the court, on motion of Mr. Gallagher awarded an alias subpoena in this case returnable first Monday of Apr., 1849. Mar. 3, 1849, alias subpoena to Apr. Term 1849 #38. Mr. Galligher was the attorney for Elizabeth Steiner.

Nov. Term 1848 #29 - Jacob Fishell vs. Mary Fishell: Sept. 12, 1848, libel in divorce presented to the court and subpoena awarded returnable first Monday of Nov. 1848. Issued. "September 22, 1848, served the within writ on Mary Fishell by reading within writ to her and handing her an attested copy of the same - so answers Thos. Jameson Shff." Nov. 8, 1848, the court appointed Monday the 12th day of Dec. 1848 at 10 o'clock, A.M. for hearing in this case. Dec. 10th rule issued to George Rice to take depositions in above case. Dec. 12, 1848, hearing in this case continued and George Rice appointed commissioner to take testimony of witnesses in Frederick

City, Md., on the part of the plaintiff. Dec. 16, 1848, rule to take testimony issued. Jan. 1, 1849, depositions filed. And now, to wit, Jan. 5, 1849, on hearing the court order and decree a divorce a vinculo matrimonii between the parties as fully and effectively as if they had never been married, according to Act of Assembly in such case made and provided. Mr. Galligher was the attorney for Jacob Fishell. Costs were $2.97 1/2 to the sheriff; $3.00 to the attorney; $1.50 for the proclamation; $4.18 3/4 to Proth. Donnell and $.50 for a copy making a total cost of $12.16 1/2. Recd. costs signed J.R. Donnell. Recd. $3.00 atty. fee signed M. Galligher.

Nov. Term 1848 #46 - Catharine Gise by her next friend John Albright vs. John Gise: alias subpoena in divorce. Original No. 8 Aug. Term 1848. "N.E.I., so answers Thos. Jameson Shff." And now, to wit, Apr. 27, 1849, the court appointed Joseph Garretson, Esq., commissioner, to take depositions of witnesses in this case. (one copy) Sept. 18, 1849, depositions filed and same day on motion of John Shelley, Esq., to court decreed a divorce a vinculo matrimonii between the parties according to Act of Assembly in such case made and provided. Messrs. Shelly and Stahle were the attorneys for Catharine Gise. Costs were $1.00 for advertising; $.18 3/4 to the sheriff; $3.00 for the attorneys; $4.50 to the proth.; $1.50 for the proclamation and $.18 3/4 to the sheriff making a total cost of $10.37 1/2 plus an additional $.50 charge making a grand total cost of $10.87 1/2.

Nov. Term 1848 #47 - Joseph Stevens vs. Elizabeth Stevens: alias subpoena in divorce. Original to Aug. Term 1848 #9. "N.E.I. so answers Thos. Jameson Shff." Mr. Stahle was the attorney for Joseph Stevens. Cost was $.18 3/4 to the sheriff.

Apr. Term 1849 #35 - Maria Catharine Stremmel by her next friend Daniel N. Lange vs. Frederick Stremmel: Mar. 2, 1849, libel in divorce presented to the Hon. Samuel C. Bonham and subpoena awarded returnable to Apr. Term 1849. Subpoena issued. "March 14, 1849, served within writ on Defendant by reading the same to him and handing him an attested copy of the same - so answers James Adams Sheriff." And now, Apr. 24, 1849, on motion of the counsel for libellant, the court appoints Jesse Faysinger, Esq., of the borough of Hanover, commissioner, to take the depositions of witnesses in the above case on May 22, 1849, on ten days notice to respondent. (one copy) Aug. 27, 1849, depositions filed. Sept. 1, 1849, the court on motion of libellant's counsel decreed divorce a vinculo matrimonii between the parties according to Act of Assembly in such case made and provided. Mr. Naille was the attorney for Maria Catharine Stremmel. Costs were $1.95 to the sheriff; $3.00 to the attorney; $4.50 to the proth.; and $.50 for a copy making a total cost of $9.95 to which was added $7.53 making a total cost of $17.48. Dec. 19, 1849 recd. above costs signed J.R. Donnell. Recd. $7.50 signed J.J.E. Naille.

Apr. Term 1849 #38 - Elizabeth Steiner by her next friend John Carman vs. George Steiner: alias subpoena in divorce original Nov. Term 1848 #28. "N.E.I. so answers James Adams Shff." Sept. 18, 1849, the court appointed Samuel Croxad, Esq., commissioner to take depositions of witnesses in this case. Mr. Galligher was the attorney for Elizabeth Steiner. Cost were $.18 3/4 to the sheriff.

Aug. Term 1849 #63 - Susanna Fickes by her next friend Daniel Bailey, Esq. vs. John Fickes: Aug. 16, 1849, libel on Divorce presented to the Hon. Daniel Durkee and subpoena awarded by him. Same day subpoena issued. "N.E.I. so answers James Adams Sheriff" alias subpoena in divorce awarded returnable to the next Term - alias subpoena No. 3 Nov. Term 1849. Mr. Fisher was the attorney for Susanna Fickes. Costs were $1.00 for the writ and $2.25 to the proth., making a total cost of $3.25.

Nov. Term 1849 #3 - Susanna Fickes by her next friend Daniel Bailey, Esq. vs. John Fickes: alias subpoena in divorce original No. 63 Aug. Term 1849. "N.E.I. so answers James Adams Sheriff." Dec. 11, 1849, on due proof made in open court that the respondent could not be found by the sheriff in his bailiwick the court order and direct that the said sheriff give notice to respondent to appear on first Monday of Jan., 1850, to answer the complaint of the libellant by publication for four successive weeks in the Democratic Press. Jan. 8, 1850, per motion the court appoints George Klinefelter, Esq., commissioner to take testimony of witnesses in this case. Feb. 25, 1850, on motion of Robert J. Fisher, Esq. attorney for libellant the court appoints Dr. George L. Shearer of Dillsburg, York County, commissioner to take testimony of witnesses in this case on behalf of the libellant. (one copy) Aug. 27, 1850, depositions filed - and now, on same day, the court on motion of R.J. Fisher, Esq., decreed a divorce a̲ vinculo matrimonii between the parties according to Act of Assembly in such case made and provided. Mr. Robert J. Fisher was the attorney for Susanna Fickes. Costs were $.18 3/4 to the sheriff; $1.50 for the proclamation; another $.18 3/4 to the sheriff; $3.00 to the attorney and $5.00 to Proth. J.R. Donnell making a total of $9.87 1/2 with additional costs of $.50 for a copy and $1.00 for advertising making a total cost of $11.37 1/2. Recd. costs signed J.R. Donnell.

Nov. Term 1849 #16 - Susan Zoller by her next friend and father Jeremiah Hess vs. Christian Zoller: libel in divorce presented to the Hon. Daniel Durkee and subpoena awarded by him. Same day issued. Nov. 14, 1849, Rule on defendant to answer in ten days notice to Messrs. Evans and Mayer at bar. Jan. 10, 1850, on motion of D.G. Barnitz, Esq., the court appoints Joseph Garretson, Esq., commissioner, to take testimony in this case. Same day respondent denies the allegations of the libel. Mr. D.G. Barnitz was the attorney for Susan Zoller. Messrs. Evans and Mayer were the attorneys for Christian Zoller. Costs were $1.00 for the sheriff; $1.25 for the writ; $2.50 for the proth., making a total cost of $3.75. Recd. my fees signed J.R. Donnell.

Jan. Term 1850 #2 - William Sponsler vs. Elizabeth Sponsler: Nov. 14, 1849, libel in divorce presented to the court and subpoena awarded. Same day subpoena issued. "Jan. 2d 1850, N.E.I. so answers James Adams, Sheriff." Jan. 7, 1850, on motion the court awarded an alias subpoena in this case returnable fourth Monday of Apr., 1850. Subpoena issued. Mr. Morris was the attorney for William Sponsler. Cost was $.18 3/4 to the sheriff.

Jan. Term 1850 #12 - John Knaub vs. Rosanna Knaub: Nov. 30, 1849, libel in divorce presented to the Hon. Daniel Durkee and subpoena awarded by him. Same day subpoena issued. "Dec. 28, 1849, served the within writ on Defendant by reading writ to her and handing her an attested copy of the same, so answers James Adams, Shff." Jan. 18, 1850, rule on defendant to plead in ten days or judgement after notice to her. (one copy) Oct. 1, 1850, It appearing to the court that the rule to plead in this case was duly served on defendant on Sept. 2, 1850, and defendant not appearing to answer, the court appoints George M. Shetter, Esq., commissioner to take testimony in this case. Mr. Shelly was the attorney for John Knaub. Costs were $1.32 to the sheriff; $1.00 for the writ; and $3.25 for Proth. J.R. Donnell making a total cost of $4.57.

Apr. Term 1850 #2 - William Sponsler vs. Elizabeth Sponsler: alias subpoena in divorce, original No. 2 Jan. Term 1850. "Feb. 27, 1850, served this writ on Elizabeth Sponsler within named by reading the same to her and handing her an attested copy of the same so answers James Adams Sheriff." May 28, 1850, the court appoints William Ilgonfritz, commissioner to take testimony of witnesses in this case. Jun. 3, 1850, depositions filed. Same day depositions read to the court, whereupon the court, on motion of William R. Morris, Esq., decreed a divorce a _vinculo_ _matrimonii_ between the parties according to the Act of Assembly in such case made and provided. Mr. William R. Morris was the attorney for William Sponsler and Mr. Galligher was the attorney for Elizabeth Sponsler. Costs were $1.00 for the sheriff and $5.00 for the proth., making a total cost of $6.00.

Apr. Term 1850 #22 - William Forster vs. Mary Forster: Feb. 28, 1850, libel in divorce presented to the Hon. Daniel Durkee, president judge of the court of common pleas, and subpoena awarded by him. Same day subpoena issued returnable fourth Monday of Apr. 1850. "March 9, 1850, served this writ on Mary Forster by reading the same to her and handing her an attested copy - so answers James Adams Shff." Apr. 25, 1850, answer of respondent filed. Messrs. Evans and Mayer were the attorneys for William Forster and Mr. Galligher was the attorney for Mary Forster. Costs were $2.28 for the sheriff; $1.00 for the writ and $1.75 for the proth., making a total cost of $5.03.

Aug. Term 1850 #6 - John M. Hoffman vs. Elizabeth Hoffman: Apr. 25, 1850, libel in divorce presented to the court and subpoena awarded. Subpoena issued. Mr. Galligher was the attorney for John M. Hoffman and Messrs. Evans and Mayer were the attorneys for Elizabeth Hoffman. Costs were $1.00 for the writ and $1.75 for the proth., making a total cost of $2.75.

Aug. Term 1850 #16 - Maria Smith by her next friend John Weber vs. Samuel Smith: Apr. 24, 1850, libel in divorce presented to the court and subpoena awarded. Subpoena issued same day. "July 29, 1850, served the within writ on respondent by reading the same to him and handing him an attested copy thereof - so answers James Adams Shff." Mr. Stahle was the attorney for Maria Smith. Cost was $1.00 to the sheriff.

Aug. Term 1850 #22 - Stephen C. Elder vs. Mary Elder: May 28, 1850, libel in divorce presented to the court and subpoena awarded returnable fourth Monday of Aug. next. Same day subpoena issued. "May 31, 1850, served the within writ on the Respondent by reading the same to her and handing her a copy thereof, so answers James Adams Shff." Oct. 3, 1850, rule on defendant to appear and plead or answer the libel or complaint of plaintiff on ten days after notice or judgment to be taken pro confesso. Nov. 4, 1850, it appearing to the court that the rule to plead in this case was duly served on defendant on Oct. 12, 1850, the court appoints John Fife, Esq., commissioner to take testimony of witnesses in this case. (one copy) Nov. 28, 1850, commission returned and depositions filed. And now, to wit, Dec. 10th 1850, upon the depositions taken in this case being read to the court, the court, on motion of Mr. Galligher, decree a divorce a vinculo matrimonii between the parties according to Act of Assembly in such case made and provided. Mr. Galligher was the attorney for Stephen C. Elder. Costs were $2.60 for the sheriff; an additional $2.10 for the sheriff; $5.00 for the proth.; $1.50 for the proclamation; $3.00 for the attorney and $.50 for a copy of the Decree making a total cost of $14.70. Recd. costs of plf. signed J.R.Donnell. Recd. attorney fee of $3.00 signed M. Galligher.

Jan. Term 1851 #2 - Philip Huber vs. Elizabeth Huber: Nov. 9, 1850, libel in divorce presented to the court and subpoena awarded returnable to next Term - same day subpoena issued. "Dec. 13, 1850, served the within writ on Respondent by reading the same to her and handing her a copy thereof - so answers James Adams Sheriff." Jan. 13, 1851, rule on respondent to answer libel in this case on ten days or judgment notice to Mr. Potts at bar. Mar. 15, 1851, judgment that the libel in this case be taken as confessed in default of an answer. May 2, 1851, Demurrer and answer of respondent to libel or complaint in this case filed. Same day libellant joins in the demurrer being No. 1 of respondent's pleadings and moves court to strike off the pleas in this case being Nos. 2, 4 and 5 of respondent's pleading and court order motion to be entered which is done. Jul. 16, 1851, demurrer and answer withdrawn by leave of court and respondent denies the facts set forth in the libel and prays issue in this case whereupon the court granted issue to be tried by a jury of the county, etc. Feb. 1852, Adjd. Ct. (J.L.) Feb. 24, 1852, trial ordered whereupon a jury of the county being called came to wit: Peter Goodling, Samuel Ziegler, John W. Schlosserr Dr. Luke Rouse, John M. Deitch, Isaac Broom, Samuel Weiser, Jacob J. Gibson, Michael Knaub, Henry Smyser, Daniel Loucks and Robert Kerr, twelve good and lawful men of the county of York, who being all sworn or affirmed according to law well and truly to try the issues joined etc. - and who upon their oaths, or affirmation aforesaid do say that they find for the plaintiff. Whereupon the court decreed a divorce a vinculo matrimonii between the said Philip Huber and Elizabeth Huber according to the Act of Assembly in such case made and provided-and the court further decreed and ordered that Elizabeth Huber the aforesaid respondent shall pay the costs in this case. Messrs. Evans and Mayer were the attorneys for Philip Huber and Mr. Potts was the attorney for Elizabeth Huber. Costs were $1.00 for the sheriff; $52.49 1/2 for the plaintiff's bill; $4.00 for the jury; $1.50 to the proth.; $3.00 for the attorney; $3.87 1/2 for Proth. Donnell and $3.76 to Proth. Garrett, making a total cost of $69.63. Recd. my costs except plaintiff's bill and Garrett's bill. Recd. my fees signed J.R. Donnell.

Apr. Term 1851 #4 - Laura M. Thomas by her next friend John Albright vs. William Thomas - Jan. 15, 1851, libel in divorce presented to the court by the plaintiff and subpoena awarded. Same day subpoena awarded as above and was issued returnable fourth Monday of Apr. 1851. "N.E.I. so answers James Adams Shff." May 2, 1851, alias subpoena awarded in this case returnable to next Aug. Term May 13, 1851. Issued to Aug. Term 1851 #11. Mr. Shelley was the attorney for Laura M. Thomas. Cost was $.18 3/4 for the sheriff.

Apr. Term 1851 #20 - Christopher Waggoner vs. Sarah Waggoner: Feb. 10, 1851, libel in divorce presented to the court and subpoena awarded by the court returnable to Apr. Term 1851. Issued. Defendant accepts service of writ which was served. Aug. 29, 1851, the court appoints Joseph Garretson, Esq., commissioner to take testimony in this case. Mr. Galligher was the attorney for Christopher Waggoner. Costs were $1.32 for the sheriff; $1.00 for the writ; and $1.75 for Proth. Donnell, making a total cost of $4.07.

Apr. Term 1851 #31 - Mary Barrows by her next friend William H. Christine vs. Thomas Barrows: Libel in divorce presented to the court and subpoena awarded. Same day subpoena issued. "N.E.I. so answers James Adams Shff." May 2, 1851, alias subpoena awarded returnable to next Aug. Term. May 13, 1851, alias subpoena issued to Aug. Term 1851 #10. Mr. Shelley was the attorney for Mary Barrows. Cost was $.18 3/4 for the sheriff.

Apr. Term 1851 #55 - Catharine Billmyer by her next friend John Albright vs. Jacob Billmyer: Apr. 9, 1851, libel in divorce presented to the Hon. Daniel Durkee and subpoena awarded. Apr. 10, 1851, subpoena issued. "April 11, 1851 subpoenaed Respondent by reading the within writ to him and handing him a copy thereof - so answers James Adams Shff." May 2, 1851, the court appointed Joseph Garretson, Esq., commissioner to take testimony in this case on ten days notice to respondent. Mr. Stahle was the attorney for Catharine Billmyer. Cost was $2.60 for the sheriff.

Aug. Term 1851 #9 - Susan Matthews by her next friend William Stough vs. Joseph Matthews: Apr. 29, 1851, libel in divorce presented to the court and subpoena awarded by the court. May 13, 1851, subpoena issued. "May 21, 1851, served the within subpoena on respondent by reading the same to him so answers James Adams, Shff." Aug. 30, 1851, the court appointed Joseph Garretson, Esq., commissioner to take the depositions of witnesses to be used in the hearing and determination of this case ex parte on ten days notice to defendant or his attorney. (one copy) Nov. 3, 1851, depositions filed. Dec. 2, 1851, marriage of parties admitted by respondent's counsel. Same day depositions read to the court, whereupon the court, on motion of libellant's counsel, decreed a divorce a vinculo matrimonii between the parties according to Act of Assembly in such case made and provided. Mr. Campbell was the attorney for Susan Matthews and Mr. Keesey was the attorney for Joseph Matthews. Costs were $2.00 for the sheriff; $3.00 for Proth. Donnell; $3.00 for the attorney; and $2.00 for Proth. Garrett, making a total cost of $10.00 to which was added $1.50 for Sheriff Adams' proclamation and $1.00 for the writ making a total cost of $12.50.

Aug. Term 1851 #10 - Mary Burrows by her next friend William H. Christian vs. Thomas Burrows: alias subpoena in divorce original No. 31 Apr. Term 1851. "N.E.I. so answers James Adams, Shff." Aug. 29, 1851, the court appointed Joseph Garretson, Esq., commissioner to take testimony of witnesses in this case. (one copy) Dec. 2, 1851, depositions filed and read to the court, whereupon the court, on motion of Mr. Shelley, attorney for libellant, the court decreed a divorce a vinculo matrimonii between the parties according to Act of Assembly in such case made and provided. Mr. Shelley was the attorney for Mary Burrows. Costs were $.18 3/4 for the sheriff; $3.00 for the attorney; $1.50 for the proclamation; $3.75 for Proth. Donnell; and $2.50 for Proth. Garrett, making a total cost of $10.93 3/4 to which was added the $.18 3/4 from the original action raising the total cost to $11.12 1/2 . Recd. my fees $3.00 signed J. Shelley. Recd. $8.12 1/2 the balance of costs signed C. Garretsen recd. $3.75 my fees in this case signed J.R. Donnell.

Aug. Term 1851 #11 - Laura M. Thomas by her next friend John Albright vs. William Thomas: alias subpoena in divorce original No. 4 Apr. Term 1851. "N.E.I. so answers James Adams Shff." Aug. 29, 1851, the court appointed Joseph Garretson, Esq., commissioner to take testimony of witnesses in this case. Mr. Shelley was the attorney for Laura M. Thomas. Cost was $.18 3/4 for the sheriff.

Nov. Term 1851 #6 - Mary Pohn by her next friend Martin Hoke vs. Joseph Pohn: Libel in divorce presented to the court and subpoena awarded returnable first Monday of Nov. 1851 and same day subpoena issued. "N.E.I. so answers James Adams, Shff." Alias subpoena awarded by the court issued to Apr. Term 1852 No. 32. Mr. C.A. Barnitz was the attorney for Mary Pohn. Costs were $.18 3/4 for the sheriff; $1.75 for the proth. and $1.00 for the writ making a total cost of $2.95 3/4.

Nov. Term 1851 #7 - Henry Layland vs. Elizabeth Layland: Aug. 28, 1851, libel in divorce presented to the court and subpoena awarded returnable first Monday of Nov. 1851 and same day subpoena issued - "Sept. 20, 1851, served the within subpoena on Defendant by reading the same to her and handing her a copy, so answers James Adams, Shff." Nov. 10, 1851, on motion of libellant's counsel the court appointed Joseph Garretson, Esq., commissioner to take testimony in this case. Dec. 2, 1851, depositions filed. Dec. 4, 1851, on motion of libellant's counsel the court appointed Isaac Beck, Esq., commissioner to take testimony of witnesses in this case. (one copy) Dec. 23, 1851, depositions filed. Jan. 8, 1852, depositions read to the court, whereupon the court, on motion of Mr. Galligher, decreed a divorce a vinculo matrimonii between the parties according to the Act of Assembly in such case made and provided. Mr. Galligher was the attorney for Henry Layland. Costs for $1.50 for the sheriff; $2.75 for Proth. Donnell; and $2.25 for Proth. G., making a total cost of $6.50.

Nov. Term 1851 #8 - Mary Glick by her next friend George Bear vs. John Glick: alias subpoena in divorce original No. 21 Aug. Term 1851 - "N.E.I. so answers James Adams, Shff." Jan. 6, 1852, the court order notice to be given by the sheriff in this case by advertisement for the stated number of time required by the Act of Assembly prior to next term - and the court at the same time appointed George M. Shetter, Esq., commissioner to take depositions of witnesses to be used on the hearing and determination of this case. Also the court appointed William Metzgar, Esq., commissioner to take depositions of witnesses in this case, etc. Sheriff gave notice accordingly. Apr. 30, 1852, depositions filed and read to the court whereupon the court decreed a divorce a vinculo matrimonii between the parties according to Acts of Assembly in such case made and provided. Messrs. Evans and Mayer were the attorneys for Mary Glick. Costs for $.18 3/4 for the sheriff; $3.00 for the attorney; $2.50 for Proth. Donnell; $2.50 for the proclamation; and $3.75 for Proth. G., making a total cost of $9.93 3/4 to which was added $1.18 3/4 for advertising and an additional cost of $1.50 for advertising bringing the total cost to $12.62 1/2.

Apr. Term 1852 #22 - Mary Pohn by her next friend Martin Hoke vs. Joseph Pohn: alias subpoena in divorce original No. 6 Nov. Term 1851. "N.E.I. so answers George Albright, Shff." May 11, 1852, the court direct the usual notice to be given by the sheriff requiring the respondent to appear at the next term to answer the complaint in this case by publication in the *York Gazette* for four successive weeks according to requirements of Act of Assembly - same day the court appointed John Weidman, Esq., commissioner to take testimony of witnesses in this case according to Act of Assembly in such case made and provided. Aug. 27, 1853, the court appointed George M. Shetter, Esq., commissioner to take testimony in this case. Mr. C.A. Barnitz was the attorney for Mary Pohn. Costs were $.18 3/4 for the sheriff; $2.50 for the proth.; $2.75 and $.66 for the original action; and $1.00 for the writ making a total cost of $7.09 3/4.

Aug. Term 1852 #21 - Elizabeth Bradley by her next friend Jacob Grass vs. Joseph Bradley: Jun. 14, 1852, libel in divorce filed and subpoena allowed by Hon. Robert J. Fisher, president judge of the Court of Common Pleas of York County. Subpoena issued returnable on fourth Monday of Aug. next. "N.E.I. so answers, Geo. Albright, Shff." Aug. 27, 1852, alias subpoena awarded returnable to next Nov. Term - same day alias subpoena issued to Nov. Term 1852 No. 9. Mr. Welsh was the attorney for Elizabeth Bradley. Cost was $.18 3/4 for the sheriff.

Aug. Term 1852 #26 - Joseph Coble vs. Margaret Ann Coble: libel in divorce presented to the Hon. Robert J. Fisher, president judge of the Court of Common Pleas of York County and subpoena awarded returnable on fourth Monday of Aug. 1852. Same day subpoena issued. "N.E.I. so answers Geo. Albright Shff." Augt. 27, 1852, alias subpoena in divorce awarded returnable to next Nov. Term. Same day alias subpoena issued to Nov. Term 1852 No. 8. Mr. Shelley was the attorney for Joseph Coble. Cost was $1.00 for the sheriff.

Aug. Term 1852 #33 - John Long, Jr., vs. Mary Ann Long: Jul. 13, 1852, libel in divorce presented to the Hon. Robert J. Fisher, president judge of the Court of Common Pleas of York County and subpoena awarded by him returnable the fourth Monday of Aug., 1852 - subpoena issued. "N.E.I. so answers Geo. Albright Shff." Aug. 27, 1852, alias subpoena in divorce awarded by the court returnable first Monday of Nov. next same issued to Nov. Term 1852 No. 7. Mr. S.M. Barnitz was the attorney for John Long, Jr. Cost was $.18 3/4 for the sheriff.

Nov. Term 1852 #6 - Mary Rupp by her next friend Jacob Zinn vs. Jacob Rupp: Aug. 27, 1852, libel in divorce presented to the court and subpoena awarded to respondent returnable on the first Monday of Nov. next - issued. "N.E.I. so answers Geo. Albright Shff." Nov. 2 1852 alias subpoena awarded returnable to the next Term alias subpoena issued to Jan. Term 1853 No. 21. Mr. Stahle was the attorney for Mary Rupp. Cost was $.18 3/4 to the sheriff.

Nov. Term 1852 #7 - John Long, Jr., vs. Mary Ann Long: alias subpoena in divorce original No. 33 Aug. Term 1852. "N.E.I. so answers Geo. Albright Shff." Nov. 2, 1852, the court appointed John A. Wilson, Esq., commissioner to take depositions in this case and the court directed the sheriff to give notice by advertisement in a newspaper printed in the borough of York according to law requiring respondent to appear at the next term to answer to the complaint of the libellant. Aug. 27, 1852. Mr. S.M. Barnitz was the attorney for John Long, Jr. Costs were $.18 3/4 for the sheriff and $2.50 for the proth.

Nov. Term 1852 #8 - Joseph Coble vs. Margaret Ann Coble: alias subpoena in divorce - original No. 26 Aug. Term 1852. "N.E.I. so answers Geo. Albright, Shff." Nov. 6, 1852, the court ordered notice to be given by the sheriff, in this case by advertisement for the stated number of times required by Act of Assembly prior to the next term. The court at the same time appointed Joseph Garretson, Esq., commissioner to take depositions of witnesses to be used on the hearing and determination of this case. Jan. 6, 1853, depositions filed and read to the court - And now same day it appearing to the court that notice was given to the respondent to appear at the court to answer the petition or complaint of the libellant in this case, and the respondent not appearing to answer etc., the court decreed a divorce a vinculo matrimonii between the parties according to Act of Assembly - in such case made and provided. Mr. Shelley was the attorney for Joseph Coble. Costs were $.18 3/4 for the sheriff; an additional $.18 3/4 for the sheriff; $1.50 for the Dr.; $3.00 for the attorney; $1.00 for advertising; and $5.00 for the proth., making a total cost of $10.87 1/2. Recd. $7.87 1/2 of costs signed E. Garretson.

Nov. Term 1852 #9 - Elizabeth Bradley by her next friend Jacob Grass vs. Joseph Bradley: Aug. 27, 1852, alias subpoena in divorce original No. 21 Aug. Term 1852. "N.E.I. so ans. Geo. Albright Shff." Jan. 10, 1853, the court, on motion of libellant's counsel, appointed John Shelley, Esq., commissioner to take testimony of witnesses in this case. Mr. Welsh was the attorney for Elizabeth Bradley. Costs were $.18 3/4 for the sheriff and $2.50 for the proth. and costs.

Jan. Term 1853 #7 - Mary Ann Sumwalt by her next friend Edie Patterson vs. Isaac H. Sumwalt: Nov. 12, 1852, libel in divorce presented to the Hon. Robert J. Fisher, president judge of the Court of Common Pleas of York County and subpoena awarded returnable to Jan. Term 1853. Same day subpoena issued. Alias subpoena to Aug. Term 1853 No. 42. "N.E.I. so answers Geo. Albright, Shff." Messrs. Dunkle and Weisler were the attorneys for Mary Ann Sumwalt. Cost was $.18 for the sheriff.

Jan. Term 1853 #21 - Mary Rupp by her next friend Jacob Zinn vs. Jacob Rupp: Dec. 3, 1852, alias subpoena in divorce - original to Nov. Term 1852 No. 6. Not served. Alias subpoena on divorce to Apr. Term 1853 No. 25. Mr. Stahle was the attorney for Mary Rupp.

Apr. Term 1853 #2 - Benjamin Grevell vs. Julia Grevell: Jan. 6, 1853, libel in divorce presented to the court and subpoena awarded returnable fourth Monday of Apr. 1853. Subpoena issued. "Apl. 2d, 1853, served the within subpoena on the defendant by reading the same to her and handing her a true and attested copy, so ans. Geo. Albright, Shff." Apr. 29, 1853, the court appointed George M. Shelter, Esq., commissioner to take depositions of witnesses in this case on ten days notice to respondent. (two copies) Jun. 7, 1853, depositions filed. And now, Jun. 9, 1853, depositions read to the court, whereupon the court, on motion of Mr. Galligher, attorney for libellant, decreed a divorce a vinculo matrimonii between the parties according to Act of Assembly in such case made and provided. Mr. Galligher was the attorney for Benjamin Grevell. Costs were $2.62 for the sheriff and $4.50 for Proth. G.

Apr. Term 1853 #3 - Eli Stern vs. Sophia Stern: Jan. 6, 1853, libel in divorce presented to the court and subpoena awarded returnable fourth Monday of Apr. 1853. Subpoena issued. "N.E.I. so ans. Geo. Albright, Sheriff" Apr. 29, 1853, alias subpoena awarded by the court returnable fourth Monday of Aug. 1853. Same day subpoena issued to Aug. Term 1853 No. 6. Mr. Galligher was the attorney for Eli Stern. Cost was $.18 3/4 for the sheriff.

Apr. Term 1853 #4 - Henrietta Bart by her next friend George Bange vs. John Bart: Jan. 7, 1853, libel in divorce presented to the court and subpoena awarded returnable fourth Monday of Apr. 1853. Issued. "January 15, 1853, served the within subpoena on Defendant by reading writ to him and handing him a true and attested copy, so ans. Geo. Albright Shff." Apl. 25, 1853, on motion of J.J. Naille, Esq. the court granted a rule to take depositions of witnesses in support of the libel in this case on ten days notice to defendant and returnable 31st May 1853. May 30, 1853, depositions filed. And now, Jun. 7, 1853, depositions read to the court - whereupon the court, on motion of Mr. Naille, atty. for the libellant, decreed a divorce a vinculo matrimonii between the parties in this case according to Act of Assembly in such case made and provided. Mr. James J.E. Naille was the attorney for Henrietta Bart. Costs were $2.44 for the sheriff; $3.00 for the attorney; $5.70 for Bill costs; $1.50 for the proclamation; and $4.75 for the proth.

Apr. Term 1853 #25 - Mary Rapp by her next friend Jacob Zinn vs. Jacob Rapp: Mar. 15, 1853, subpoena in divorce original No. 6 Nov. Term, 1852, - alias No. 21, Jan. Term, 1853. "March 17, 1853, served the within subpoena on Defendant by leaving a copy at his residence with an adult of his family, with whom he resides - the said defendant being absent. So answers Geo. Albright, Shff." May 3, 1853, the court appointed John Shelley, Esq., commissioner to take depositions of witnesses in this case to be used on the hearing and determination thereof on the part of the libellant. Aug. 31, 1853, the court rescinded the appointment of John Shelley, Esq., as commissioner in this case and appointed in his place and stead, John A. Wilson, Esq., commissioner to take testimony of witnesses in this case. (one copy) And now, Nov. 10, 1853, depositions filed and read to the court - whereupon the court, on motion of Gen. Stahle, libellant's counsel, decreed a divorce a vinculo matrimonii between the parties according to Act of Assembly in such case made and provided. Mr. Stahle was the attorney for Mary Rapp. Costs were $1.94 for the sheriff and $5.50 for Proth. G., making a total cost of $7.44. Recd. signed E. Garretson.

Aug. Term 1853 #3 - Dorothy Ann Gardner by her next friend James Curran vs. David Gardner: Apr. 28, 1853, libel in divorce presented to the court and subpoena awarded returnable fourth Monday of Aug. 1853. Subpoena issued. "N.E.I. so answ. Geo. Albright, Sheriff." Aug. 27, 1853, on proof having been made that the respondent is not in the bailiwick of the sheriff of this county, and that therefore the subpoena in divorce could not be served on him, the court awarded an alias subpoena returnable on first Monday of Nov. 1853. Same day alias subpoena issued to Nov. Term 1853 No. 6. Messrs. Evans and Mayer were the attorneys for Dorothy Ann Gardner.

Aug. Term 1853 #4 - Louisa Becker by her next friend Jacob Gross vs. John Becker: Apr. 28, 1853, libel in divorce presented to the court and subpoena awarded returnable fourth Monday of Aug. 1853. Subpoena issued. "Mr. Potts appears for Defendant so answer Geo. Albright, Sheriff." Aug. 31, 1853, the court appointed John A. Wilson, Esq., commissioner to take testimony of witnesses in this case. (one copy) Nov. 19, 1853, depositions filed and read to the court - whereupon the court, on motion of Gen. Stahle, decreed a divorce a vinculo matrimonii between the parties according to Act of Assembly in such case made and provided. Gen. Stahle was the attorney for Louisa Becker. Mr. Potts was the attorney for John Becker. Costs were $.18 3/4 for the sheriff; $3.00 for the attorney; $1.50 for the proclamation; and $4.25 for Proth. G., making a total cost of $8.93 3/4. Costs paid by E. Smith, signed E. Garrettson. $3.00 attorney fees paid signed J. S. Stahle.

Aug. Term 1853 #5 - Adaline S. Blakeslee by her next friend Charles Hildebrand vs. Amaziah Blakeslee: Apr. 28, 1853, libel in divorce presented to the court and subpoena awarded returnable fourth Monday of Aug. 1853. Subpoena issued. "N.E.I. so ans. Geo. Albright, Shff." Aug. 27, 1853, alias subpoena in divorce awarded by the court returnable first Monday of Nov. 1853. Same day subpoena issued. Nov. 7, 1853, sheriff returned alias subpoena issued in this case. "N.E.I. so ans. Geo. Albright Sheriff." Jan. 6, 1854, on motion of the plaintiff's counsel, the court appointed John A. Wilson, Esq., commissioner to take testimony of witnesses in this case according to Act of Assembly. Jan. 28, 1854, depositions filed and read to the court, whereupon the court, on motion of libellant's counsel decreed a divorce a vinculo matrimonii between the parties in this case according to the Act of Assembly in such case made and provided.

Mr. Stahle was the attorney for Adaline S. Blakeslee. Costs were $.18 3/4 for the sheriff; an additional $.18 3/4 for the sheriff; $1.50 for the proclamation; $3.00 for the attorney; $4.50 for Proth. G. and $2.00 for advertising making a total cost of $11.37 1/2. Rec. costs signed E. Garrettson. Recd. my fees $1.87 1/2 and advertising a total cost of $3.87 1/2. signed Geo. Albright.

Aug. Term 1853 #6 - Eli Stern vs. Sophia Stern: Apr. 29, 1853, alias subpoena in divorce original No. 3 Apr. Term 1853. "N.E.I. so ans. Geo. Albright, Shff." Aug. 26, 1853, the court appointed Gustav Reinak, Esq., commissioner to take testimony in this case in the city of Philadelphia and George M. Shetter, Esq., appointed commissioner to take testimony in this case at York and the court directed the sheriff to give notice to respondent by advertisement in one newspaper printed in the borough of York according to Act of Assembly in such case made and provided. (two copies) Mar. 13, 1854, depositions filed and read to the court - whereupon the court, on motion of General Stahle, counsel for libellant, the court decreed a divorce in this case between the parties a vinculo matrimonii according to the Acts of Assembly in such case made and provided. Mr. Galligher was the attorney for Eli Stern. Costs were $.18 3/4 for the sheriff; an additional $.18 3/4 for the sheriff; $2.00 for advertising; $1.50 for the proclamation; $3.00 for the attorney; and $5.25 for Proth. G. making a total cost of $12.14 1/2. Recd. costs signed E. Garrettson and J.S. Stahle.

Aug. Term 1853 #42 - Mary Ann Sumwalt by her next friend Edie Patterson vs. Isaac H. Sumwalt: alias subpoena in divorce - original to Jan. Term 1853 No. 7. "August 6, 1853, served the within subpoena on the Respondent by reading writ to him and handing him a true and attested copy thereof - so ans. Geo. Albright, Sheriff." Oct. 4, 1853, on motion of libellant's counsel the county granted a rule to take depositions of witnesses in support of the libel in this case on ten days notice to respondent. Nov. 19, 1853, depositions filed and read to the court - whereupon the court, on motion of libellant's counsel decreed a divorce a vinculo matrimonii between the parties according to the Act of Assembly in such case made and provided. Messrs. Durkee and (Horace S.) Weiser were the attorneys for Mary Ann Sumwalt. Costs were $2.72 for the sheriff; $1.50 for the proclamation; $3.00 for the attorney and $5.25 for Proth. G., making a total cost of $12.47 with an additional charge of $.18 for the sheriff for the original action making a new total of $12.65 due.

Nov. Term 1853 #5 - John Summer vs. Dorothy Summer: Aug. 27, 1853, libel in divorce presented to the court and subpoena awarded returnable to Nov. Term 1853. Same day subpoena issued. "N.E.I. so answers Geo. Albright Shff." Nov. 10, 1853, on motion of

H.L. Fisher, Esq. atty. for libellant, the court awarded an alias subpoena in divorce in this case returnable first Monday of Jan. 1854. Alias subpoena issued to Jan. Term 1854 #5. Mr. Galligher was the attorney for John Summer and Mr. H.L. Fisher, Esq. was the attorney for Dorothy Summer. Cost was $.18 3/4 for the sheriff.

Nov. Term 1853 #6 - Dorothy Ann Gardner by her next friend James Curran vs. David Gardner: alias subpoena in divorce original No. 3 of Aug. Term 1853. "N.E.I. so ans. Geo. Albright, Sheriff." Feb. 7, 1854, the court appointed Joseph Garretson, Esq., commissioner to take depositions in support of the libel in this case. (one copy) And now, Apr. 26, 1854, depositions taken by Joseph Garretson, Esq., persuant to the above appointment were filed and read to the court whereupon the court, on motion of Messrs. Evans & Mayer, decreed a divorce a vinculo matrimonii between the parties in this case according to Act of Assembly in such case made and provided. Messrs. Evans & Mayer were the attorneys for Dorothy Ann Gardner. Costs were $.18 for the sheriff; $3.00 for the attorneys; $1.50 for advertising; $1.50 for the proclamation; and $4.50 for Proth. G., making a total cost of $10.68. Recd. $7.68 of above costs for I. Evans signed C.B. Wallace.

Nov. Term 1853 #31 - Mary Ann Becker by her next friend Martin Heiner vs. John Becker: Oct. 17, 1853, libel in divorce presented to the court and subpoena awarded by the court returnable on the first Monday of Nov. next. Same day subpoena issued. "N.E.I. so answ. Geo. Albright, Shff." Nov. 7, 1854, alias subpoena awarded by the court returnable first Monday of Jan. 1854. Issued. Jan. 2, 1854, alias subpoena returned by sheriff thus endorsed "N.E.I. so answ. Geo. Albright, Sheriff." Nov. 10, 1854, the court appointed John A. Wilson, Esq., commissioner to take testimony of witnesses in this case. And now, Dec. 1, 1854, depositions filed and read to the court whereupon the court, on motion of libellant's counsel, decreed a divorce a vinculo matrimonii between the parties in this case according to the Act of Assembly in such case made and provided. Mr. Stahle was the attorney for Mary Ann Becker. Costs were $.18 for the sheriff; $2.87 for Proth. G.; $1.50 for advertising; $1.50 for sheriff G.; $1.50 for Proth. H.; and $3.00 for the attorney a total cost of $10.55

Jan. Term 1854 #5 - John Summer vs. Dorothy Summer: Nov. 12, 1853, alias subpoena in divorce. Original No. 5 Nov. Term 1853. "Dec. 9, 1853, served the within subpoena on Respondant by reading the same to her and handing her a true and attested copy so ans. Geo. Albright, Shff." Jan. 2, 1854, the court appointed Thomas A. Ziegle, Esq., commissioner to take testimony in this case - ten days notice to be given of time and place. (one copy) Feb. 7, 1854, depositions filed and read to the court whereupon the court, on motion of libellant's counsel, H.L. Fisher, Esq., decreed a divorce a vinculo matrimonii between the parties in this case according to the Acts of Assembly in such case made and provided and the court direct the respondent to pay the costs. Mr. H.L. Fisher was the attorney for John Summer and Mr. Wilton was the attorney for Dorothy Summer. Costs were $2.42 for the sheriff; $.18 3/4 additional cost for sheriff; $1.50 for the proclamation; $3.00 for the attorney (Recd. signed H.L. Fisher); and $4.50 for Proth. G., making a total cost of $11.60 3/4 with an additional cost of $.50 for Proth. G., making a grand total cost of $12.10 3/4. Costs paid by libellant signed E. Garretson.

Apr. Term 1854 #4 - Catharine Grove by her next friend George Coleman vs. John Grove: libel in divorce presented to the court and subpoena awarded returnable fourth Monday of Apr. 1854. Same day subpoena issued. "N.E.I. so answ. Geo. Albright, Shff." Apr. 28, 1854, alias subpoena awarded by the court returnable fourth Monday of Aug. 1854. Apr. 29, 1854, subpoena issued to Aug. Term 1854 #10. Mr. Stahle was the attorney for Catharine Grove. Cost was $.18 3/4 to the sheriff.

Apr. Term 1854 #18 - John Kise vs. Catharine Kise: Feb. 20, 1854, libel in divorce presented to the court and subpoena awarded to be directed to respondent returnable fourth Monday of Apr. 1854. Same day subpoena issued. "March 9, 1854, served the within subpoena on the Defendant by reading the same to her and handing her a true and attested copy thereof - so ans. Geo. Albright, Sheriff." Apr. 28, 1854, the court on motion of Mr. Stahle appointed John A. Wilson, Esq., commissioner to take testimony in this case. May 31, 1854, depositions filed and read to the court whereupon the court, on motion of libellant's counsel, decreed a divorce in this case between the parties a vinculo matrimonii according to the Act of Assembly in such case made and provided and the court directed the libellant to pay the costs. Mr. Stahle was the attorney for John Kise. Costs were $2.31 to the sheriff; $3.00 to the attorney; $1.50 for the proclamation and $4.00 to the proth., making a total of $10.81. Recd. costs signed E. Garretson and J.S. Stahle.

Apr. Term 1854 #28 - Elijah Barnhart vs. Catharine Barnhart: Mar. 22, 1854, libel in divorce presented to the Hon. Robert J. Fisher, president judge of the Court of Common Pleas of York County, and subpoena awarded to respondent returnable to Apr. Term 1854. Subpoena issued. "1 Apl. (sic) 1854, served the within subpoena on the Defendant by reading the same to her and handing her a true and attested copy thereof - so ans. Geo. Albright, Shff." Messrs. Evans and Mayer were the attorneys for Elijah Barnhart. Costs were

$1.75 to the sheriff and $2.50 to the proth., making a total cost of $4.25.

Aug. Term 1854 #8 - Hiram Koons vs. Hannah Koons: Apr. 22, 1854, libel in divorce presented to the court and subpoena awarded to be directed to the defendant returnable fourth Monday of Aug., 1854. Subpoena issued. "N.E.I. so answ. Geo. Albright, Shff." Jan. 5, 1855, the court appointed John A. Wilson, commissioner to take depositions of witnesses in this case. Mr. Stahle was the attorney for Hiram Koons. Costs were $.18 to the sheriff and $.75 for the writ a total cost of $.93.

Aug. Term 1854 #9 - Gabriel Rice vs. Catharine Rice: Apr. 28, 1854, libel in divorce presented to the court and subpoena awarded to be directed to respondent returnable fourth Monday of Aug. 1854. Subpoena issued. "N.E.I. so ans. Geo. Albright, Shff." Aug. 31, 1854, alias subpoena awarded to respondent returnable first Monday of Nov., 1854. Sept. 2, 1854, alias subpoena issued to Nov. Term 1854 No. 7. Mr. Wallace was the attorney for Gabriel Rice. Cost was $.18 to the sheriff.

Aug. Term 1854 #10 - Catharine Grove by her next friend George Coleman vs. John Grove: Apr. 29, 1854, alias subpoena in divorce. Original No. 4 Apr. Term 1854. "May 5, 1854, served the within subpoena on Defendant by reading the same to him and handing him a true and attested copy thereof - so ans. Geo. Albright, Shff." Sept. 2, 1854, the court appointed John A. Wilson, Esq., commissioner to take depositions in this case. Mr. Stahle was the attorney for Catharine Grove. Costs were $1.25 to the sheriff; $.75 for the writ; and $2.75 for the proth., making a total cost of $4.75.

Aug. Term 1854 #12 - Leah Martha Fahs by her next friend Martin Basehore vs. David Fahs: libel in divorce presented to the Hon. Robert J. Fisher, president judge of the Court of Common Pleas of York County - and subpoena awarded by him to be directed to the respondent returnable fourth Monday of Aug. 1854. Issued. "June 2d, 1854, served the within subpoena on defendant by reading writ to him and handing him a true and attested copy thereof - so ans. Geo. Albright, Shff." Sept. 2, 1854, the court appointed Thomas A. Ziegler, Esq., commissioner to take testimony in this case. Aug. 31, 1855, depositions filed and read to the court, whereupon, the court on motion of E.H. Weiser, Esq. decreed a divorce a vinculo matrimonii between the parties according to the Act of Assembly in such case made and provided and the court direct the costs to be paid by the respondent. Messrs. Durkee and Weiser were the attorneys for Leah Martha Fahs. Mr. H.L. Fisher was the attorney for David Fahs. Costs were $1.37 to the sheriff; $2.25 for the proth. and writ (released see paper filed with subpoena released $1.00); $2.00 to Proth. H.; $3.00 to the attorneys; $1.50 for advertising and $1.50 for the proclamation, making a total cost of $11.62. Recd. atty. fee $3.00 signed E.H. Weiser. Recd. $2.50 of sheriff's fees signed C.B. Wallace.

Aug. Term 1854 #34 - John Shettel vs. Mary Shettel: Jul. 3, 1854, libel in divorce presented to the Hon. Robert J. Fisher, president judge of the Court of Common Pleas of York County who awarded a subpoena to respondent returnable fourth Monday of Aug. 1854 - same day subpoena issued. "Aug. 9, 1854, served the within subpoena on the Respondent by reading writ to her and handing her a true and attested copy thereof - so ans. Geo. Albright, Shff." Sept. 2, 1854, the court appointed Joseph Garretson, Esq., commissioner to take testimony of witnesses in this case. Commission issued. Oct. 3, 1854, Commission returned and depositions filed and read to the court whereupon the court, on motion of libellant's counsel, decreed a divorce a vinculo matrimonii between the parties according to the Act of Assembly in such case made and provided. Messrs. Evans and Mayer were the attorneys for John Shettel. Costs were $2.40 to the sheriff; $3.00 to the attorney; $1.50 for the proclamation and $4.41 1/4 making a total cost of $11.31 1/4 Recd. $8.31 signed E. Garretson.

Aug. Term 1854 #35 - Margaret Douglass by her next friend Joseph J.E. Reed vs. James H. Douglass: libel in divorce presented to the Hon. Robert J. Fisher, president judge of the Court of Common Pleas of York County who awarded a subpoena to respondent returnable fourth Monday of Aug. 1854. Same day subpoena issued. "Aug. 5, 1854, served the within writ on Respondent by reading the same to him and handing him a true and attested copy thereof - so ans. Geo. Albright, Shff." Sept. 4, 1854, rule on defendant to file his answer to plaintiff's libel in fifteen days or bill to be taken pro confesso - notice to Mr. Keesey at bar. Mr. Cochran was the attorney for Margaret Douglass and Mr. Keesey was the attorney for James H. Douglass. Costs were $3.02 for the sheriff and $1.85 for Proth. G., making a total cost of $4.87.

Aug. Term 1854 #39 - Sarah Fishel by her next friend John Albright vs. Granville Fishel: Jul. 27, 1854, libel in divorce a vinculo matrimonii presented to the Hon. Robert J. Fisher, president judge of the Court of Common Pleas of York County who awarded a subpoena to respondent returnable fourth Monday of Aug. 1854. Same day subpoena issued. "N.E.I. so ans. Geo. Albright, Shff." Sept. 2, 1854, alias subpoena awarded to the respondent returnable first Monday of Nov. 1854. Alias subpoena issued this Sept. 2, 1854, to Nov. Term 1854 No. 6. Jan. 5, 1855, the court appointed John A.

Wilson, Esq., commissioner to take depositions of witnesses in this case. (one copy) Jan. 22, 1855, depositions filed and read to the court, whereupon the court, on motion of libellant's counsel, decreed a divorce a vinculo matrimonii between the parties according to the Act of Assembly in such case made and provided. Mr. Keesey was the attorney for Sarah Fishel. Costs were $.18 for the sheriff and other costs which were not recorded in the docket book apparently.

Aug. Term 1854 #40 - John Fry vs. Elizabeth Fry: Jul. 27, 1854, libel in divorce presented to the Hon. Robert J. Fisher, president judge of the Court of Common Pleas of York County who awarded a subpoena to the respondent returnable fourth Monday of Aug. 1854. Same day subpoena issued. "July 3d 1854, served the within subpoena on the defendant by reading the same to her and handing her a true and attested copy thereof - so ans. Geo. Albright, Shff." Sept. 4, 1854, rule on defendant to file his answer to plaintiff's libel in fifteen days or bill to be taken pro confesso on notice to Mr. Fisher at bar. Sept. 19, 1854, respondent's answer filed. Feb. 7, 1855, the court appointed John Gibson, Esq., commissioner to take testimony in this case on the part of the libellant and respondent. All the facts alleged in respondent's answer except the marriage is denied by libellant. Mar. 6, 1855, deposition filed and read to the court whereupon the court, on motion of libellant's counsel, decreed a vinculo matrimonii between the parties according to the Act of Assembly in such cases made and provided. Mr. Keesey was the attorney for John Fry and Mr. H.L. Fisher was the attorney for Elizabeth Fry. Costs were $2.50 for the sheriff; $1.85 for the proth.; $10.00 for the commissioner; $2.00 for Proth. H. and $3.00 for the attorney making a total cost of $19.35. Recd. of Mr. Keesey the above costs signed C.B. Wallace. Recd. atty. fee signed (T.K.K.?). Recd. commissioner's fee signed John Gibson. Recd. my fee $1.85 signed E. Garretson. Recd. of C.B. Wallace my fees signed (J. Holland?).

Nov. Term 1854 #6 - Sarah Fishell by her next friend John Albright vs. Granville Fishell. Alias subpoena in divorce, original No. 39 of Aug. Term 1854. "N.E.I. so ans. Geo. Albright, Sheriff." And now, to wit, Jan. 5, 1855, the court appoints John A. Wilson, Esq., commissioner to take depositions in this case. (one copy) Jan. 22, 1855, depositions filed and read to the court whereupon the court, on motion of libellant's counsel, decreed a divorce a vinculo matrimonii between the parties, according to the Act of Assembly in such cases made and provided. Mr. Keesey was the attorney for Sarah Fishell. Costs were $.18 3/4 for the sheriff; $2.50 for the proth.; $1.50 for Proth. H.; $3.00 for the attorney; $1.00 for advertising; $1.50 for the proclamation; $.18 3/4 for the sheriff on the original writ and an additional cost of $.50 (what this was for went unrecorded) making a total cost of $10.37 1/2. Recd. the above costs of V.K. Keesey signed C.B. Wallace. Recd. atty. fees signed V.K.K. Recd. my fees signed E.G. (E. Garretson).

Nov. Term 1854 #7 - Gabriel Rice vs. Elizabeth Rice: Sept. 2, 1854 alias subpoena in divorce original No. 9 Aug. Term 1854. "N.E.I. so ans. Geo. Albright, Shff." Feb. 7, 1855, on motion of libellant's counsel the court appointed Robert W. Smith, Esq., commissioner to take testimony in this case. Commission issued. Apr. 27, 1855, depositions filed and read to the court. Whereupon the court, on motion of libellant's counsel, decreed a divorce a vinculo matrimonii between the parties, according to the Act of Assembly in such cases made and provided. Mr. Wallace was the attorney for Gabriel Rice. Costs were $.18 for the sheriff; $2.50 for the proclamation and writ; $1.50 for Proth. H.; $3.00 for the attorney and $1.50 for advertising making a total cost of $8.68.

Nov. Term 1854 #22 - Hiram Koons vs. Hannah Koons: alias subpoena in divorce. Original to Aug. Term 1854 No. 8. "N.E.I. so ans. Geo. Albright, Shff." Jan. 5, 1855, the court appointed John A. Wilson, Esq., commissioner to take depositions in this case. And now, Jan. 5, 1855, depositions filed and read to the court - whereupon the court, on motion of Mr. Stahle, attorney for libellant, decreed a divorce a vinculo matrimonii between the parties in this case according to the Act of Assembly in such case made and provided. Mr. Stahle was the attorney for Hiram Koons. Costs were $.18 for the sheriff; $2.50 for the proclamation and writ; $1.87 for Proth. H.; $1.50 for advertising; $1.50 for Proth. G. and $3.00 for the attorney making a total cost of $10.55.

Nov. Term 1854 #26 - Henry McFadden vs. Jane McFadden: Oct. 6, 1854, libel in divorce presented to the Hon. Robert J. Fisher, president judge of the Court of Common Pleas of York County who awarded a subpoena to respondent returnable first Monday of Nov. 1854. Subpoena issued. "October 7, 1854, served the within subpoena on Defendant by reading writ to her and handing her a true and attested copy thereof, so ans. Geo. Albright, Shff." Nov. 10, 1854, court appointed John A. Wilson, Esq., commissioner to take testimony of witnesses in this case. Nov. 27, 1854, depositions read to the court, the court on motion of John G. Campbell, Esq., decreed a divorce a vinculo matrimonii between the parties in this case according to the Act of Assembly in such cases made and provided. Mr. Campbell was the attorney for Henry McFadden. Costs were $1.37 1/2 for the sheriff; $4.00 for the proth.; $3.00 for the attorney and $1.50 for the proclamation, making a total cost of $9.87 1/2.

Jan. Term 1855 #3 - Mary LeFevre by her next friend George Neiman vs. Samuel LeFevre: Nov. 6, 1854, libel in divorce presented to the court and subpoena awarded. Subpoena issued. "N.E.I. so answers Daniel Ginder, Sheriff." Jan. 1, 1855, alias subpoena awarded returnable fourth Monday of Apr. 1855. Issued to Apr. Term 1855 No. 2. Mr. H.S. Weiser was the attorney for Mary LeFevre. No costs were listed.

Jan. Term 1855 #11 - Mary Gray by her next friend John Schuarts vs. William Gray: Nov. 25, 1854, libel in divorce presented to Hon. John Reiman an associate judge of the Court of Common Pleas of York County and subpoena awarded returnable first Monday of Jan. 1855. Same day subpoena issued, Dec. 26, 1854. "N.E.I. so answers Danl. Ginder, Sheriff." Jan. 5, 1855, alias subpoena awarded returnable the fourth Monday of Apr. 1855. Issued to Apr. Term 1855, No. 6. Messrs. Evans and Mayer were the attorneys for Mary Gray. Costs were $1.30 for Pro. G.; and $.18 3/4 for Sheriff Ginder making a total cost of $1.51 3/4.

Jan. Term 1855 #20 - Eliza Boyer by her next friend Elijah Garretson vs. John Boyer: libel in divorce presented to the court and subpoena awarded, returnable first Monday of Jan. 1855. Same day subpoena issued. Dec. 26, 1854, N.E.I. so answers Daniel Ginder, Sheriff. Jan. 1, 1855, alias subpoena awarded returnable the fourth Monday of Apr. 1855. Issued to Apr. Term 1855 No. 1. Mr. Keesey was the attorney for Eliza Boyer. Costs were $.18 3/4 to Sheriff Ginder and $.75 for the writ making a total cost of $.93 3/4.

Apr. Term 1855 #1 - Eliza Boyer by her next friend Elijah Garretson vs. John Boyer: alias subpoena in divorce. Original No. 20 Jan. Term 1855. "N.E.I. so answers Daniel Ginder, Shrff." Aug. 30, 1855, on motion of V.K. Keesey, Esq. the court appointed Adam Stevens, Esq. to take testimony in this case. (one copy) Sept. 29, 1855, depositions filed and read to the court, whereupon the court, on motion of V.K. Keesey, Esq., decreed a divorce a vinculo matrimonii between the parties according to the Act of Assembly in such case made and provided. Mr. V.K. Keesey, Esq. was the attorney for Eliza Boyer. Costs were $.18 3/4 for Sheriff Ginder; $3.00 for the attorney; $1.50 for advertising; $1.50 for the proclamation; $.18 3/4 for the sheriff; and $4.25 for Pro. H. making a total cost of $10.62 1/2 after which an additional cost of $.50 was added for an unmarked reason making a grand total cost of $11.12 1/2. Recd. the above costs of Mr. Keesey signed C.B. Wallace. Recd. attorney fee signed V.K.K. (V.K. Keesey, Esq.). Recd. my fees signed D. Ginder.

Apr. Term 1855 #2 - Mary LeFever by her next friend George Neiman vs. Samuel LeFever. Alias subpoena in divorce original to

Jan. Term 1855 No. 3. "N.E.I., so answers, Daniel Ginder, Shrff." Aug. 27, 1855, on motion of H.S. Weiser, Esq. the court appointed John A. Wilson, Esq., commissioner to take testimony in this case. (one copy) Aug. 31, 1855, depositions filed and read to the court, whereupon the court, on motion of E.H. Weiser, Esq., decreed a divorce a vinculo matrimonii between the parties according to the Act of Assembly in such cases made and provided. Costs were $.18 3/4 for Sheriff Ginder; $1.50 for advertising; $3.00 for the attorney; $1.50 for the proclamation; $4.50 for Pro. H. (Pro. Joseph Holland) making a total cost of $10.87 1/2. Recd. of H.S. Weiser, Esq. $6.37 1/2 of the above costs signed C.B. Wallace. H.S. Weiser, Esq. assures the payment of advertising in this case. Recd. my fees signed D. Ginder.

Apr. Term 1855 #6 - Mary Gray by her next friend John Swartz vs. William Gray: alias subpoena in divorce. Original No. 11 Jan. Term 1855. "N.E.I. so answers Daniel Ginder, Shrff." Sept. 3, 1855, on motion of Messrs. Evans & Mayer the court appointed John A. Wilson, Esq., commissioner to take testimony in this case. (one copy) Oct. 4, 1855, depositions filed and read to the court - whereupon the court, on motion of libellant's counsel, decreed a divorce a vinculo matrimonii, between the parties according to the Act of Assembly in such case made and provided. Messrs. Evans & Mayer were the attorneys for Mary Gray. Costs were $.18 3/4 to Sheriff Ginder - $1.50 for advertising; $1.50 for the proclamation; another $.18 3/4 for Sheriff Ginder; $3.00 for the attorney and $4.50 to the proth., making a total cost of $10.87 1/2. Recd. the above costs signed C.B. Wallace. Recd. atty. fee signed Jno. Evans. Recd. my fees signed D. Ginder.

Apr. Term 1855 #26 - Sarah Strader by her next friend Frederick Kassabaum vs. Charles F. Strader: libel in divorce presented to the Hon. Robert J. Fisher, president judge of the Court of Common Pleas of York County, who awarded a subpoena to respondent returnable the fourth Monday of Apr. 1855. Mar. 6, 1855, on motion of libellant's counsel the court appointed George M. Sheffer, Esq., commissioner to take testimony on the part of the libellant on ten day's notice to the respondent. (one copy) Mar. 10, 1855, served the within subpoena on defendant by reading the same to him and handing him a true and attested copy thereof so answers Daniel Ginder, shrff. Apr. 26, 1855, commission returned and depositions filed and read to the court. Whereupon the court, on motion of libellant's counsel, decreed a divorce a vinculo matrimonii between the parties according to the Act of Assembly in such cases made and provided. Mr. H.L. Fisher was the attorney for Sarah Strader. Costs were $1.50 for the sheriff; $3.00 for the attorney; $1.50 for the proclamation; $3.75 for Proth. H., making a total of $9.75 with an additional cost of $.50 for a grand total cost of $10.25. Recd. sheriff and Proth. H. fees of $7.25 signed C.B. Wallace. Recd. my fees signed D. Ginder.

Apr. Term 1855 #42 - John H. Carl vs. Mary Carl: libel in divorce presented to the Hon. John Reiman, an associate judge of the Court of Common Pleas of York County, who awarded a subpoena to respondent returnable the fourth Monday of Apr. 1855. Same day subpoena issued. "N.E.I. so answers Daniel Ginder, Shrff." Alias subpoena awarded by the court. Issued to Aug. Term 1855 No. 3. Messrs. Evans & Mayer were the attorneys for John H. Carl. Costs were $.18 3/4 for the sheriff and $.75 for the writ making a total cost of $.93 3/4.

Aug. Term 1855 #3 - John Carl vs. Mary Carl: Apr. 26, 1855, alias subpoena in divorce, original No. 42 Apr. Term 1855. Jul. 10, 1855, served the within writ on respondent by reading the same to her and handing her an attested copy thereof, so answers Daniel Ginder, Shrff. Aug. 31, 1855, on motion of Mr. Evans, the court appointed Joseph Garretson, Esq., commissioner to take testimony in this case. Oct. 4, 1855, depositions filed and read to the court. Whereupon the court, on motion of Messrs. Evans & Mayer, decreed a divorce a vinculo matrimonii between the parties according to the Act of Assembly in such case made and provided. Messrs. Evans & Mayer were the attorneys for John Carl. Costs were $2.17 for the sheriff; $.75 for the writ; $3.00 for the attorneys; $1.50 for the proclamation; another $.18 3/4 for the sheriff; and $3.25 for Proth. H. making a total of $10.85 3/4 to which was added an additional cost of $.50 making a total of $11.35 to which $4.10 was subtracted making a grand total cost of $7.25. Recd. the above costs $7.25 signed C.B. Wallace. Recd. $1.00 atty. fee the rest released signed Jno. Evans. Recd. my fees signed D. Ginder. Deduct atty. fee $2.00; Sheriff Ginder $1.60 and $.50 for the proclamation, making a total deduction of $4.10.

Nov. Term 1855 #13 - Sarah Wagner by her next friend William Hamilton vs. James Wagner: Sept. 5, 1855, libel in divorce presented to the Hon. Robert J. Fisher, president judge of the Court of Common Pleas of York County and subpoena awarded returnable to Nov. Term 1855 issue. Nov. 3, 1855, - Nihil as to defendant - so answers Daniel Ginder, shrff. Nov. 12, 1855, alias subpoena awarded returnable first Monday of Jan. 1856 - Issued to Jan. Term 1856 No. 6. Mr. Campbell was the attorney for Sarah Wagner. Costs were $.18 3/4 to Sheriff Ginder; $.75 for the writ; and $1.22 for the proclamation making a total cost of $2.15 3/4.

Nov. Term 1855 #34 - Mary Ann Ebersole by her next friend William Schmuck vs. Jesse Ebersole: Oct. 2, 1855, libel in divorce presented to the court and subpoena awarded returnable first Monday of Nov. 1855. Nov. 3, 1855, served the within writ on defendant by reading the same to him and handing him a true and attested copy thereof. So answers Daniel Ginder, shrff. Nov. 12, 1855, on motion of Mr. Galligher, the court appointed John A. Wilson, commissioner to take testimony in this case. Jan. 9, 1856, depositions filed. Jan. 14, 1856, depositions read to the court, whereupon the court, on motion of libellant's counsel, decreed a divorce a vinculo matrimonii, between the parties according to the Act of Assembly in such case made and provided etc. etc. Mr. Galligher was the attorney for Mary Ann Ebersole. Costs were $2.34 to the sheriff; $.75 for the writ; $3.00 for the attorney; $1.50 for the advertising; $1.00 for the proclamation; and $3.50 for Pro. H. making a total of $12.09 minus $1.50 changing the total to $10.59. Recd. $7.59 above costs signed C.B. Wallace. Recd. my fees D. Ginder.

Jan. Term 1856 #1 - Ann Secrist by her next friend Andrew Diehl vs. George Secrist: Nov. 9, 1855, libel in divorce presented to the court and subpoena awarded to respondent returnable first Monday of Jan. 1856, same day subpoena issued. Nov. 26, 1855, on motion of W.C. Chapman, Esq. the court appointed Joseph Garretson, Esq., commissioner to take testimony in this case. Dec. 19, 1855, depositions filed. Nov. 19, 1855, served the within writ on defendant by reading the same to him and handing him a true and attested copy thereof so answers Daniel Ginder, sheriff. May 2, 1856, depositions read to the court whereupon the court, on motion of William C. Chapman, Esq., decreed a divorce a vinculo matrimonii, between the parties according to the Act of Assembly in such case made and provided - court directed respondent to pay costs. Mr. William C. Chapman, Esq. was the attorney for Ann Secrist. Costs were $1.37 to Sheriff Ginder; $1.50 for the commissioner; $3.00 for the attorney and $4.00 for Pro. H. making a total cost of $9.87.

Jan. Term 1856 #6 - Sarah Wagner by her next friend William Hamilton vs. James Wagner: alias subpoena in divorce original No. 13 Nov. Term 1855 "Nihil as to defendant" so answers Daniel Ginder, shrff. Mr. Campbell was the attorney for Sarah Wagner. Costs were $.18 3/4 for the sheriff; $.75 for the writ; and $1.22 for Proth. H., making a total cost of $2.15 3/4.

Apr. Term 1856 #5 - Elizabeth Kochenour by her next friend Robert Morrison vs. Samuel Kochenour: Jan. 9, 1856, libel in divorce presented to the court and subpoena awarded to be presented to the court and subpoena awarded to be directed to the respondent, returnable fourth Monday of Apr. 1856. Subpoena issued. Feb. 13, 1856, "on motion of H.L. Fisher, Esq., the court appointed George M. Shetter, Esq. Commissioner, to take testimony in this case - on ten days notice to Respondent or his counsel. (one copy) April 12, 1856, served the within subpoena on Samuel Kochenour, defendant by reading the same to him and handing him a true and attested copy thereof, so answers Daniel Ginder, shrff. Mr. H.L. Fisher, Esq. was the attorney for Elizabeth Kochenour. Costs were $1.24 to Sheriff Daniel Ginder and $2.72 for Proth. H., making a total cost of $3.96.

Apr. Term 1856 #7 - Maria Bear by her next friend Gabriel Stover, Esq. vs. John R. Bear: Jan. 11, 1856, libel in divorce presented to the court and subpoena awarded to respondent returnable fourth Monday of Apr. 1856. Same day subpoena issued. Mar. 3, 1856, served the within subpoena on John R. Bear, by reading the same to him and handing him a true and attested copy thereof - so answers Daniel Ginder, shrff. May 5, 1856, court appointed George M. Shetter, Esq., commissioner to take testimony in this case. May 31, 1856, depositions filed. Jun. 10, 1856, depositions read to the court whereupon the court, on motion of libellant's counsel, decreed a divorce a vinculo matrimonii, between the parties, according to the Act of Assembly in such case made and provided. The court directed respondent to pay costs. Messrs. Evans & Mayer were the attorneys for Maria Bear. Costs were $1.31 for the sheriff; $3.00 for the attorney; 1.50 for the proclamation; and $3.50 for Proth. H., making a total cost of $9.31. Recd. the above costs signed C.B. Wallace. Recd. atty. fee signed Jno. Evans. Recd. my fees signed D. Ginder.

Apr. Term 1856 #13 - Eliza Shenberger by her next friend William Herbst vs. Henry Shenberger: Jan. 19, 1856, libel in divorce presented to the Hon. Robert J. Fisher, president judge of the Court of Common Pleas of York County, and subpoena awarded returnable fourth Monday of Apr. 1856. Same day subpoena issued - "N.E.I." so answers Daniel Ginder, shff. May 3, 1856, alias subpoena awarded to respondent returnable fourth Monday of Aug. 1856, - same day subpoena issued to Aug. Term 1856 No. 9. Mr. Keesey was the attorney for Eliza Shenberger. Costs were $.18 3/4 for the sheriff.

Apr. Term 1856 #15 - John Raugkrat vs. Lydia Raugkrat: Jan. 24, 1856, libel in divorce presented to the Hon. John Reiman, one of the associate judges of the Court of Common Pleas of York County, and subpoena awarded returnable fourth Monday of Apr. 1856. Same day subpoena issued. "N.E.I. so answers Daniel Ginder, Sheff." Apr. 30, 1856, alias subpoena awarded to respondent returnable fourth Monday of Aug. 1856. Same day subpoena issued to

Aug. Term 1856 No. 6. Messrs. Gibson & Alleman were the attorneys for John Raugkrat. Cost was $.18 3/4 for the sheriff.

Aug. Term 1856 #6 - John Raugkrat vs. Lydia Raugkrat: alias subpoena in divorce original No. 15 Apr. Term 1856. "N.E.I. so answers Daniel Ginder, Sheff." Aug. 29, 1856, the court appointed John A. Wilson, Esq., commissioner to take testimony in this case. Messrs. Gibson & Alleman were the attorneys for John Raugkrat. Costs were $.18 3/4 for the sheriff; another .18 3/4 for the sheriff; another $1.50 for the sheriff; $2.25 for the proclamation; and $3.00 for the attorneys making a total of $7.12 1/2. Recd. of Mr. Alleman the above costs except attorney fee. signed C.B. Wallace. Recd. my fees signed D. Ginder.

Aug. Term 1856 #9 - Eliza Shenberger by her next friend William Herbst vs. Henry Shenberger: May 3, 1856, alias subpoena in divorce original #13 Apr. Term 1856. "N.E.I." so answers Daniel Ginder, shff. Dec. 11, 1856, court on motion of V.K. Keesey, Esq. appoints John A. Wilson, Esq., commissioner to take testimony in this case. Mar. 27, 1857, depositions filed and read to the.court and it appearing to the court to have been advertised according to law, the court on motion of V.K. Keesey, Esq. decreed a divorce a vinculo matrimonii between the parties according to the Act of Assembly in such cases made and provided. Mr. V.K. Keesey, Esq. was the attorney for Eliza Shenberger. Costs were $.18 3/4 for the sheriff; $3.00 for the attorney; another $.18 3/4 for the sheriff; $1.50 for advertising; $3.50 for Proth. H.; and $.50 for a copy making a total of $8.62 1/2. Recd. of Mr. Keesey the above costs signed C.B. Wallace. Recd. attorney fees - $3.00 plus $1.00 a total of $4.00 signed V.K.K. Recd. my fees signed Daniel Ginder.

Aug. Term 1856 #10 - Anna Mary Vannatten by her next friend John Zimmerman vs. Peter Vannatten: alias subpoena in divorce original No. 54 Apr. Term 1856. "N.E.I." so answers Daniel Ginder, sheff. Nov. 7, 1856, the court appointed Henry C. Stroman, Esq., commissioner to take testimony in this case. May 2, 1857, depositions filed and read to the court whereupon the court, on motion of G.A. Barnitz, Esq., decreed a divorce a vinculo matrimonii between the parties, according to the Act of Assembly in such case made and provided. Mr. G.A. Barntiz, Esq. was the attorney for Anna Mary Vannatten. Costs were $.18 3/4 for the sheriff; another $.18 3/4 for the sheriff; $1.50 for the proclamation; $3.00 for the attorney and $3.75 for the proth. a total cost of $10.12 1/2.

Aug. Term 1856 #24 - Mary Black by her next friend Daniel Snyder vs. Samuel Black: May 26, 1856, libel in divorce presented to the Hon. John Kerman one of the associate judges of the Court of

Common Pleas of York County and subpoena awarded returnable fourth Monday of Aug. 1856 - "N.E.I. so answers Daniel Ginder, Shrff." Aug. 28, 1856, alias subpoena awarded to respondent returnable first Monday of Nov. 1856. Same day subpoena issued to Nov. Term 1856 #4. Mr. Detweiler was the attorney for Mary Black. Cost was $.18 3/4 for the sheriff.

Nov. Term 1856 #4 - Mary Black by her next friend Daniel Snyder vs. Samuel Black: alias subpoena in divorce original No. 24 Aug. Term 1856, "N.E.I. so answers Daniel Ginder, Sheff." Nov. 7, 1856, the court appointed William Metzgar, Esq., commissioner to take testimony in this case. Jan. 9, 1857, depositions filed and read to the court, whereupon the court decreed a divorce a vinculo matri-monii between the parties according to the Act of Assembly in such case made and provided. Mr. Detweiler was the attorney for Mary Black. Costs were $.18 3/4 for the sheriff; $3.00 for the attorney; $1.50 for advertising; another $.18 3/4 for the sheriff; $1.50 for the proclamation; $3.75 for Proth. H; and $.50 for a copy of the rule making a total cost of $10.62 1/2.

Nov. Term 1856 #16 - Sophia Kettler by her next friend Henry Grothe vs. William Kettler: Sept. 10, 1856, libel in divorce presented to the Hon. Robert J. Fisher, president judge of the Court of Common Pleas of York County and subpoena awarded returnable first Monday of Nov. 1856. Sept. 12, 1856, subpoena issued. N.E.I. so answers Daniel Ginder, shff. Nov. 6, 1856, alias subpoena awarded returnable first Monday of Jan. 1857. Issued to Jan. Term 1857 No. 3. Mr. Fisher was the attorney for Sophia Kettler. Cost was $.18 3/4 to the sheriff.

Nov. Term 1856 #18 - Nancy Law by her next friend Samuel Spangler vs. Israel Law: Sept. 13, 1856, libel in divorce presented to the Hon. Robert J. Fisher, president judge of the Court of Common Pleas of York County and subpoena awarded, returnable first Monday of Nov., 1856. Sept. 16, 1856, subpoena issued. Oct. 22, 1856, served the within subpoena on Israel Law, by leaving a true and attested copy at his residence, so answers Daniel Ginder, shff. Nov. 7, 1856, the court, on motion of libellant's counsel, appointed George M. Shetter, Esq., commissioner to take testimony in this case. Jan. 3, 1857, depositions filed. Jan. 8, 1857, depositions read to the court whereupon the court, on motion of libellant's counsel, decreed a divorce a vinculo matrimonii between the parties according to the Act of Assembly in such case made and provided and the court ordered the respondent to pay the costs of this suit. Mr. Alleman was the attorney for Nancy Law. Costs were $1.61 for the sheriff; $.75 for the writ; $3.00 for the attorney; $1.75 for the proclamation; and $2.00 for the commissioner making a total cost of $9.11.

Nov. Term 1856 #19 - Louisa Menough by her next friend Benjamin Myers vs. Samuel Menough: Sept. 15, 1856, libel in divorce presented to the Hon. Robert J. Fisher, president judge of the Court of Common Pleas of York County and subpoena awarded returnable first Monday of Nov. 1856. Sept. 16, 1856, subpoena issued. "N.E.I. so answers Danl. Ginder, Sheff." Nov. 6, 1856, subpoena awarded returnable first Monday of Jan. 1857. Issued to Jan. Term 1857 No. 4. Mr. Weiser was the attorney for Louisa Menough. Cost was $.18 3/4 for the sheriff.

Nov. Term 1856 #20 - Nancy Hoke by her next friend James McClellan vs. Michael Hoke: Sept. 3, 1856, libel in divorce presented to the Hon. Robert J. Fisher, president judge of the Court of Common Pleas of York County and subpoena awarded returnable first Monday of Nov. 1856. Mr. Ziegle was the attorney for Nancy Hoke and Mr. Alleman was the attorney for Michael Hoke. Cost was $1.98 for Proth. H.

Nov. Term 1856 #23 - Matthias Haak vs. Sophia Haak: Sept. 29, 1856, libel in divorce presented to the Hon. Robert J. Fisher, president judge of the Court of Common Pleas of York County and subpoena awarded returnable first Monday of Nov. 1856. Same day subpoena issued. N.E.I. so answers Daniel Ginder, shff. Mr. Galligher was the attorney for Matthias Haak. Costs were $.18 3/4 for the sheriff, $.75 for the writ and $1.22 for the proclamation making a total cost of $2.15 3/4.

Jan. Term 1857 #3 - Sophia Kettler by her next friend Henry Grothe vs. William Kettler: Nov. 6, 1856, alias subpoena in divorce. Original No. 16 Nov. Term 1856. Dec. 11, 1856, the court appoints George M. Shetter, Esq., commissioner to take testimony in this case. Nov. 18, 1856, served the within subpoena on William Kettler by reading the same to him and handing him a true and attested copy thereof - so answers Daniel Ginder, shff. Mr. Fisher was the attorney for Sophia Kettler. Costs were $1.12 1/2 for the sheriff; $1.00 for the writ and $1.75 for Proth. H., making a total cost of $3.87 1/2.

Jan. Term 1856 #4 - Louisa Menough by her next friend Benjamin Myers vs. Samuel Menough: alias subpoena in divorce. Original No. 19 Nov. Term 1856. "N.E.I. so answers Daniel Ginder, Sheff. April 27, 1857, I Samuel H. Menough appear to the above suit and waive any irregularity in the proceeding." (see paper filed) Apr. 29, 1857, the court appoints T.A. Ziegle, Esq., commissioner to take testimony in this case and direct five days notice to be given to the respondent. May 5, 1857, depositions read to the court, whereupon the court, on motion of E.H. Weiser, Esq., decreed a divorce <u>a vinculo matrimonii</u> between the parties according to the Act of Assembly in such case made and provided. Mr. E.H. Weiser, Esq., was the attorney for Louisa Menough. Costs were $.18 3/4 for the sheriff; another $.18 3/4 for the sheriff; $1.50 for the proclamation; $3.00 for the attorney; $3.75 for the proth.; and $5.00 for the commissioner making a total cost of $13.62 1/2. Recd. the above costs signed C.B. Wallace. Recd. costs as commissioner signed Thos. Ziegle. Recd. atty. fee $3.00 signed E.H. Weiser. Recd. my fees signed D. Ginder.

Jan. Term 1856 #17 - Nancy Hoke by her next friend James McClellan vs. Michael Hoke: Dec. 2, 1856, libel in divorce presented to the Hon. Adam Ebaugh, Esq. one of the associate judges of the Court of Common Pleas of York County, and subpoena awarded returnable first Monday of Jan. 1857. Issued. "Dec. 11, 1856, served the within writ on Michael Hoke by reading the same to him and handing him a true and attested copy thereof so answers Daniel Ginder, Sheff." Jan. 9, 1857, court appointed John S. Detweiler, Esq., commissioner to take testimony in this case. Jan. 12, 1857, defendant's answer filed. Feb. 6, 1857, depositions filed. Mar. 27, 1857, the court refused to grant a divorce in this case and direct each party to pay his and her own costs. Mr. Ziegle was the attorney for Nancy Hoke and Mr. Alleman was the attorney for Michael Hoke. Costs were $1.84 to the sheriff; $3.00 to the attorney and $3.50 to Proth. H., making a total cost of $8.34.

Jan. Term 1857 #19 - Eve Kalkreider by her next friend Jacob Hittett vs. Samuel Kalkreider: Dec. 5, 1856, libel in divorce presented to the Hon. Robert J. Fisher, president judge of the Court of Common Pleas of York County and subpoena awarded returnable first Monday of Jan. next (1857). Issued. "Dec. 24, 1856, served the within subpoena on defendant by leaving a true and attested copy at his residence with an adult member of his family, so answers Daniel Ginder, Sheff." Jan. 7, 1857, the court appointed Abraham M. Hershey, Esq., commissioner to take testimony in this case. Mar. 5, 1857, depositions filed. Whereupon the court, on motion of Mr. Naille, decreed a divorce <u>a vinculo matrimonii</u> between the parties according to the Acts of Assembly in such case made and provided. Court ordered the respondent to pay the costs of this suit. Mr. Naille was the attorney for Eve Kalkreider. Costs were $2.85 for the sheriff; $3.00 for the attorney; and $3.50 for the proth. making a total cost of $9.35. Recd. the above costs except atty. fee signed C.B. Wallace. Recd. my fee signed D. Ginder.

Apr. Term 1857 #20 - Stephen B. Miles vs. Hannah S. Miles: Feb. 23, 1857, libel in divorce presented to the Court of Common Pleas of York County, and subpoena awarded returnable fourth Monday of Apr. 1857. Subpoena issued. N.E.I. so answers Daniel Ginder, shff. Aug. 3, 1857, alias subpoena awarded returnable fourth Monday of Aug. Instant subpoena issued to No. 48 Aug. Term 1857. Mr. Chapin was the attorney for Stephen B. Miles. Cost was $.18 3/4 to the sheriff.

Aug. Term 1857 #42 - Mary Ann Stevens by her next friend Jeremiah Collison vs. Thomas Hoffman Stevens: Jul. 23, 1857, libel in divorce presented to the Hon. John Reiman, one of the associate judges of the Court of Common Pleas of York County and subpoena awarded returnable fourth Monday of Aug. 1857. Subpoena issued. Jul. 30, 1857, served the within writ of subpoena on defendant by reading the same to him and handing him a true and attested copy thereof, so answers Daniel Ginder, shff. Aug. 31, 1857, court appointed John S. Detweiler, Esq., commissioner to take testimony in this case. Sept. 29, 1857, depositions filed and read to the court whereupon the court, on motion of libellant's counsel, decreed a divorce a vinculo matrimonii between the parties, according to the Acts of Assembly in such case made and provided. Mr. Ziegle was the attorney for Mary Ann Stevens. Costs were $1.00 for the sheriff; $.75 for the writ; $3.00 for the attorney; $1.75 for the proclamation; $.50 for a copy making a total cost of $7.00 from which the $1.00 for the sheriff was taken off leaving a total cost of $6.00. Recd. $5.00 of the above costs signed C.B. Wallace. Recd. $2.00 atty. fee signed Thos. Ziegle.

Aug. Term 1857 #48 - Stephen B. Miles vs. Hannah S. Miles: alias subpoena in divorce - original No. 20 Apr. Term 1857. N.E.I. so answers Daniel Ginder, shff. Dec. 8, 1858, on motion of E. Chapin, Esq., the court appointed Robert Ramsey (Tanner), of Peach Bottom Twp., commissioner to take depositions to be used on the part of the plaintiff on the hearing of the above case. Feb. 10, 1859, depositions filed. And now, to wit, Feb. 15, 1859, depositions read to the court, whereupon the court, on motion of Mr. Chapin, decreed a divorce a vinculo matrimonii between the parties in this case according to the Act of Assembly in such case made and provided. Mr. E. Chapin, Esq., was the attorney for Stephen B. Miles and Messrs. Evans & Meyer were the attorneys for Hannah S. Miles and they appeared for the defendant Nov. 7, 1857. Costs were $.18 3/4 for the sheriff; $1.75 for Proth. H.; another $1.75 for Proth. H. on the original action; $1.50 for the proclamation; $3.00 for the attorney; and $3.20 for Proth. B. with two additional charges of $.63 1/4 and .18 for some unstated expenses making a total cost of $12.19. Pd. signed

W. Ilg. Recd. $3.87 shff. G. and Proth. H. per (*sic*) signed C.B. Wallace.

Nov. Term 1857 #7 - William R. Nebinger vs. Martha Nebinger: Aug. 29, 1857, libel in divorce presented to the Court of Common Pleas of York County and subpoena awarded returnable first Monday of Nov. 1857. N.E.I. so answers Daniel Ginder, shff. Alias subpoena awarded to Jan. Term 1858 No. 9. Mr. Gibson was the attorney for William P. Nebinger. Costs were $.18 3/4 for the sheriff; $.75 for the writ; and $1.25 for Proth. H., making a total cost of $2.18 3/4.

Nov. Term 1857 #8 - Catharine Eaton by her next friend Jacob Eichelberger vs. Ross Eaton: Aug. 29, 1857, libel in divorce was presented to the Court of Common Pleas of York County and subpoena awarded returnable first Monday of Nov., 1857. "October 31, 1857, N.E.I. so answers Daniel Ginder, Sheff." Alias subpoena No. 10 Jan. Term 1858. Mr. Keesey was the attorney for Catharine Eaton. Costs were $.18 3/4 for the sheriff; $.75 for the writ; and $1.25 for Proth. H., making a total cost of $2.18 3/4.

Jan. Term 1858 #9 - William P. Nebinger vs. Martha Nebinger: alias subpoena in divorce original No. 7 Nov. Term 1857. "December 1, 1857, served the within writ on Defendant by reading the same to her and handing her a true and attested copy thereof, so answers Samuel Forscht, Sheriff." Mar. 1, 1858, on motion of Mr. Gibson the court appointed George M. Shetter, Esq., commissioner to take testimony in this case. Nov. 5, 1860, depositions filed and read to the court, whereupon the court, on motion of John Gibson, Esq., decreed a divorce a vinculo matrimonii between the parties in this case pursuant to the Acts of Assembly in such case made and provided. Mr. John Gibson, Esq. was the attorney for William P. Nebinger. Mr. Keesey was the attorney for Martha Nebinger. Costs were $.75 for the writ; $.55 for Proth. H.; $2.65 for Sheriff Samuel Forscht; $1.50 for the proclamation; $3.00 for the attorney; and $2.50 for Proth. H., making a total of $10.95 to which was added $2.18 on the original action changing the total to $13.13. Costs pd. by plaintiff signed W. Ilgenfertz. Recd. my fees signed Saml. Forscht Recd. my fees signed John Gibson.

Jan. Term 1858 #10 - Catharine Eaton by her next friend Jacob Eichelberger vs. Ross Eaton: Nov. 1857 alias subpoena in divorce original No. 8 Nov. Term 1857 "Non Est Inventus - so answers Samuel Forscht, Sheriff." Nov. 1, 1858, it appearing to the court that the sheriff gave notice of advertisement as directed by the Act of Assembly, the court appointed John H. Wilson, Esq., commissioner to take testimony in this case. Mr. Keesey was the attorney for

Catharine Eaton. Costs were $.75 for the writ; $.55 for Proth. H.; $.18 3/4 for Sheriff Forscht; and $1.50 for Proth. B., making a total cost of $2.98 3/4.

Jan. Term 1858 #21 - William H. Shetley vs. Susan Shetley: Nov. 23, 1857, libel in divorce presented to the Court of Common Pleas of York County and subpoena awarded returnable first Monday of Jan. 1858 issued. "Non Est Inventus - so ans. Saml. Forscht, Shff." Jan. 6, 1858, on motion of Mr. Keesey the court awarded an alias subpoena in divorce in this case returnable fourth Monday of Apr., 1858. Subpoena issued. Apr. 19, 1858, alias subpoena returned "N.E.I. - so answ. Saml. Forscht, Shff." Nov. 1, 1858, it appearing to the court that the sheriff gave notice by advertisement in the manner directed by the Act of Assembly, the court appointed John A. Wilson, Esq., commissioner, to take testimony in this case. (1 copy) Nov. 6, 1858, depositions filed and read to the court, whereupon the court, on motion of V.K. Keesey, Esq., decreed a divorce a vinculo matrimonii between the parties according to the Act of Assembly in such case made and provided. Mr. Keesey was the attorney for William H. Shetley. Costs were $.75 for the writ; $.55 for Proth. H.; $.18 for Sheriff Forscht; another $.18 for Sheriff Forscht; $1.50 for the advertisement; $3.75 for Proth. B.; $1.50 for the proclamation; and $3.00 for the attorney making a total cost of $11.41. Recd. my fee signed W. Ilg. Recd. my first advertisement signed Saml. Forscht. Recd. atty. fee signed V.K.K. Recd. fees $1.30 signed C.B. Wallace.

Apr. Term 1858 #4 - Cordelia Martin by her next friend Andrew Kump vs. William L. Martin: libel in divorce presented to the court and filed - court awarded a subpoena returnable the fourth Monday of Apr. 1858, requiring the defendant to appear and answer to the complaint in this case, etc. Same day subpoena issued. "Non Est Inventus - so answers Saml. Forscht, Shff. Apr. 28, 1858, on motion of the plaintiff's counsel the court awarded an alias subpoena returnable the fourth Monday of Aug. 1858. Subpoena issued. Aug. 23, 1858, sheriff returned alias subpoena. "N.E.I. so answers Saml. Forscht, Sheriff." Nov. 4, 1858, it appearing that the sheriff of York Co. had given the required notice to the respondent in the *Hanover Spectator* for four successive weeks previous to the first day of this term, the court grants a rule to take depositions of witnesses to be read in this case in behalf of the libellant before John A. Aulabaugh, Esq., of Hanover. (1 copy) Nov. 30, 1858, depositions filed. Dec. 7, 1858, depositions read to the court and it appearing to the court that due notice was given by publication to the respondent as required by law, whereupon the court, on due consideration, decreed a divorce between the parties a vinculo matrimonii according to the Act of Assembly in such case made and provided. Mr. Naille was the attorney for Cordelia Martin. Costs were $.18 for the sheriff; an additional $.18 for the sheriff; $3.00 for the attorney; $1.50 for the proclamation; and $4.66 for Proth. B., making a total cost of $9.52.

Apr. Term 1858 #7 - Albertus Hibner vs. Margaret Hibner: Jan. 8, 1858, libel in divorce presented to the court and filed - and the court awarded a subpoena returnable the fourth Monday of Apr. 1858, requiring respondent to appear and answer the complaint of petitioner in this case, etc. Subpoena issued. "Feby. (*sic*) 18, 1858, served the within writ of subpoena on the defendant by leaving a true and attested copy at her residence with her father she being absent - so answers Saml. Forscht, Shff." Jun. 1, 1858, on motion of Mr. Ziegle, the court appointed Oscar K. Harris, Esq., commissioner to take depositions in the above case. And now, Aug. 28, 1858, depositions taken by the commissioner in this case were filed and read to the court whereupon the court, on due consideration, decreed a divorce a vinculo matrimonii between the parties according to the Act of Assembly in such case made and provided. Court directed costs to be paid by plaintiff. Mr. Ziegle was the attorney for Albertus Hibner. Costs were $3.06 for the sheriff; an additional $2.75 for the sheriff; $3.00 for the attorney; $1.50 for the proclamation; $4.50 for Proth. H. and $5.00 for the commissioner making a total cost of $19.81. Recd. my fees signed Saml. Forscht. Recd. $9.00 signed W. Ilg. Recd. my fees signed Thos. Ziegle.

Apr. Term 1858 #22 - Nancy Hoke by her next friend Noah Martin vs. Michael Hoke: Jan. 27, 1858, libel in divorce presented to the court and filed, whereupon the court awarded a subpoena to the respondent requiring him to appear before the court on the fourth Monday of Apr. 1858 to answer the complaint of the libellant. Subpoena issued. "Feby.(*sic*) 17, 1858, served the within subpoena on the Defendant by reading the same to him and handing him a true and attested copy thereof - so answers Saml. Forscht, Shff." Apr. 30, 1858, on motion of plaintiff's counsel the court appointed M.F. Mulgrew, Esq., commissioner to take depositions of witnesses in this case on ten days notice to respondent. Mr. Thomas Ziegle was the attorney for Nancy Hoke and Mr. Vincent K. Keesey was the attorney for Michael Hoke. Costs were $1.96 for the sheriff; $1.80 for the rule; and $2.75 for Proth. B., making a total cost of $6.51. Above costs paid by W. Bittenger, Esq. signed W. Ilg. Recd. of W. Ilgcufutz my fees signed Saml. Forscht.

Apr. Term 1858 #58 - Lavinia Morthland by her next friend John Weaver vs. Michael Morthland: Mar. 13, 1858, libel in divorce presented to the Hon. John Reiman and subpoena awarded by him to respondent returnable fourth Monday of Apr. 1858 (see petition filed) Subpoena issued. "April 5, 1858, served the within subpoena on defendant by reading it to him and handing him a true and attested copy thereof - so ans. Saml. Forscht, Shff." Apr. 30, 1858, the court appointed John A. Wilson, Esq., commissioner to take testimony in this case. (1 copy) and now, Jun. 1, 1858, the depositions taken in this case by the commissioner were filed and read to the court, whereupon the court, on due consideration, decreed a divorce a vinculo matrimonii between the parties in this case according to the Act of Assembly in such case made and provided. Messrs. Evans and Mayer were the attorneys for Lavinia Morthland. Costs were $2.36 for the sheriff; $1.50 for the proclamation; $3.00 for the attorneys; $4.22 for Proth. B. and $1.50 for the commissioner making a total cost of $12.50. Costs paid signed W. Ilg. Recd. my fees signed Saml. Forscht. Recd. my fees signed John A. Wilson.

Apr. Term 1858 #66 - William Englesberger vs. Rebecca J. Englesberger: Mar. 19, 1858, libel in divorce presented to the Hon. John Reiman, one of the judges of the Court of Common Pleas of York County and subpoena awarded by him to the respondent returnable fourth Monday of Apr. 1858. Subpoena issued. April 6, 1858, served the within writ on defendant by reading writ to her and handing her a true and attested copy thereof - so ans. Saml. Forscht, Shff." Apr. 30, 1858, the court appointed M.F. Mulgrew, Esq., commissioner to take depositions in this case on ten days notice to respondent. Mr. Thomas Ziegle was the attorney for William Englesberger. Costs were $1.25 for the sheriff and $2.25 for Proth. B. making a total cost of $3.50.

Aug. Term 1858 #1 - Josephine Hyberger by her next friend George Myers vs. John Hyberger: Apr. 27, 1858, libel in divorce presented to the court and filed. Court awarded a subpoena to respondent returnable fourth Monday of Aug. 1858 at 2:00 o'clock, A.M. Same day subpoena issued - Jun. 10, 1858, on motion of Mr. Chapman the court granted rule to take depositions to be read on the hearing of this case on ten days notice of the time and place being given to respondent and the court appointed Henry Stehman, Esq., of Dauphin Co., commissioner to take said depositions. (2 copies) "July 1, 1858, served the within writ on Defendant by reading it to him and handing him a true and attested copy thereof, so ans. Saml. Forscht, Shff." Aug. 13, 1858, depositions filed. And now, to wit, Feb. 15, 1859, depositions filed and read to the court, whereupon the court, on motion of William C. Chapman, Esq., one of the attorneys of this court, on due consideration, decreed a divorce a vinculo matrimonii between the parties in this case according to the Act of Assembly in such case made and provided. Mr. Chapman was the attorney for Josephine Hyberger. Costs were $1.25 for the sheriff; $1.50 for the proclamation; and $2.25 for the proth. making a total cost of $5.00. Recd. of Mr. Chapman $5.00 signed W. Ilg. Recd. my fees signed Saml. Forscht.

Aug. Term 1858 #36 - Eliza Ann Shariffe by her next friend David Starry vs. Solomon Shariffe: Jun. 1, 1858, libel in divorce presented to the court and subpoena awarded to the respondent returnable fourth Monday of Aug. 1858. Subpoena issued - Jun. 10, 1858, on motion of Mr. Chapman the court granted a rule to take depositions to be read on the hearing of this case on ten days notice of the time and place being given to the respondent and the court appointed John A. Wilson, Esq., commissioner to take said depositions. (2 copies) Sheriff returned writ "July 30, 1858, served the within subpoena on Respondent by reading within writ to him and handing him a true and attested copy thereof - so ans. Saml. Forscht, Shff." Aug. 13, 1858, depositions filed - Aug. 28, 1858, depositions read to the court whereupon the court, on due consideration of this case, decreed a divorce a vinculo matrimonii between the parties according to the Acts of Assembly in such case made and provided. Mr. Chapman was the attorney for Eliza Ann Shariffe. Costs were $1.50 for the sheriff; $3.00 for the attorney; and $3.50 for the proth., making a total cost of $8.00. $4.00 recd. signed W. Ilg.

Nov. Term 1858 #3 - Sarah Bisder by her next friend Catharine Blessing vs. Matthias Bisder: Aug. 28, 1858, libel in divorce from bed and board and for maintenance and alimony, etc. Subpoena awarded by the court returnable first Monday of Nov. 1858, requiring respondent to appear and answer to complaint etc. Subpoena issued Oct. 14, 1858, settled and costs paid (see app. docket). Mr. Weiser was the attorney for Sarah Bisder and Messrs. Evans & Mayer were the attorneys for Matthias Bisder.

Nov. Term 1858 #29 - Thomas Siechrist vs. Catharine Siechrist: Sept. 25, 1858, libel in divorce presented to the Hon. Robert J. Fisher, president judge of the court of common pleas who awarded a subpoena to the respondent returnable first Monday of Nov. 1858, requiring her to answer the complaint of libellant, etc. subpoena issued accordingly Oct. 8, 1858, the court appointed John A. Wilson, Esq., commissioner to take testimony in this case. Writ returned thus "Oct. 4, 1858, served the within subpoena on the Respondent by reading it to her and handing her a true and attested copy thereof - so ans. Sam. Forscht, Shff." Jan. 27, 1868, depositions in this case were read to the court and filed. And it further appearing to the court that due notice has been given by the sheriff of York Co., to the respondent, requiring her to answer the complaint in this case, and no answer having been filed, the court thereupon, on motion of libellant's counsel, decreed a divorce a vinculo matrimonii between the parties according to Act of Assembly of the Commonwealth in such case made and provided and the court orders respondent to pay costs. (copy) Mr. Wallace was the attorney for Thomas Siechrist.

Costs were $1.50 for the sheriff; $2.75 for Proth. B.; $2.50 for the proth.; $3.00 for the attorney; and $.75 for the certificate making a total cost of $10.50.

Nov. Term 1858 #36 - John Paul vs. Mary Ann Paul: libel in divorce presented to the court and subpoena awarded to respondent returnable first Monday of Nov. 1858. Subpoena issued - writ returned thus - "N.E.I. so ans. Saml. Forscht, Sheriff" Nov. 6, 1858, alias subpoena awarded to respondent returnable first Monday of Jan. 1859 - issued - Returned "N.E.I. so ans. Samuel Forscht, Sheriff" Dec. 8, 1858, on motion of Mr. Chapman the court appointed John A. Wilson, Esq. of the borough of York and Henry Beader, Esq. of the borough of Harrisburg, or any or either of them, Commissioners, to take depositions of witnesses in this case. (1 copy) Mr. Chapman was the attorney for John Paul. Costs were $.20 for the sheriff and $2.75 for Proth. B., making a total cost of $2.95.

Jan. Term 1859 #2 - Charles Glessner vs. Sarah Glessner: libel in divorce presented to the court - court awarded a subpoena to respondent returnable first Monday of Jan. 1859. Same day subpoena issued. "Nov. 30, 1858, served the within writ on Defendant by reading it to her and handing her a true and attested copy thereof - so ans. Saml. Forscht, Shff." Jan. 7, 1859, on motion of Thomas A. Ziegle, Esq. attorney for plf., the court appointed Oscar K. Harris, Esq., commissioner, to take testimony in the above case on five days notice. And now, Oct. 15, 1861, depositions taken on this case filed and read to the court, whereupon the court, on due consideration, decreed a divorce a vinculo matrimonii between the parties according to the Act of Assembly on such case made and provided. Respondent ordered to pay costs. Mr. Thomas A. Ziegle, Esq. was the attorney for Charles Glessner. Costs were $1.00 for the sheriff; $1.50 for the proclamation; $5.00 for the commissioner; $.50 for the notice; $4.00 for the proth.; and $3.00 for the attorney making a total cost of $15.00. Recd. $7.00 of fee signed W. Ilg.

Apr. Term 1859 #19 - Henry Brose vs. Maria Brose: Feb. 2, 1859, libel in divorce presented to the court and subpoena awarded to the respondent returnable fourth Monday of Apr. 1859. Same day subpoena issued. Apr. 9, 1850, answer of respondent filed. The sheriff made return as follows "Feby. (sic) 28, 1859, served the within writ on Defendant by reading writ to her and handing her a true and attested copy thereof - so answers Saml. Forscht, Shff." Apr. 30, 1859, the court granted a rule in this case on the defendant to plead in ten days or judgment pro confesso with notice to Mr. Chapman at bar. Mar. 18, 1862, the court appointed B.F. Koller, Esq., commissioner to take testimony in this case. (1 copy) on ten days notice to respondent of her counsel of record. Sept. 1, 1862, depositions filed. And now, Nov. 10, 1862, the depositions taken in this case were read to the court whereupon the court, on due consideration, decreed a divorce a vinculo matrimonii between the parties according to the Act of Assembly in such case made and provided. Mr. Keesey was the attorney for Henry Brose and Mr. Chapman was the attorney for Maria Brose. Costs were $2.60 to the sheriff; $3.75 for Proth. B.; $1.25 for the writ; $3.00 for the attorney; $1.50 for the proclamation and $.50 for the copy making a total cost of $12.60.

Apr. Term 1859 #28 - Joseph K. Sharp vs. Cassandra Sharp: libel in divorce presented to the court and awarded to the respondent returnable fourth Monday of Apr. 1859. Subpoena issued. The sheriff returned writ on the defendant by reading it to her and handing her a true and attested copy thereof so answers Saml. Forscht, Shff." Apr. 30, 1859, the court appointed George M. Shetter, Esq., commissioner to take testimony in this case. May 31, 1859, depositions filed and read to the court whereupon the court, on motion of John Evans, Esq., attorney for the libellant, decreed a divorce a vinculo matrimonii between the parties in the above case according to the Act of Assembly in such case made and provided. Messrs. Evans & Mayer were the attorneys for Joseph K. Sharp. Costs were $1.25 for the sheriff; $3.00 for the attorneys; $1.50 for the proclamation and $4.00 for the proth., making a total cost of $9.75.

Apr. Term 1859 #51 - Catharine Ford by her next friend Henry Turner vs. Benjamin Ford: Mar. 18, 1859, libel in divorce presented to the court and subpoena awarded to the respondent returnable to the court and subpoena awarded to the respondent returnable fourth Monday of Apr. 1859. Subpoena issued. The sheriff made return of the writ in this case as follows "March 22, 1859, served the within writ on defendant by reading it to him and handing him a true and attested copy thereof - so answers Saml. Forscht, Shff." Apr. 30, 1859, the court appointed Jacob Glessner, Esq., commissioner to take testimony in this case. Exit Commission. Messrs. Evans & Mayer were the attorneys for Catharine Ford. Costs were $3.20 for the sheriff and $3.00 for Proth. B., making a total cost of $6.20.

Apr. Term 1859 #57 - Barbara Thomas by her next friend Henry Reinicka vs. John Rudolph Thomas: Mar. 23, 1859, libel in divorce presented to the Hon. Robert J. Fisher, president judge of the Court of Common Pleas of York County. Subpoena awarded to the respondent returnable fourth Monday of Apr. 1859. Mar. 23, 1859, subpoena issued. The sheriff returned the writ as follows "March 25, 1859, served the within writ on the defendant by reading it to him and handing him a true and attested copy thereof - so answers

Saml. Forscht, Sheriff." Apr. 30, 1859, the court appointed Jacob Glessner, Esq., commissioner, to take testimony in this case. Exit Commission. May 31, 1859, depositions filed. And now, Jun. 2, 1859, depositions read to the court, whereupon the court, on motion of Vincent K. Keesey, Esq., decreed a divorce a vinculo matrimonii between the parties according to the Act of Assembly in such case made and provided. Mr. Vincent K. Keesey was the attorney for Barbara Thomas. Costs were $1.00 for the writ; $1.90 for the sheriff; $1.50 for the proclamation; $3.00 for the attorney and $3.00 for the proth., making a total cost of $10.40. Recd. costs except atty. fee signed W. Ilg. Recd. my fee signed Saml. Forscht. Recd. atty. fee signed V.K.K.

Aug. Term 1859 #3 - James Riley Schmidt vs. Caroline Schmidt: Apr. 28, 1859, libel in divorce presented to the court and filed, whereupon the court awarded a subpoena to respondent returnable fourth Monday of Aug. 1859. Subpoena issued. "Non Est Inventus - so ans. Sam. Forscht, Sheriff." Aug. 29, 1859, the court awarded an alias subpoena to respondent returnable first Monday of Nov. 1859. Same day alias subpoena issued. Alias subpoena returned "Non Est Inventus - so ans. Saml. Forscht, Sheriff." Jan. 2, 1860, on motion of plaintiff's counsel the court appointed James J. Naille, Esq., commissioner to take testimony in this case. (1 copy) Jan. 14, 1860, depositions filed and same day, on motion of plaintiff's counsel and after reading depositions to the court, the court decreed a divorce a vinculo matrimonii between the parties in this case according to the Acts of Assembly in such case made and provided. Mr. Lewis was the attorney for James Riley Schmidt. Costs were $.20 for the sheriff; another $.20 for the sheriff; $1.50 for the writ; $2.50 for the proth.; $3.00 for the attorney; $1.50 for the proclamation and $1.50 for advertising plus $.50 for a copy making a total cost of $10.90.

Aug. Term 1859 #44 - Lydia E. Eckert by her next friend Hiram Dill vs. George Eckert: Jul. 2, 1859, subpoena in divorce from bed and board and alimony presented to the Hon. John Reiman and subpoena awarded to respondent by said judge returnable fourth Monday of Aug. 1859. Subpoena issued - "July 13, 1859, Served the within subpoena on defendant by reading it to him and handing him a true and attested copy thereof - so ans. Saml. Forscht, Shff." Nov. 21, 1859, rule on respondent to answer libel of plaintiff in ten days after notice to counsel of record of judgment. (2 copies) Dec. 1, 1860, answer of respondent filed. Dec. 31, 1860, Adjd. Court (J.L.) Dec. 3, 1860, continued by consent. Dec. 6, 1860, plaintiff's counsel moved the court to strike out the second plea of defendant in this case - to be argued and disposed of at Jan. Term 1861 - and defendant to take notice of trial for fourth day of Feb. 1861. Jan. 31, 1861, court striked of second plea in this case. Feb. 1861, Adjd. Ct. (J.L.), Feb.

4, 1861, continued by consent. Dec. 1861, Adjd. Ct. (J.L.), Dec. 16, 1861, cont'd. Jan. 1862. Adjd. Ct. (J.L.) Jan. 28, 1862, the libellant in this case upon afft. filed moves the court to grant an order on the respondent to pay her a suitable sum of money at this time to defray the expenses of this suit and to enable her to carry on the same etc. - the sum of $2.50 being now required (2 copies). Jan. 30, 1862, Contd. by the court. Same day court filed on Feb. 14, 1862, for hearing argument of this motion in this case and rule to take depositions by either party on five days notice to counsel. Feb. 17, 1862, depositions taken on behalf of plf. filed. Mar. 1862, Argt. list. Mar. 14, 1862, contd. 1863, Feb. Adjd. Ct. (J.S.) Feb. 16, 1863, contd. Attorneys for Lydia E. Eckert were Messrs. Evans & Mayer and Mr. Keesey was the attorney for George Eckert. Costs were $2.21 for the sheriff and $5.50 for the proth. making a total cost of $7.71. Recd. $7.71 of Mr. Mayer, signed W. Ilg. Recd. my fee, signed Samuel Forscht.

Nov. Term 1859 #2 - George M. Kehr vs. Sarah Kehr: libel in divorce presented to the court and subpoena awarded to respondent returnable first Monday of Nov. 1859. Same day subpoena issued. "N.E.I. so ans. Saml. Forscht, Sheriff." 11 Nov. 1859, alias subpoena awarded returnable first Monday of Jan. 1860 - issued to Jan. Term 1860 No. 11. Mr. Green was the attorney for George M. Kehr. Cost was $1.76 for the sheriff.

Nov. Term 1859 #6 - Thomas Miller vs. Catharine Miller: libel in divorce presented to the court. Court awarded a subpoena to respondent returnable on first Monday of Nov. 1859 to appear and answer the complaint in this case. Same day - subpoena issued. "Oct. 19, 1859, served the within subpoena on Respondent by reading it to her and handing her a true and attested copy thereof, so answ. Saml. Forscht, Sheriff." Nov. 9, 1859, on motion of Mr. Hay, the court appointed Horace Bonham, Esq., commissioner to take testimony in this case. (1 copy) Dec. 27, 1859, depositions filed. And now, Jan. 6, 1860, on proof of due service of notice on respondent of time and place of taking depositions in this case and after reading depositions to the court, the court on due consideration decree a divorce a vinculo matrimonii between the parties in this case according to the Acts of Assembly of this Commonwealth in such case made and provided. Mr. Hay was the attorney for Thomas Miller. Costs were $1.20 for the sheriff; $3.00 for the attorney; $1.50 for the proclamation; $3.50 for the proth.; and $.50 for a copy making a total costof 49.70 to which was added $5.00 for the commissioner making a total cost of $14.70.

Nov. Term 1859 #10 - Henry Landis vs. Rachel Landis: libel in divorce presented to the Court of Common Pleas of York County.

Court awarded a subpoena to the respondent returnable first Monday of Nov. 1859 to appear and answer the complaint in this case etc. - Aug. 29, 1859, subpoena issued. "Oct. 18, 1859, served the within writ on Respondent by leaving a true and attested copy at the residence with her mother - so answers Saml. Forscht, Sheriff." Nov. 11, 1859, on motion of Mr. Weiser, the court appointed John A. Wilson, Esq., commissioner to take testimony of witnesses in this case on ten days notice. Dec. 6, 1859, answer of respondent filed by leave of court Mar. 1860. Aug. Term - Mar. 21, 1860, depositions filed and read to the court. After reading depositions to the court respondent's counsel prayed the court to direct an issue in this case - objected to by Counsel for petitioner. Prayer and objections filed. And now, Jun. 5, 1860, the court enter judgment for the respondent and further order and decree that each party pay his own costs. Mr. Weiser was the attorney for Henry Landis and Mr. Green was the attorney for Rachel Landis. Costs were $2.12 for the sheriff; $3.94 for Proth. B. and $4.75 for the writ making a total cost of $10.81.

Jan. Term 1860 #1 - Rachel Bingaman by her next friend David Paters vs. James Bingaman: libel in divorce presented to the court Nov. 7, 1859. Same day subpoena awarded by the court to the respondent returnable first Monday of Jan. "N.E.I. so ans. Saml. Forscht, Shff." Jan. 7, 1860, alias subpoena awarded to the respondent returnable first next Term. Jan. 10, 1860, alias subpoena issued. Mr. Weeser was the attorney for Rachel Bingaman. Costs were $.32 for the sheriff and $3.25 for the proth. making a total cost of $3.57.

Jan. Term 1860 #7 - Catharine Nace by her next friend Jacob Stably vs. Ephraim Nace: Nov. 11, 1859, libel in divorce presented to the court and subpoena awarded to the respondent to answer the complaint in this case. Returnable first Monday of Jan., 1860 - issued. "N.E.I. so ans. Saml. Forscht, Shff." Alias subpoena issued to Aug. Term 1860 No. 80. Mr. Green was the attorney for Catharine Nace. Cost was $.20 for the sheriff.

Jan. Term 1860 #11 - George M. Kehr vs. Sarah Kehr: Nov. 18, 1859 alias subpoena in divorce. Original No. 2 Nov. Term 1859. "N.E.I. so ans. Samuel Forscht, Shff." Apr. 30, 1860, on motion of the plaintiff's counsel the court appointed George Fisher, Esq., commissioner to take testimony in this case according to the Act of Assembly in such case made and provided. (Exit copy) Aug. 29, 1860, depositions filed and read to the court whereupon the court, on motion of A.N. Green, Esq., attorney for libellant, decreed a divorce between the parties in this case a vinculo matrimonii according to the Act of Assembly in such case made and provided. Mr. A.N. Green, Esq., was the attorney for George M. Kehr and Mr. Waser was the attorney for Sarah Kehr. Costs were $.32 for the sheriff; $1.76 for the sheriff on the original action; $1.50 for the proclamation; $3.00 for the attorney and $4.37 for the writ making a total cost of $10.95. Def.'s bill $17.02 1/2. Recd. proth. and sheriff's fees of Mr. Green, signed W. Ilg. Recd. my fees signed Saml. Forscht. Added note - And the court order the defendant to pay the cost. Sept. 1, 1860, decree vacated and court order that the case be finally heard on the Oct. 16, 1860. Either party to take depositions on ten days notice or rebutting testimony on five days notice to counsel on record. Reasons filed. Sept. 27, 1860, depositions. Oct. 11, 1860, depositions taken on part of plaintiff filed. And now, Dec. 11, 1860, the court upon due consideration of this case decreed a divorce between the parties a vinculo matrimonii according to the Acts of Assembly in such case made and provided and libellant is ordered to pay the costs of these proceedings.

Jan. Term 1860 #22 - John Lehr vs. Isabella Lehr: libel in divorce presented to the court. Court awarded a subpoena to the respondent returnable first Monday of Jan. 1860 to answer petition or complaint in this case-issued. "Dec. 10, 1859, served the within subpoena on Defendant by reading it to her and handing her a true and attested copy thereof - so answ. Saml. Forscht, Shff." Jan. 6, 1860, on motion of the plaintiff's counsel, the court appointed David J. Williams, Esq., commissioner to take testimony in this case on ten days notice to respondent. Jan. 10, 1862, depositions filed and read to the court, whereupon the court, on due consideration, decreed a divorce a vinculo matrimonii between the parties in this case according to the Act of Assembly in such case made and provided. Mr. Green was the attorney for John Lehr. Costs were $3.00 for the attorney; $1.60 for the sheriff; $4.50 for the proth. and $1.50 for the proclamation making a total cost of $10.60.

Apr. Term 1860 #9 - William Cocklin vs. Mary Cocklin: Jan. 6, 1860, libel in divorce presented to the court and ordered to be filed which is accordingly done and the court awarded a subpoena to be issued to the respondent after the 20th day of Mar. 1860 - returnable fourth Monday of Apr. 1860. Mar. 21, 1860, subpoena issued. "March 29, 1860, served the within writ on defendant by reading it to her and handing her a true and attested copy thereof - so ans. Saml. Forscht, Shff." Apr. 30, 1860, on motion of plaintiff's counsel the court appointed N. Green, Esq., commissioner to take testimony in this case. (EX. 1 copy). Aug. 28, 1860, depositions filed and read to the court, whereupon the court, on motion of D.S. Williams, Esq., one of the attorneys of this court, decreed a divorce between the parties in this case a vinculo matrimonii according to the Act of Assembly in such case made and provided. Mr. D.W. Williams, Esq. was the attorney for William Cocklin. Costs were $2.80 for the sheriff; $3.00 for the attorney; $1.50 for the proclamation; and $4.53 for Proth. B., making a total cost of $11.83. Recd. of Mr. Williams $8.83 signed W. Ilg. Recd. my fees signed Saml. Forscht.

Apr. Term 1860 #10 - Rebecca McCracken by her next friend George Pollinger vs. William McCracken: libel in divorce presented to the court - court awarded a subpoena to the respondent returnable fourth Monday of Apr. 1860. Subpoena issued. "N.E.I. so ans. Saml. Forscht, Shff." Jun. 6, 1860, the court awarded an alias subpoena to the respondent returnable fourth Monday of Aug., 1860 - alias subpoena issued to Aug. Term 1860 No. 52. Mr. Williams was the attorney for Rebecca McCracken. Cost was $1.92 for the sheriff.

Apr. Term 1860 #55 - Henry Wilt vs. Rachel Wilt: Feb. 25, 1860, libel in divorce presented to one of the judges of the Court of Common Pleas of York County. Subpoena awarded returnable fourth Monday of Apr. 1860, and subpoena issued accordingly to the respondent. Subpoena issued. "Feby, 25, 1860, served the within writ on Defendant by reading it to her and handing her a true and attested copy thereof - so ans. Saml. Forscht, Shff." May 5, 1860, on motion of the plaintiff's counsel the court appointed John A. Wilson, Esq., commissioner to take testimony of witnesses in this case on five days notice to the respondent. Mr. Weiser was the attorney for Henry Wilt. Costs were $1.25 for the sheriff and $2.50 to Proth. B., making a total cost of $3.75. Received above costs from Mr. Weiser, signed Jas. B. Ziegler. Received my fees, signed Saml. Forscht. Received my fee signed H.G. Brissey.

Apr. Term 1860 #65 - William Butler vs. Amelia Butler: Mar. 12, 1860, libel in divorce presented to the court and subpoena awarded to the respondent returnable 4th Monday of Apr., 1860. Subpoena issued. "N.E.I. so ans. Saml. Forscht, Sheriff" alias Subpoena No. 65 Aug. Term 1860. Mr. Lewis was the attorney for William Butler. Cost was $.40 for the sheriff.

Aug. Term 1860 #1 - Joseph Wagner Vs. Mary Ann Wagner: Apr. 22, 1860, libel in divorce presented to the court and filed. Court awarded a subpoena to respondent returnable on 4th Monday of Aug. 1860. Apr. 23, 1860, subpoena issued. "June 9, 1860, served the within subpoena on Defendant by reading writ to her and handing her a true and attested copy thereof - so ans. Saml. Forscht, Sheriff." Aug. 28, 1860, on motion of plaintiff's counsel the court appointed D.J. Williams, Esq., commissioner to take testimony of witnesses in this case on ten days notice to respondent or her counsel of record. Mr. Green was the attorney for Joseph Wagner and Messrs. Evans & Mayer were the attorneys for Mary Ann Wagner.

Costs were $1.50 for the sheriff and $2.50 for Proth. B., making a total cost of $4.00.

Aug. Term 1860 #6 - Thomas Sayer vs. Lenah Sayer: Apr. 25, 1860, libel in divorce presented to the court and filed. Court awarded a subpoena to the respondent returnable fourth Monday of Aug. 1860. Subpoena issued. "Aug. 6, 1860, served the within writ on the Respondent by reading it to her and handing her a true and attested copy thereof - so ans. Saml. Forscht, Shff." Aug. 27, 1860, on motion of plaintiff's counsel the court appointed John Gibson, Esq., commissioner to take testimony of witnesses in this case. May 2, 1863, depositions filed and read to the court whereupon the court decreed a divorce a vinculo matrimonii between the parties according the Acts of Assembly in such case made and provided. Mr. Mulgreed was the attorney for Thomas Sayer and Mr. Green was the attorney for Lenah Sayer. Costs were $5.00 for the commissioner; $2.92 for the sheriff; $3.00 for the attorney; $1.50 for the proclamation and $3.75 for the proth. and copy, making a total cost of $16.17.

Aug. Term 1860 #7 - John Aughey vs. Mary Aughey: Apr. 25, 1860, libel in divorce presented to the court and filed. court awarded a subpoena to the respondent returnable fourth Monday of Aug., 1860. Subpoena issued. "N.E.I. so ans. Saml. Forscht, Shff." Aug. 31, 1860, alias subpoena awarded to the respondent returnable first Monday of Nov. 1860. Alias subpoena in divorce No. 5, Nov. Term, 1860. Mr. Keesey was the attorney for John Aughey. Cost was $.20 for the sheriff.

Aug. Term 1860 #11 - Susanna Clark by her next friend George Spangler vs. Edward A. Clark: Apr. 27, 1860, alias subpoena in divorce. Origl. No. 75 Apr. Term 1860. "N.E.I. so ans. Samuel Forscht, Shff." Messrs. Evans & Mayer were the attorneys for Susanna Clark. Costs were $.20 for the sheriff; $3.00 for the attorney; $3.50 for the proth. and an additional cost of $.32 making a total cost of $7.02. Recd. proth. and sheriff's fees, signed W. Ilg. Recd. my fees, signed Samuel Forscht.

Aug. Term 1860 #19 - Mary E. Meredith by her next friend Daniel Jacobs vs. Marion Meredith: May 4, 1860, libel in divorce presented to the court and filed - and the court on motion of plaintiff's cousel awards a subpoena to the respondent returnable fourth Monday of Aug. 1860. Subpoena issued. "N.E.I. so ans. Saml. Forscht, Shff." Aug. 31, 1860, alias subpoena awarded to the respondent returnable on first Monday of Nov. 1860. Alias subpoena No. 9 Nov. Term 1860. Messrs. Cochran & Hay were the attorneys for Mary E. Meredith. Cost was $.20 for the sheriff.

Aug. Term 1860 #20 - Edward Kipp vs. Lavinia Kipp: libel in divorce presented to the court and filed and the court, on motion of plaintiff's counsel awards a subpoena to the respondent returnable fourth Monday of Aug. 1860. Subpoena issued. "Aug. 12, 1860, served the within writ on Defendant by reading it to her and handing her a true and attested copy thereof - so ans. Saml. Forscht, Shff." Aug. 27, 1860, on motion of plaintiff's counsel the court appointed John A. Wilson, Esq., commissioner to take testimony in this case. Mr. Lewis was the attorney for Edward Kipp. Costs were $1.60 for the sheriff and $3.00 for Proth. B., making a total cost of $4.60.

Aug. Term 1860 #52 - Rebecca McCracken by her next friend George Pollinger vs. William McCracken: alias subpoena in divorce origl. 10 Ap. Term 1860 "N.E.I. so ans. Saml. Forscht, Shff." Oct. 2, 1860, on motion of Mr. Williams the court directs the sheriff to cause notice to be published in some newspapers of this county requiring ahove named defendant to appear as required by Act (sic) of Assembly. Oct. 18, 1860, on motion the court appointed George Fisher, Esq., commissioner to take testimony of witnesses in this case. And now, Dec. 11, 1860, depositions filed and read to the court whereupon the court, on motion of plaintiff's counsel, decreed a divorce between the parties in this case a vinculo matrimonii according to the Acts of Assembly in such case made and provided - and further the court orders the respondent to pay the costs of these proceedings. Mr. Williams was the attorney for Rebecca McCracken. Costs were $3.85 for the proth.; $3.00 for the attorney; $1.50 for the proclamation; $2.00 for the writ and $2.00 for advertising making a total cost of $12.35.

Aug. Term 1860 #65 - William Butler vs. Amelia Butler: Jun. 25, 1860, alias subpoena in divorce - origl. No. 65 Apr. Term 1860. "N.E.I. so ans. Saml. Forscht, Shff." Aug. 27, 1860, on motion of plaintiff's counsel the court appointed Joseph Wilson, Esq., commissioner to take testimony in this case. And now, Nov. 12, 1860, it appearing to the court that notice was given to the respondent in this case by the late sheriff, as directed by Act (sic) of Assembly, in a newspaper printed in the borough of York for four successive weeks prior to the first day of this term and the testimony taken by the commissioner being filed this day and read to the court, the court on motion of libellant's counsel decreed a divorce between the parties in this case a vinculo matrimonii according to the Acts of Assembly in such case made and provided. Mr. Lewis was the attorney for William Rutler. Costs were $2.06 for the sheriff; $3.00 for the attorney; $.40 for a copy; $1.50 for the proclamation and $4.00 for the proth., making a total cost of $10.96. Recd. costs of A.E. Lewis, Esq. signed W. Ilg. Recd. atty. fee signed A.E. Lewis. Recd. my fees signed Saml. Forscht.

Aug. Term 1860 #74 - Wennetta Hambright by her next friend Frederick Kuntz vs. Charles Frederick Hambright: libel in divorce presented to the Hon. Robert J. Fisher, president judge of the Common Pleas of York County who awarded a subpoena to the respondent returnable fourth Monday of Aug. 1860. Subpoena issued. "N.E.I. so ans. Saml. Forscht, Shff." Aug. 31, 1860, alias subpoena awarded to the respondent returnable first Monday of Nov., 1860. Alias subpoena issued to Nov. Term 1860 No. 6. Mr. Fisher was the attorney for Wennetta Hambright. Cost was $.32 1/2 for the sheriff.

Aug. Term 1860 #80 - Catharine Nace by her next friend Jacob Stably vs. Ephraim Nace: alias subpoena in divorce original No. 7 Jan. Term 1860. "N.E.I. so ans. Saml. Forscht, Shff." Nov. 12, 1860, on motion the court appointed George Wehrly, Esq., commissioner to take testimony in this case. Feb. 2, 1861, depositions filed. Feb. 14, 1861, depositions taken in this case were read to the court and it further appearing to the court that due and legal notice has been given by the sheriff of this county for four successive weeks prior to the first Monday of Nov. 1860, in a newspaper printed in the borough of York requiring respondent to appear on said day to answer the complaint in this case, and he not having appeared as required, the court now, upon due consideration, decreed a divorce a vinculo matrimonii between the said parties according to the Act of Assembly in such case made and provided. Court orders respondent to pay the costs of these proceedings. Mr. Green was the attorney for Catharine Nace. Costs were $.20 & and $.32 for the sheriff; $3.00 for the attorney; $2.00 for the writ; $3.12 for the proth.; $1.50 for the proclamation; and $1.50 for advertising making a total cost of $11.65.

Nov. Term 1860 #5 - John Aughey vs. Mary Aughey: Aug. 31, 1860 alias subpoena in divorce original No. 7 Aug. Term 1860. "N.E.I. so ans. Samuel Forscht, Shff." Jan. 8, 1861, the court appointed John A. Wilson, Esq., commissioner to take testimony of witnesses in this case. (1 copy) Jan. 11, 1861, depositions filed and read to the court and it appearing to the court that due notice has been given by the sheriff of York County as required by law for respondent to appear at this court to answer the complaint in this case and the respondent not appearing the court thereupon decreed a divorce a vinculo matrimonii between the parties in pursuance of the Act of Assembly of this Commonwealth in such case made and provided. Mr. Keesey was the attorney for John Aughey. Costs were $.20 for the sheriff; an additional $.20 for the sheriff; $1.50 for the proclamation; $3.00 for the attorney; $2.00 for something illegible and $5.00 for something illegible making a total cost of $11.40.

Recd. costs signed W. Ilg. Recd. atty. fee signed V.K.K. Recd. my fees signed William Martin. Recd. my fees signed Saml. Forscht.

Nov. Term 1860 #6 - Wennetta Hambright by her next friend Frederick Kuntz vs. Charles Frederick Hambright: alias subpoena in divorce - original 74 Aug. Term 1860. "N.E.I. so ans. Saml. Forscht, Shff." Jan. 12, 1861, the court on motion of plf.'s counsel, appointed George Wehrly, Esq., commissioner to take testimony of witnesses in this case. Jan. 31, 1861, depositions filed and read to the court and it further appearing to the court that due legal notice has been given by the sheriff of this county for four successive weeks prior to the first day of Jan. Term 1861, in a newspaper printed in the borough of York requiring the respondent to appear on the said day to answer the complaint in this case, and he not appearing, the court decreed a divorce between the parties in this case a vinculo matrimonii according to the Act of Assembly in such case made and provided - and the court make and order that the respondent pay the costs. Mr. Fisher was the attorney for Wennetta Hambright. Costs were $.20 and $.32 for the sheriff; $1.50 for the proclamation; $3.00 for the attorney; $1.50 for advertising. $4.75 for proth. and $5.00 for the commissioner making a total cost of $16.27 to which was added a $.50 charge for a copy making the total cost $16.77.

Nov. Term 1860 #9 - Mary E. Meredith by her next friend Daniel Jacobs vs. Marion Meredith: Sept. 1, 1860, alias subpoena in divorce original 19 Aug. Term 1860. "N.E.I. so ans. Saml. Forscht, Shff." Nov. 9, 1860, on motion of libellant's counsel the court directs the sheriff to publish notice to respondent as required by Act of Assembly - and appoint James W. Latimer, Esq., commissioner to take testimony in this case. Jan. 11, 1861, depositions taken in this case filed and read to the court, and it further appearing to the court that notice has been given to the respondent to appear at this court to answer the complaint in this case according to the requirements of the Act of Assembly in such case made etc. - the court decreed a divorce a vinculo matrimonii between the parties in this case pursuant to the Act of Assembly of this Commonwealth in such case made and provided. Messrs. Cochran & Hay were the attorneys for Mary E. Meredith. Costs were $.20 and $.20 for the sheriff; $5.00 for the commissioner; $3.00 for the attorneys; $1.50 for the proclamation; $4.00 for the proth. and $.75 for a copy making a total cost of $14.65. Recd. sheriff & attorneys fees, signed W. Ilg.

Nov. Term 1860 #25 - Elizabeth Meckley by her next friend Jacob Eichelberger vs. Emanuel Meckley: Oct. 4, 1860, libel in divorce presented to the Hon. Adam Ebaugh, and filed. Subpoena granted to the respondent returnable first Monday of Nov. 1860. Issued. "N.E.I. so ans. Saml. Forscht, Shff." Dec. 3, 1860, on motion of plaintiff's counsel the court awarded an alias subpoena to respondent returnable first Monday of Jan. 1861. Alias subpoena issued to Jan. Term 1861 No. 22. Mr. Keesey was the attorney for Elizabeth Meckley. Costs was $.20 for the sheriff.

Nov. Term 1860 #28 - Peter Stambaugh vs. Levanna Stambaugh: libel in divorce presented to the court and subpoena awarded to the respondent returnable first Monday of Nov. 1860, see petition filed. Same day subpoena issued. Oct. 16, 1860, on motion of Mr. Chapman the court appointed George M. Shelter, Esq., commissioner to take depositions in the above case on five days notice of time and place of taking the same to the opposite party or her counsel of record. "October 13, 1860, served the within subpoena on the Respondent by reading it to her and handing her a true and attested copy thereof so ans. Saml. Forscht, Shff." Nov. 3, 1860, depositions filed. Nov. 6, 1860, depositions read to the court, and upon motion of Mr. Chapman atty. for libellant, the court decreed a divorce a vinculo matrimonii between the parties in this case according to the Act of Assembly in such case made and provided. Mr. Chapman was the attorney for Peter Stambaugh. Costs were $1.76 for the sheriff; $3.00 for the attorney; $1.50 for the proclamation; $3.12 for the proth.; and $1.60 for the record making a total cost of 10.68. Recd. by Mr. Chapman signed W. Ilg.

Surname Index

ADAMS, 93 118 125 126 128-135
AGNEW, 2
ALBRIGHT, 117 126 128 132-146
ALDERICE, 98
ALLEMAN, 152-155
ALLEN, 105 106
ALWARD, 23
ANSTINE, 120
ARCHER, 99
ARNOLD, 113
ASH, 2 5
ASTON, 89
ATTLEE, 2
AUGHENBACH, 105
AUGHEY, 169 171
AUGHINBACH, 94
AULABAUGH, 158
BACHMAN, 107
BAHN, 108 116 118 119
BAILEY, 96 102 121 129
BAIR, 96 100
BAKER, 16
BANGE, 138
BARKER, 11
BARNHART, 142
BARNITZ, 113-118 123 125 130 134-136 152
BARR, 110
BARRET, 20
BARROWS, 133
BART, 138
BASKINS, 21
BATTIS, 33
BAUGHER, 88 99

BAYLY, 95
BEADER, 162
BEALER, 6
BEALERT, 5 6
BEAR, 100-102 135 151
BEARD, 92
BECHTOLD, 32
BECK, 127
BECKER, 139 141
BEHLER, 122
BEIDLEMAN, 109
BELL, 96 97
BEOKEL, 112 114
BERGER, 106
BERKHEIMER, 127
BERNHART, 83
BIGLER, 17
BILLMEYER, 83
BILLMYER, 133
BINGAMAN, 166
BISDER, 161
BITTENGER, 159
BIXBY, 25
BLACK, 87 152 153
BLAKESLEE, 139 140
BLESSING, 161
BOAK, 105
BOHN, 119
BOLLINGER, 102-104
BONHAM, 111 121 123 125-128 165
BORTNER, 105
BOSSLER, 1-3
BOWERMAN, 13
BOYER, 22 147
BRADLEY, 135-137